The Infancy Gospels of James and Thomas

THE
SCHOLARS
BIBLE

The Infancy Gospels of James and Thomas

RONALD F. HOCK

*with Introduction, Notes, and Original Text
featuring the NEW Scholars Version Translation*

SANTA ROSA CALIFORNIA

Copyright © 1995 Polebridge Press

All rights reserved. No part of this publication may be reproduced, stored in a retrieval system, or transmitted in any form or by any means, electronic or otherwise, without prior permission of the copyright owner.

Library of Congress Cataloging-in-Publication Data
Gospel of James (Infancy Gospel). English & Greek.
    The Infancy Gospels of James and Thomas : with introduction, notes, and original text featuring the New Scholars Version translation / Ronald F. Hock.
       p.   cm. — (The Scholars Bible ; vol. 2)
    Includes bibliographical references.
    ISBN 0-944344-46-1. —ISBN 0-944344-47-X (pbk.)
    1. Gospel of James (Infancy Gospel)—Introductions. 2. Gospel of Thomas (Infancy Gospel)—Introductions. I. Hock, Ronald F., 1944-.   II. Gospel of Thomas (Infancy Gospel). English & Greek.
BS2860.J2A3   1995
229'.8–dc20   95-38112
                                                     CIP

Printed in the United States of America

Contents

The Scholars Version

Editor in Chief

Robert W. Funk
Westar Institute

<table>
<tr><td>

General Editors

Daryl D. Schmidt
Texas Christian University

Julian V. Hills
Marquette University

</td><td>

Editors, Apocryphal Gospels

Ron Cameron
Wesleyan University

Karen L. King
Occidental College

</td></tr>
</table>

Translation Panel

Harold Attridge, *University of Notre Dame*
Edward F. Beutner, *Las Positas College*
J. Dominic Crossan, *DePaul University*
Jon B. Daniels, *Defiance College*
Arthur J. Dewey, *Xavier University*
Robert T. Fortna, *Vassar College*
Ronald F. Hock, *University of Southern California*
Roy W. Hoover, *Whitman College*
Arland D. Jacobson, *Concordia College*
John S. Kloppenborg, *University of St. Michael's College*
Helmut Koester, *Harvard University*
Lane C. McGaughy, *Willamette University*
Marvin W. Meyer, *Chapman College*
Robert J. Miller, *Midway College*
Stephen J. Patterson, *Eden Theological Seminary*
Bernard Brandon Scott, *Phillips Graduate Seminary*
Philip Sellew, *University of Minnesota*
Chris Shea, *Ball State University*
Mahlon H. Smith, *Rutgers University*

vi

Preface

This book grew out of the classroom and my efforts at trying to make sense of the historically dubious but immensely popular stories of the birth of Jesus in the Gospels of Matthew and Luke. Trying to explain these stories that are so different in terms of characters, events, and presumed dates and geographical movements led to a history of traditions approach which meant reconstructing a history of these birth stories back to earlier statements about Jesus' birth (Gal 4:4) and his divine sonship (Mark 1:1) as well as forward to the second century when Christians seem to have had a special interest in Jesus' birth, his mother Mary, and his childhood. The consequence of these interests was the development and revision of the canonical stories into books that are now known as the Infancy Gospels. Of these the most important are the Infancy Gospels of James and Thomas. The canonical stories have received sustained and sophisticated study, but the Infancy Gospels, unfortunately, have not.

Consequently, I was delighted when Professor Robert W. Funk of the Westar Institute/Polebridge Press invited me to include the Infancy Gospels of James and Thomas in The Scholars Bible series being published by Polebridge Press. My thanks to Bob for the invitation and to him and the editorial board of The Scholars Bible, especially Professor Julian V. Hills of Marquette University and Robert J. Miller of Midway College, for their careful reading of my translation and for their many suggestions for its improvement.

Others who deserve my gratitude are my students at the University of Southern California, in particular Geoffrey Black, Marla Echeverria, Luna Gorlick, Sharon Parker, and Pamela Sullivan. Their questions, enthusiasm, and insights were of more help to me than they probably ever realized. In addition, I wish to thank Mary Hollerich and her staff at the Interlibrary Loan/Global Express department of the USC Library. Their help in securing many obscure books and articles is much appreciated. I also wish to express special thanks to Professor C. Clifton Black of Southern Methodist University for his help in securing virtually overnight a journal article that came to my attention only at the last minute.

Thanks also to the staff at Polebridge Press, especially to Char Matejovsky as well as to Geneviève Duboscq, John Leech, and Mary Lowe.

vii

Their prompt, careful, and efficient handling of a complex manuscript is greatly appreciated.

Finally, a heartfelt expression of gratitude to my family: to my children, Jennifer and David, who also helped to secure several articles for me at their libraries at Yale and Cornell before coming home, and to my wife Carol for her lifelong support and encouragement.

Abbreviations

Biblical & Early Christian Writings

Acts	Acts of the Apostles, New Testament
Amos	Amos, Old Testament
2 Chron	2 Chronicles, Old Testament
Col	Colossians, New Testament
1 Cor	1 Corinthians, New Testament
Deut	Deuteronomy, Old Testament
Exod	Exodus, Old Testament
Ezek	Ezekiel, Old Testament
Gal	Galatians, New Testament
Gen	Genesis, Old Testament
Heb	Hebrews, New Testament
Hos	Hosea, Old Testament
Inf James	Infancy Gospel of James, NT Apocrypha
Inf Thom	Infancy Gospel of Thomas, NT Apocrypha
Joel	Joel, Old Testament
John	Gospel of John, New Testament
Jud	Judith, OT Apocrypha
1 Kgs	1 Kings, Old Testament
Lev	Leviticus, Old Testament
Luke	Gospel of Luke, New Testament
Mark	Gospel of Mark, New Testament
Matt	Gospel of Matthew, New Testament
Mic	Micah, Old Testament
Neh	Nehemiah, Old Testament
Num	Numbers, Old Testament
1 Pet	1 Peter, New Testament
Phil	Philippians, New Testament
Prov	Proverbs, Old Testament
Ps	Psalms, Old Testament
Rev	Revelation, New Testament
Ruth	Ruth, Old Testament
1 Sam	1 Samuel, Old Testament
Sir	Sirach (Ecclesiasticus), OT Apocrypha
Sus	Susanna, OT Apocrypha
2 Tim	2 Timothy, New Testament
Tob	Tobit, OT Apocrypha

General Abbreviations

An Boll	*Analecta Bollandiana*
ANRW	*Aufstieg und Niedergang der römischen Welt*
CBQ	*Catholic Biblical Quarterly*
FRLANT	Forschungen zur Religion und Literatur des Alten und Neuen Testaments
JHS	*Journal of Hellenic Studies*
JTS	*Journal of Theological Studies*
NGS	New Gospel Studies
ODB	*Oxford Dictionary of Byzantium*
PTS	Patristische Texte und Studien
SBFA	Studium Biblicum Franciscanum Analecta
SBLSBS	Society of Biblical Literature Sources for Biblical Study
SHG	Subsidia Hagiographica
SHR	Studies in the History of Religion
SNTU	Studien zum Neuen Testament und seiner Umwelt
TU	Texte und Untersuchungen
ZNW	*Zeitschrift für die neutestamentliche Wissenschaft*

The Infancy
Gospel
of James

INTRODUCTION

1. Infancy Gospels

Advent candles and Christmas cards, nativity scenes and Christmas carols, gift giving and Christmas trees, holiday travel and Christmas decorations— these and many more traditions make the celebration of the birth of Christ the richest and perhaps the most meaningful time of the Christian year. But such intense interest in Christ's birth was not always the case, and certainly not for the Christians of the New Testament period. They focused their attention instead on the other end of Christ's life, on his death and resurrection, as is clear from such pre-Pauline traditions as the creed which Paul recalled for the Corinthians (1 Cor 15:3–5) and the hymn which he quoted for the Philippians (Phil 2:6–11).

Paul himself had the same focus with his emphasis on preaching 'Christ crucified' (1 Cor 1:23; Gal 3:1), but he also provides us with our earliest reference to the birth of Christ. Writing to the churches of Galatia in the mid-50's of the first century, Paul makes a brief aside about that birth in an argument on another topic, saying that Christ 'was born of a woman, born under law' (Gal 4:4). This statement is not only brief. More important, it assumes nothing extraordinary about Jesus' birth, for all people are born of women and born under the customs, norms, and laws of their respective communities. That Paul can make such an assumption is all the more remarkable since he also says that while in Jerusalem he had met with 'James, the brother of the Lord' (Gal 1:19). Presumably, James would have informed Paul about any extraordinary circumstances at Jesus' birth.

In any case, even when the Jesus traditions are first given narrative form about the year 70 by the author of the Gospel of Mark there is not a word about his birth. Jesus first appears in this gospel as a young man about to be baptized (Mark 1:9). It is only later—about 80 for the Gospel of Luke and 90 for the Gospel of Matthew—that the narrative is extended back to include accounts of Jesus' birth (Matt 1–2; Luke 1–2). These accounts thus appear nearly a century after the events they purport to narrate.

The reason that the authors of Matthew and Luke extended their narratives back to the time of Jesus' birth is not readily apparent, but it may have been prompted by one of their sources, i.e., the Gospel of Mark, which opens with these words: 'The beginning of the Gospel of Jesus Christ, the Son of God' (Mark 1:1). In this gospel the theme of sonship is treated only functionally, designating Jesus' tasks as those of the one who would precede the coming judgment of God (see 1:9–15). When the authors of Matthew and Luke read this reference to Jesus as the Son of God, they may have been prompted to ask how it came to be that Jesus was in fact the Son of God.

But whatever the reason Matthew's and Luke's gospels start their stories with the circumstances of Jesus' birth.[1] More important, in the following decades these stories generated further interest in that birth and raised even more questions: Why was Mary chosen to be the mother of Christ? What in her life qualified her for this role? How did the infant John escape the murderous soldiers of Herod? What was Jesus doing between the time he and his parents returned from Egypt and the time he went at age twelve to the Temple in Jerusalem?

Questions like these were not likely to go unanswered because Greco-Roman narrative conventions required that only plausibility, not accuracy, of information be maintained when writing history. Consequently, starting in the second century, a whole new set of Christian writings arose to answer these questions. Scholars have called these writings Infancy Gospels, as 'they tell of events in the life of Jesus prior to his public ministry and of his parentage.'[2] This convenient, if not always appropriate, label will be retained here, and of the many that were written the two earliest and most important ones, the Infancy Gospel of James and the Infancy Gospel of Thomas, are the subjects of this volume of The Scholars Bible. The former extends the canonical birth accounts back to the circumstances of Mary's birth and childhood and ends shortly after she gives birth to Jesus and the astrologers make their visit which prompts Herod's murder of the infants (cf. Matt 2:16–18). The latter takes up the story when Jesus is a child, beginning with him as a five year old and continuing until Jesus visits the Temple in Jerusalem at age twelve (cf. Luke 2:42–51). The other Infancy Gospels are not only much later, but they are also usually dependent on

---

1. For the standard treatment of the canonical birth stories, see Brown, *Birth of the Messiah*.
2. Elliott, *Apocryphal New Testament*, 46.

these two,[3] thereby providing justification for limiting this study to the Infancy Gospels of James and Thomas.

2. The Infancy Gospel of James

2.1 Title

The name 'Infancy Gospel of James' is a rather loose rendering of the traditional Latin title for this work: *Protevangelium Jacobi.* But even this title, while long familiar to scholars ever since the Frenchman Guillaume Postel re-introduced this document in Latin dress to the West in 1552, is itself not original.[4] The Greek MS from which Postel made his Latin translation has long since been lost, so that we do not know whether Postel simply rendered the title in the MS. But the possibility is remote, as such a title occurs nowhere in the many MSS that are extant. The MSS in fact display a bewildering array of titles, some of them quite long.[5] One popular title, though with many variants, reads: 'An Account of James regarding the Birth of the exceedingly pure Mother of God.' But the oldest MS now available, the early 4th c. Papyrus Bodmer V, has a simpler title: Birth of Mary, Revelation of James,' and its most recent editor argues that only the first half is original.[6]

This short title has gained widespread support,[7] but it is hardly adequate to characterize the document as a whole and is of little help to establish the genre or to analyze its contents. Consequently, the traditional title, in its Anglicized form, will be retained here, although more for the sake of convenience than for any claim to originality or analytical value.[8]

2.2 Summary of the Contents

The Infancy Gospel of James, as we have seen, extends the canonical birth stories back to the circumstances surrounding the birth of Mary and her childhood and ends shortly after the birth of Jesus with its own version of Matthew's account of the murder of the infants. But this dependence on Matthew's account is not the only instance. In fact, the Infancy Gospel of James assumes, reworks, or develops both Matthew's and Luke's stories at

---

3. For other, later Infancy Gospels, including the Gospel of Pseudo-Matthew, the Arabic Infancy Gospel, and the History of Joseph the Carpenter, see Elliott, *Apocryphal New Testament*, 84–122.

4. For fuller discussion of Postel's re-introduction of the Infancy Gospel of James to the West, see Bouwsma, *Concordia Mundi*, 16–17 and 36.

5. For sample titles, see Daniels, *Manuscript Tradition*, 1.2–6.

6. de Strycker, *Protévangile*, 208–16.

7. See, e.g., Vielhauer, *Geschichte*, 668; Pratscher, *Herrenbruder Jakobus*, 221; Cothenet, "Protévangile," 4253.

8. Titles, to be sure, are not without significance, as Vorster ("Intertextuality," 270–71) shows for this very document, noting that "Protevangelium" places the emphasis on the birth of Jesus, while "Birth of Mary" clearly puts the focus on Mary and her story.

many points throughout the narrative. Consequently, a summary of the contents of the Infancy Gospel of James will help to sort out traditional and new elements and so aid the following discussion and analysis.

For purposes of this summary, the Infancy Gospel of James is divided into roughly three equal sections. The first section (1:1–8:2)[9] begins with the circumstances of Mary's conception and birth and ends with her about to become a woman. As the story opens we learn of the plight of Joachim and Anna, a wealthy and prominent Jewish couple (1:1). They are also childless and therein lies their plight. Joachim is publicly chastised for his childlessness when he is told that he alone among the righteous in Israel has had no offspring (1:5). He responds by going to the wilderness where he fasts and prays in order to learn from God why he is childless (1:9–11).

Meanwhile, Anna is rebuked privately by her slave for being childless (2:6). She responds by going to her garden where a nest of sparrows prompts a poignant lament in which she sees herself as the only one in all creation who is not fruitful (3:1–8). At this point, however, a heavenly messenger appears and informs her that her prayer has been heard and that she will bear a child after all—a child in fact who will be known throughout the world (4:1). Out of joy at such news Anna vows to give the child to God for life-long service (4:2). Joachim is informed of Anna's pregnancy (4:3–4) and returns home to celebrate their paradoxical blessing: a barren woman has conceived (4:9).

In time Anna gives birth to a girl and names her Mary (5:5–9). At six months, after Mary has taken her first steps, Anna transforms her bedroom into a virtual sanctuary where nothing unclean can touch her (6:1–5). Then, Mary's first birthday is celebrated with a magnificent banquet during which the priests bless the child (6:6–9) and Anna can finally gain a measure of vindication when she says, 'Listen, listen, you twelve tribes of Israel: Anna has a child at her breast!' (6:13).

When Mary is two years old, Joachim and Anna discuss the vow that Anna had made but decide not to give the child to God at that time (7:1–3). But at age three they do take her to the Temple where she spends the rest of her childhood, loved by the whole house of Israel and fed by the hand of a heavenly messenger (7:4–8:2).

The second section (8:3–16:8) opens with Mary at twelve years of age and about to become a woman and hence a threat to the purity of the Temple. The priests inform the high priest Zechariah about the problem posed by Mary's continued presence in the temple and ask him to seek divine guidance (8:3–5). Incidentally, this mention of Zechariah is the first

---

9. References to the Infancy Gospel of James use the traditional chapter numbers, but the verse numbers have been changed. The verses now mark smaller portions of the text than Tischendorf's. The increased number of verses will allow for more precise identification.

instance in which the Infancy Gospel of James reveals knowledge of the canonical birth accounts, although there Zechariah is not the high priest, but only a priest (see Luke 1:5). In any case, Zechariah enters the holy of holies to pray and is soon visited by a heavenly messenger who instructs him to summon all widowers. They are to bring their staffs, and a sign, he is told, will determine which widower is to receive Mary as his wife (8:6-8).

The widowers assemble, Joseph among them (8:9-9:1), which is surprising, since he is not so characterized in the canonical accounts. Less surprising, however, is the outcome, for Joseph's staff provides a a sign—a dove flying out of it—that prompts the high priest to give Mary to him, though now only as his ward, not as his wife (9:6-7; cf. 8:8). Joseph at first objects, saying that he is an old man and already has sons (9:8)—a further departure from the canonical characterization of him. He soon complies, however, when reminded of the consequences of flouting the will of God (9:9-11).

But as soon as Joseph takes Mary home he leaves her to build houses and trusts to God to protect her during his absence (9:12). Shortly thereafter, Mary is put to work when the priests assign her and seven other virgins the task of making a veil for the Temple (10:1-7). While working on her portion of the task, the scarlet and purple threads, Mary goes out briefly to fill a water jar and hears a voice saying, 'Greetings, favored one! The Lord is with you. Blessed are you among women' (11:1-2). Frightened, Mary returns home and quickly resumes her spinning, but she is soon visited again by a heavenly messenger who announces that she has found favor with the Lord and will conceive by means of his word. In addition, she is to call the child Jesus, who, as son of the Most High, will save his people from their sins (11:5-8). This scene clearly recalls the annunciation in Luke 1:26-38, though not without echoes from Matt 1:21. The overall impression, however, is of an original and more vivid narrative.

At any rate, when Mary finishes her part in making the veil (12:1-2), she leaves to visit her relative Elizabeth who herself is pregnant with the future baptist John (13:3-6), an episode which follows Luke 1:39-56 rather closely, if also more briefly. After three months she returns home and by the time she is six months pregnant Joseph returns, too (12:7-13:1). When he finds her pregnant he laments his failure to protect her and asks her why she did it (13:2-7). Mary, however, protests her innocence: 'I'm innocent, for I've not had sex with any man' (13:8). Joseph is at a loss about what to do with her (14:1-3), and he even has thoughts of divorcing her quietly (14:4), thoughts which recall the situation in Matt 1:19. But a dream in which a heavenly messenger appears to him resolves his doubts. He is told that her child, to be called Jesus, will save his people from their sins (14:5-7; cf. Matt 1:21). Consequently, Joseph awakens with a renewed commitment to protect Mary (14:8).

That commitment is soon tested, however, when a visitor to Joseph's house notices Mary's condition and reports it to the high priest (15:1-8).

The high priest summons them and questions them both, but their protestations of innocence do not satisfy him (15:9–18). As a result, the high priest orders that Mary be returned to the Temple (16:1), but he relents when Joseph breaks into tears (16:2). Instead, the high priest orders a test to establish their innocence or guilt (16:3). This test involves taking a drink and then going off into the wilderness. When they return unharmed, the high priest publicly pronounces them innocent (16:4–7) and Joseph then takes Mary home (16:8).

The third section (17:1–24:14) covers ground familiar from the canonical accounts: Joseph's and Mary's trip to Bethlehem, the birth of Jesus, the visit of the astrologers, and Herod's attempt on Jesus' life by murdering all infants under two years of age. But while the basic story line is taken from Matt 2:1–18 and Luke 2:1–7, the many changes, expansions, and additions to this familiar story create a surprisingly fresh account of the events associated with the birth of Christ.

The section opens in familiar fashion with Joseph and Mary traveling to Bethlehem for the census (17:1; cf. Luke 2:1–5). But not only is the census restricted to Judea in contrast to the whole world (see Luke 2:1), but Joseph also takes his sons along (17:5), and they never do reach Bethlehem before it is time for Mary to give birth (17:10). She is placed in a cave (18:1), and the story is then considerably expanded by a vision Joseph has while in search of a midwife (18:2). This vision, which presumably occurs while Mary is giving to birth to Jesus, involves a temporary suspension of time in which everything—from the heavens to men and animals on earth—is brought to a stop (18:3–11). All creation thus dutifully notes what is happening in the cave.

Once things resume their natural course, however, Joseph finds a midwife (19:1), and when the two arrive back at the cave (19:12), Mary already has Jesus at her breast (19:16). The midwife has thus arrived too late to be of assistance, but she does make the principal confession of the entire narrative. Thus when another woman, named Salome, arrives, the midwife confesses: 'A virgin has given birth' (19:18). Salome is skeptical, however, and performs a physical examination of Mary (19:19–20:2). But such skepticism only brings disaster, as Salome cries out that her hand is being consumed by flames (20:4). Her desperate prayer for help is heard, though, when a heavenly messenger instructs her to pick up the infant Jesus (20:5–9). She does as she is told and is immediately healed (20:10–11).

Once again the story reverts to the canonical accounts. The visit of the astrologers (21:1–12) is, of course, taken from Matt 2:1–12. In contrast to the Lukan trip to Bethlehem, however, it is handled rather faithfully, although there are some departures from Matthew. For example, the astrologers follow the star until it stopped over the cave where Jesus had been born (21:10; contrast Matt 2:10–11: house), but they offer the infant the familiar gifts of gold, pure incense, and myrrh before being told by a heavenly messenger to return by another route (21:11–12; cf. Matt 2:11–12).

It is only after the astrologers leave that the Infancy Gospel of James departs dramatically from the Matthean story. The brief account in Matthew of the murder of the infants by Herod (Matt 2:16–18) is changed in key respects and considerably expanded. For example, Jesus is saved from Herod's soldiers not by Joseph's flight to Egypt (so Matt 2:13–15), but by Mary's wrapping him in strips of cloth and then hiding him in a feeding trough (22:3–4)—narrative details taken from another context in Luke 2:7.

More significant than this change is the addition of a lengthy account of the threat posed by Herod to the infant John (22:5–24:14). Elizabeth tries to protect him by fleeing to the nearby hills, but fatigue overtakes her (22:5–7). Her prayer for help is heard, and mother and child are saved by a mountain opening up and hiding them (22:8–9). John's father, the high priest Zechariah, however, is not so lucky. Herod's agents question him regarding the whereabouts of his son, but are met with a courageous, if also fatal, refusal to answer (23:1–9).

Zechariah's murder is probably based on the author's equating him with another Zechariah who was murdered near the altar (see Matt 23:35), but in any event the whole narrative draws to a close with the priests discovering the murder and then, after mourning three days for Zechariah, appointing a new high priest, a certain Simeon (24:1–14), a figure known from Luke 2:25–26.

The Infancy Gospel of James concludes with a brief epilogue about the author and the circumstances in which he composed his account (25:1–3).

3. Authorship, Dating, and Provenance

3.1 The Epilogue

The Infancy Gospel of James is unusually explicit about its origins. The last chapter provides information about the author as well as the circumstances surrounding the composition of this gospel. The author begins by saying, 'Now I, James, am the one who wrote this account at the time when an uproar arose in Jerusalem at the death of Herod' (25:1).

The purpose of these closing remarks is clearly to secure the truth of the account which the reader has just finished. The simple name 'James' (25:1) doubtlessly refers to James, the brother of Jesus (Matt 13:55; Mark 6:3; Gal 1:19), thereby establishing the author as an eyewitness of much of the story he has narrated. Who better to write such a story than a knowledgeable family member (9:8; 17:5; 18:1) and eventual 'pillar' of the Jerusalem church (Gal 2:9; Acts 12:17; 15:13; 21:18)?

The truth of the account is further enhanced by the remarks about the time and place of writing. The Herod mentioned (25:1) is clearly King Herod, who died in 4 B.C.E., so that this gospel is not only an eyewitness account but a near contemporary one as well, and the composition of this account in the wilderness outside Jerusalem (25:2) keeps the author close to the scene of the events he is narrating.

If true, these claims would make the Infancy Gospel of James extraordinarily important, antedating even the earliest writings of the New Testament by over fifty years. Postel believed the claims to be true,[10] but scholars since then have recognized that they are a literary fiction. In fact, the claims do not bear the simplest scrutiny.

A comparison with the birth stories in Matthew and Luke is decisive in revealing the fiction. The previous summary of the Infancy Gospel of James has shown various points of contact between this gospel and the canonical accounts, and only literary dependence can explain the similarities.[11] That the Infancy Gospel of James is dependent on the canonical stories (and not the other way around) is assured, however, by the following reasoning.

The Infancy Gospel of James answers a question that arises only if one has both the Matthean and Lukan stories in mind. Matthew's birth narrative contains Herod's murder of the infants and has Jesus saved by Joseph's flight to Egypt (Matt 2:13–18). The Lukan birth narrative contains an account of Elizabeth's pregnancy with John, which precedes Mary's by only a few months (Luke 1:13–17; 39–45, 57–66). Taken singly, these narratives are not problematic. But when read together they are, for they raise this question: If John and Jesus were born only months apart (so Luke), and if Jesus had to escape Herod's murderous soldiers (so Matthew), how, then, did the infant John escape the soldiers? The Infancy Gospel of James answers this question with its stories of Elizabeth fleeing to the hills with John and of Zechariah refusing to disclose the whereabouts of his son (22:5–23:9).

But by answering this question, the author also reveals the fiction of the epilogue (25:1–3). In other words, since the question of John's fate could have arisen only after the Gospels of Matthew and Luke were written, that is, after 80–90, and since James himself died in 62,[12] he could not, therefore, have composed this document that is attributed to him. Once the epilogue is revealed to be a fiction, however, scholars have had to seek more credible answers to the questions of authorship, dating, and provenance.

3.2 Authorship

Once the Infancy Gospel of James is seen to be a pseudonymous writing, the chances of knowing much about the author are minimal. In fact, even statements about the author's cultural background and literary abilities, at

---

10. See further, Daniels, *Manuscript Tradition*, 1.2–4.
11. For the case for literary dependence, see Massaux, *Influence*, 2.227–36.
12. On the death of James, see Josephus, *Ant.* 20.200, and Pratscher, *Herrenbruder Jakobus*, 231.

least as they can be inferred from the document itself, are often vague and seldom conclusive. For example, a Jewish background is often assumed, based on the author's extensive use of the Septuagint, or Greek version of the Old Testament, which is apparent right from the beginning, as the names Joachim (1:1) and Anna (2:1), for example, are taken from Sus 4 and 1 Sam 1:2. Indeed, P.A. van Stempvoort considers the Septuagint to be the key to the author's sources and cites many parallels in thought and wording from the stories of Susanna, Judith, and Tobit, as well as further borrowings from the lives of the patriarchs, especially Abraham and Sarah.[13]

The author's use of the Septuagint is undeniable, and specific parallels will be indicated at many points in the Notes to the Translation (see also below 5.1). But the author's background was not so focused on Jewish scriptures and stories that the author should be characterized as writing a 'Christian midrash.'[14] Indeed, the author himself hardly came from a Jewish milieu, as there are not only problems with Palestinian geography (see below 3.4) but also little knowledge of Jewish life and customs that does not come from the Septuagint (see below 5.1).[15] The author in fact betrays a much wider cultural awareness. For example, other scholars have noted various contacts with the broader Greco-Roman world, including the birth myths of Dionysos and Mithras[16] as well as popular Greek novels.[17] Recently, Z. Thundy has even pointed out some contacts with Indian traditions about the Buddha.[18]

In addition to a wide cultural awareness, the author of the Infancy Gospel of James displays some literary talent and training. To be sure, his story is not without its problems (see below 4.1), but overall the literary judgment has been positive. Thus scholars point to the author's clear and simple language as being appropriate for a story of innocence and birth,[19] and others see stylistic artistry in the way in which the author has treated parallel themes.[20] More specifically, the lament of Anna (3:2-8) is almost poetic, and even some rhetorical training shines through in the use of antithesis (4:9; 19:18), comparison (1:8; 2:9; 13:5), and dialogue (13:6-10; 15:1-18; 19:1-11; 23:1-8).

---

13. See van Stempvoort, "Protevangelium," 415-20. See also Cothenet, "Protévangile," 4261-63.
14. See Cothenet, "Protévangile," 4259.
15. That the author was not a Jewish Christian is widely held today (see, e.g., Pratscher, *Herrenbruder Jakobus*, 224; Cullmann, "Protevangelium," 423-24; Elliott, *Apocryphal New Testament*, 49), although a Jewish milieu was often assumed previously (see, e.g., de Strycker, "Protévangile," 353; Smid, *Commentary*, 21; and esp. Cothenet, "Protévangile," 4267).
16. See, e.g., Michaelis, *Apokryphen Schriften*, 70, and Vielhauer, *Geschichte*, 671.
17. See, e.g., van Stempvoort, "Protevangelium," 416 n. 2.
18. See now Thundy, *Buddha and Christ*, 75-155.
19. See Cothenet, "Protévangile," 4256.
20. See van Stempvoort, "Protevangelium," 411.

In other words, the author of the Infancy Gospel of James emerges as a figure of some literary ability and training who possessed a bookish acquaintance with Judaism but also an awareness of many cultural traditions.

3.3 Dating

Although the characterization of the author of the Infancy Gospel of James remains frustratingly vague, merely a figure of wide experience and some literary talent and training, the matter of dating this gospel can be resolved with greater satisfaction. To be sure, dates for the Infancy Gospel of James have ranged widely over the years—from the mid-second century to as late as the fifth.[21] The later end of this range was proposed by scholars at the beginning of this century, but the earlier centuries are preferred by scholars today.

This shift to an earlier dating has come about in large part because papyrus discoveries rule out the later dates. For example, Papyrus Bodmer V dates from the early fourth century.[22] In addition, scholars have shown that the Infancy Gospel of James was probably known to Christian writers of the third century. Origin (d. 253/54), for example, refers to the brothers of Jesus as sons of Joseph by a previous marriage (*Comm. in Matt.* 10.17), a view in accord with the Infancy Gospel of James (9:8). Clement of Alexandria (d. before 212) even more clearly knows this gospel, as he speaks of a midwife who attended Mary and proclaimed her to be a virgin (*Strom.* 7.16.93), precisely what is said in the Infancy Gospel of James (19:16–18). Consequently, allowing some time for this gospel to become known to Christians, scholars now favor the late second century as the most likely dating for the Infancy Gospel of James.[23]

One scholar in particular has tried to secure a more precise dating. P. A. van Stempvoort places the composition of the Infancy Gospel of James between the years 178 and 204.[24] The earlier date is the year Celsus wrote his *True Doctrine*, in which Mary is attacked on several fronts—for her poverty and low social status, which Celsus illustrated by claiming that she had made her living from spinning; and for her lack of purity, which, he said, resulted in her having been convicted of adultery.[25] The author of the Infancy Gospel of James, van Stempvoort claims, directly meets these attacks, making the gospel an apologetic writing in which the attacks on Mary are refuted by portraying her as having been born into a wealthy and socially prominent family (1:1; 6:6) and raised in the absolute purity of the

---

21. See the discussion in de Strycker, *Protévangile*, 6–12 and 412–18.
22. On the dating of this important ms, see now de Strycker, "Handschriften," 579.
23. See, e.g., de Strycker, *Protévangile*, 418; Pratscher, *Herrenbruder Jakobus*, 224 n. 69; Cothenet, "Protévangile," 4257; and Cullmann, "Protevangelium," 423.
24. See van Stempvoort, "Protevangelium," 413–23.
25. For Celsus' attacks, see Hoffmann, *Celsus*, 57.

Temple itself (8:2); and if she did spin, she did so only as a specially selected virgin and only in order to make a new veil for the Temple (10:1–8).[26]

The other date, namely 204, is the likely year Hippolytus wrote his homily on Susanna which he incorporated into his commentary on the book of Daniel. This homily attests to the popularity of the figure of Susanna among Christians in the first years of the third century, and this popularity, van Stempvoort argues, explains the clear parallels between Susanna and the portrayals of Anna and Mary in the Infancy Gospel of James.[27]

While van Stempvoort's dating largely confirms the scholarly consensus, it must still be asked if his dating is not too precise, especially at the lower end. On the one hand, it is not clear that the Infancy Gospel of James is directly answering Celsus' charges since they hardly started with him.[28] On the other, it is also not clear that the Infancy Gospel of James is to be regarded as primarily apologetic in origin and aim, a point that will be taken up later (see below 4.3). In short, the upper limit of about 200 has little to commend it, and even the lower limit of 180 should be pushed back to, say, 160, if the gospel is dependent on Justin Martyr's *Dialogue with Trypho*, written about 155, which refers to Jesus' birth in a cave (*Dial.* 78.5), or even to 150, if G. Zervos is correct in seeing Justin Martyr as being dependent on the Infancy Gospel of James.[29]

3.4 Provenance

The question of provenance for the Infancy Gospel of James is the most difficult to answer, and perhaps only negative answers are possible. Scholars have long been confident that the author was not from Palestine since he displays 'an astonishing ignorance,' to use J. Quasten's language, of Palestinian geography.[30] He is confused about the relation of Jerusalem, Judea, and Bethlehem (21:1), and he seems to place the wilderness too close to Jerusalem (4:5; 25:1).[31] In addition, some scholars rule out the Greek mainland, the Greek islands, and the Greek cities of western Asia Minor on the grounds that the Greek of the Infancy Gospel of James is too impoverished in vocabulary and syntax to have come from such centers of Greek language and culture.[32] Consequently, only Egypt, Syria, and interior Asia Minor remain, but arguments favoring any of these areas are tenuous at

26. See van Stempvoort, "Protevangelium," 413–15.
27. See van Stempvoort, "Protevangelium," 415–23.
28. See Shaberg, *Illegitimacy of Jesus*, 22–24.
29. See Zervos, "Dating," 432–34.
30. See Quasten, *Patrology*, 121. Quasten's judgment is often repeated: Michaelis, *Apokryphen Schriften*, 71; de Strycker, *Protévangile*, 353; Cothenet, "Protévangile," 4267; Cullmann, "Protevangelium," 423–24; and Elliott, *Apocryphal New Testament*, 49.
31. See further de Strycker, *Protévangile*, 419–21.
32. See de Strycker, *Protévangile*, 421–23.

best. For example, the laurel tree in Anna's garden (2:8) has led some scholars to see a connection with Syrian Antioch, which was known as the laurel city.[33] Likewise, the identity of mountains and wilderness (1:9; 4:5) has led others to posit Egypt where such an identity holds.[34] But neither connection is convincing, so that it is still necessary to be content with the negative answer that the author did not write in Palestine.[35]

But even this seemingly minimal and safe answer has been challenged recently, at least in a preliminary way. M. Lowe notes that the wilderness does begin on the eastern slopes of the mountains adjoining Jerusalem, so that the identity of mountains and wilderness holds for Palestine as well.[36] He also points out that the author consistently refers to Jews as a Palestinian writer would have, namely by using the term 'Israel' rather than 'Judeans,' the term preferred by writers outside Palestine.[37] But even Lowe must resort to excision at 21:1 in order to save the author from the confusion of going from Bethlehem into Judea (when Bethlehem is already in the area called Judea).[38] Therefore, while the widely-held negative answer of 'not Palestine' has not been ruled out, it may be best at present to withhold judgment on the matter of provenance, at least until new evidence or arguments are forthcoming.

4. The Literary Unity and Purpose of the Infancy Gospel of James

4.1 Questions about Literary Unity

Every reader of the Infancy Gospel of James has noted the various peculiarities in style, structure, and details that have raised questions about the unity of the work. The one stylistic peculiarity that is especially noticeable is the abrupt shift in narrative style from third to first person. This shift begins with the opening of Joseph's vision (18:3) and does not end until well into Joseph's conversation with the midwife (19:9). Another peculiarity is structural. Mary is clearly the central character of the story, but she is eventually eclipsed by Joseph from the moment he goes off in search of a midwife and has his vision (18:1–19:9). In fact, both Joseph and Mary recede into the background as the two midwives and the parents of John become the focus of attention in the later chapters of the gospel. Finally, several problematic details have drawn scholars' queries. For example, Joseph is said to have received Mary from the Temple when she was twelve

---

33. See Smid, *Commentary*, 175–76.
34. See de Strycker, *Protévangile*, 353–54 and 422–23.
35. See, e.g., Michaelis, *Apokryphen Schriften*, 71.
36. See Lowe, "IOYΔAIOI," 62 n. 24.
37. See Lowe, "IOYΔAIOI," 59–62.
38. See Lowe, "IOYΔAIOI," 62 n. 24.

years old (8:3). He leaves her at his home shortly afterwards, and even though Mary conceives when she is sixteen (12:3), Joseph on his return home is personally held responsible for her being pregnant (15:4–6).[39]

Given the nineteenth century penchant to resolve literary anomalies by proposing multiple sources, it is not surprising that earlier scholars proposed various sources to explain the peculiarities in the Infancy Gospel of James. Thus, A. Hilgenfeld explained the shift to a first person narrative style by positing a separate source,[40] and A. Berendts did likewise for the peculiar prominence of Zechariah at the end of the gospel.[41] But it was A. von Harnack who, in 1897, offered a comprehensive source theory and literary history.[42] He identified three sources: one about Mary (chaps 1–17), a second about Joseph (18–20), and a third about Zechariah (22–24). All were combined, Harnack claimed, sometime before the mid-fourth century.

Harnack's source theory has proved influential, for, even if some parts of it no longer commend themselves, such as the late dating, many scholars still regard the Infancy Gospel of James to be a composite work.[43] Nevertheless, Harnack's influence is waning today, in part because the penchant for source theories has declined but also because the case for literary unity is argued more effectively. For example, inconsistencies in detail are now explained by appeal to varying oral traditions available to the author.[44] Similarly, the shift to the first person narrative seems less abrupt once parallel instances are gathered and the rhetorical function appreciated.[45] In addition, the extensive attention in the final chapters to Elizabeth and Zechariah is not as problematic as might appear at first sight, for their actions are also related to Mary's giving birth to Jesus.[46] Especially noteworthy is the overall consistency in vocabulary and syntax which also argues in favor of literary unity.[47] And further arguments favoring unity will emerge in the course of this analysis (see below 4.3).

4.2 Mary's Purity—The Unifying Theme

If recent scholarship favors the literary unity of the Infancy Gospel of James, there is still the matter of defining that unity more precisely—both thematically and structurally—so that an understanding of the author's

---

39. For a convenient summary of various problematic details, see Elliott, *Apocryphal New Testament*, 51 and n. 2.
40. See Hilgenfeld, *Untersuchungen*, 153–61.
41. See Berendts, *Studien*, 23–47.
42. See von Harnack, *Chronologie*, 600–3.
43. See, e.g., Michaelis, *Apokryphen Schriften*, 65–66; Koester, "Evangelienliteratur," 1484; Pratscher, *Herrenbruder Jakobus*, 222; and Cullman, "Protevangelium," 424.
44. See Vielhauer, *Geschichte*, 669–70.
45. See Bovon, "Suspension of Time," 395.
46. See Smid, *Commentary*, 179–80.
47. See de Strycker, *Protévangile*, 6–13, and Elliott, *Apocryphal New Testament*, 50.

purpose in writing it can emerge. And what unifies the narrative is the theme of Mary's purity. This purity is especially evident in the claims that Mary was a virgin before, during, and after the birth of Jesus (see esp. 10:2–4; 16:7; 19:18), but the theme is in fact present throughout the gospel. Note how much of the story can be attributed to this theme: Anna's miraculous conception and attention to ritual purity after Mary's birth (4:1, 4; 5:9); Anna's decision, after Mary's first steps, to keep her from touching even the ground (6:3); Anna's transformation of her bedroom into a sanctuary (6:4); Anna's insistence on raising Mary on a ritually pure diet with only unde- filed daughters of the Hebrews as her companions (6:4–5); Mary's child- hood years, from three to twelve years of age, spent in the meticulously pure Temple, where she is fed by the hand of a heavenly messenger (7:7–8:2); Mary's stay at Joseph's house where he immediately absents himself (9:11–12); Mary's being engaged, with other virgins, in that most virtuous of women's tasks, that of spinning thread for a new veil for the Temple (10:1–8); Joseph's characterization as an old man and widower and hence as having no interest in Mary as a woman (9:8); Jesus' brothers, and presu- mably the other children of Mary (see Matt 13:55–56), being assigned to Joseph's earlier marriage (17:2–3; 19:9); and the high priest's public proc- lamation of Mary's innocence and purity (16:7). In short, it is difficult to imagine anyone more pure than Mary.

4.3 Apologetic or Encomiastic Purpose?

With purity such a prominent theme in the Infancy Gospel of James, many scholars have tried to account for it by postulating an apologetic purpose for the writing as a whole. Indeed, the author, it is claimed, seems to be protesting too much and hence must have been defending Mary against attacks on her character, such as those already identified above in Celsus' *True Doctrine* (see above 3.3). An apologetic purpose, therefore, is widely presumed among scholars.[48]

An apologetic reading of the Infancy Gospel of James has much to commend it. The test of Mary and Joseph that leads to the high priest's public exoneration of her (15:10–16:7) as well as Salome's physical exam- ination of Mary after she has given birth to Jesus (19:19–20:3) seem especially susceptible to such a reading. Moreover, given the general currency of slanders against Mary and Jesus,[49] apologetic designs cannot be ruled out entirely.

But apology hardly needs to be the principal purpose. It does not explain the gospel as a whole, and even passages that do admit an apologetic

48. See, e.g., van Stempvoort, "Protevangelium," 410; Smid, *Commentary*, 15–17; Pratscher, *Herrenbruder Jakobus*, 223; Cothenet, "Protévangile," 4268; Allen, "Prot- evangelium," 515–17; and Elliott, *Aprocryphal New Testament*, 49–50.
49. See Hoffmann, *Jesus*, 36–60.

reading permit another one. For example, Mary's role in spinning the scarlet and purple threads for the Temple veil (10:8–10; 11:4; 12:1) functions less to counter the attack that she spun for a living than to underscore Mary's virtue, not to mention pointing ahead to the ironic coincidence that the very veil she had helped to make was split in two at Jesus' death (cf. Matt 27:51).

In fact, instead of an apologetic purpose for the Infancy Gospel of James, an encomiastic one is worth considering. In other words, when viewed from this perspective, defending Mary becomes a secondary, even incidental, purpose; rather, the author's primary purpose was to praise Mary. Such a purpose and especially its implications for the structure of the Infancy Gospel of James have not been developed sufficiently and so require rather detailed discussion.[50]

Praise of a person, object, event or whatever was a standard subject in the educational curriculum of the Greco-Roman world. Specifically, students learned how to compose a praise, or ἐγκώμιον, during their instruction in pre-rhetorical composition.[51] Fortunately, the very instructions for praising a person have been preserved in teaching manuals called *Progymnasmata*.[52] These manuals contain a graded series of fourteen compositional exercises, and each exercise is defined, classified into sub-types, and provided with instructions on the structure and style appropriate for that particular composition. Midway through this series of exercises is the ἐγκώμιον, which is defined as 'a composition that sets forth the excellent qualities of its subject,' to cite Hermogenes,[53] whose *Progymnasmata* are contemporary with the Infancy Gospel of James. He then sub-divides the ἐγκώμιον into those of people, things, animals, plants, and places.[54] Of special interest to us are the instructions regarding the structure and topics of an ἐγκώμιον whose subject is a person. Aphthonius, another writer of *Progymnasmata*, gives the following structure for an ἐγκώμιον: It begins with an introduction, and then discusses family background, upbringing, adult pursuits, and especially the deeds that illustrate the person's virtues; then a comparison with someone of equal or greater virtue is provided; and it ends with a conclusion that is rather more like a prayer.[55] Hermogenes and Aphthonius also provide specific instructions for filling in this formal outline, such as

50. See the statement of Cullmann ("Protevangelium," 425): The Infancy Gospel of James "was written for the glorification of Mary." But the statement is not developed in terms of the structure of the gospel.

51. On this portion of the educational curriculum, see Bonner, *Education*, 250–76, esp. 264–67.

52. On the *Progymnasmata*, see Kennedy, *Rhetoric*, 52–73, and esp. Hunger, *Literatur*, 1.92–120. The best introduction to the rhetorical culture that so dominated these centuries is Russell, *Declamation*.

53. Hermogenes, *Progymn.* 7 (p. 14, 17–18 Rabe).

54. See Hermogenes, *Progymn.* 7 (pp. 14, 20 - 15, 2 Rabe).

55. See Aphthonius, *Progymn.* 8 (p. 22, 1–11 Rabe).

including an account of the person's birth, especially if marvels attended it;[56] organizing the deeds around the four cardinal virtues or presenting them chronologically in narrative form;[57] and including the manner of death, the subsequent renown of the person, or the fame of the descendants, if they are appropriate.[58]

The Infancy Gospel of James, of course, is not an ἐγκώμιον as would have been written in a classroom. For one thing it is not a speech, as is envisioned in the *Progymnasmata*. For another, the author identifies his work as an ἱστορία, or 'history' (25:1; cf. 1:1; 25:3), not as an ἐγκώμιον. Scholars have recognized the importance of the word ἱστορία for analyzing this gospel, but their emphasis has been too much on content, especially on this gospel's similarities with the 'histories' of such Jewish figures as Susanna, Tobit, and Judith.[59] This emphasis has meant a neglect of the formal significance of the word ἱστορία, including its relation with the ἐγκώμιον.

Since the relation between ἱστορία and ἐγκώμιον is not immediately obvious, a short digression is necessary here. The term ἱστορία recalls one of the other *progymnasmata*, namely διήγημα, or 'narrative,' one of whose sub-types is the διήγημα ἱστορικόν, or 'historical narrative.'[60] Such narratives, in contrast to mythical, fictional, and judicial ones, set forth events that happened in the past.[61] The historical narrative, however, was developing in a certain way during the very period when the Infancy Gospel of James was written. A contemporary of the author, the satirist Lucian of Samosata, in a short account on how to write history, notes, to his dismay, that historians of his day were writing almost entirely with an encomiastic purpose in view.[62] In other words, ἱστορία was becoming ἐγκώμιον. Consequently, although the author of the Infancy Gospel of James used the term ἱστορία to characterize his writing, that does not mean that the conventions regarding the ἐγκώμιον become irrelevant. Lucian's lament suggests the opposite, and in fact it will soon become apparent that the Infancy Gospel of James follows closely the instructions for writing an encomium, and those instructions will provide us with clear signals to the author's intent, namely, to praise his subject, Mary.

The first topic of an ἐγκώμιον is family background, beginning with the general notion of race (γένος) and then moving on to nationality (ἔθνος),

56. See Hermogenes, *Progymn.* 7 (p. 15, 20–21 Rabe).
57. See Aphthonius, *Progymn.* 8 (p. 22, 6–9 Rabe).
58. See Hermogenes, *Progymn.* 7 (pp. 16, 23 - 17, 4 Rabe).
59. See, e.g., van Stempvoort, "Protevangelium," 415–19, and esp. Allen, "Protevangelium," 513–15.
60. See Hermogenes, *Progymn.* 2 (p. 4, 16–20 Rabe).
61. See Aphthonius, *Progymn.* 2 (p. 2, 19–22 Rabe).
62. See Lucian, *How to Write History*, 7–8, and Georgiadou and Larmour, "Historiography," 1450–78, esp. 1460–62 ("History and Encomium").

region (πατρίς), ancestors (πρόγονοι), and parents (πατέρες).[63] If we turn to the Infancy Gospel of James we recognize that the opening chapters are devoted to this encomiastic topic of γένος. In fact, the initial phrase 'According to the records of the twelve tribes of Israel' (1:1) identifies Mary's γένος, and the following narrative focuses on her πατέρες, though not without some mention of πρόγονοι. Thus her parents, Joachim and Anna, easily redound to Mary's credit because they are portrayed as being prosperous, prominent, and pious (1:1–5), and in the course of narrating their efforts to have a child, there are also references to illustrious ancestors, such as Abraham (1:8) and Sarah (2:9). Attentive readers, moreover, would recognize allusions to other ancestors, such as Joachim being modeled on his namesake from the story of Susanna (1:1; cf. Sus 4) and Anna on the mother of the prophet Samuel (4:2; cf. 1 Sam 1–2). In addition, marvels attend the conception, if not the birth, of Mary, as both Joachim and Anna receive divine messages that Anna is pregnant (4:1, 4), and Joachim gets additional confirmation of God's mercy regarding his wife's pregnancy in the revelatory mirror that adorns the priest's clothing (5:1–3). Mary clearly has illustrious ancestors and family.

Upbringing or nurture (ἀνατροφή) is the next topic of an ἐγκώμιον, and Mary's extraordinary ἀνατροφή receives detailed treatment. Special attention, for example, is given to the efforts of Anna to raise her daughter in purity by transforming her bedroom into a sanctuary (6:4–5), and this purity is only intensified when Mary is taken at three years of age to the Temple (7:4–10), where, until she is twelve, she is fed by the hand of a heavenly messenger (8:2). This divine ἀνατροφή, in fact, is especially praiseworthy and receives special emphasis because it becomes thematic, used throughout the narrative as a shorthand way of referring to her extraordinary upbringing (13:7; 15:11; 19:8).

Mary's childhood upbringing ends, of course, when at age twelve she is no longer able to stay in the Temple (8:3–4), and the priests must find a husband, or at least a guardian, for her. With divine guidance Joseph is selected as the guardian (8:5–9:11). At this point, therefore, the author takes up the next encomiastic topic: Mary's adult pursuits, skills, and habits (ἐπιτηδεύματα καὶ τέχνη καὶ νόμοι).[64] Accordingly, we read of Mary's being selected, along with other virgins, to help in making a new veil for the Temple (10:1–5); she is assigned the purple and scarlet threads (10:8) and is depicted as responsibly using her domestic skill to carry out this adult pursuit (10:10; 11:4; 12:1–2).

The most important part of an ἐγκώμιον, however, is the presentation of

---

63. See Aphthonius, *Progymn.* 8 (p. 22, 2–3 Rabe).
64. See Aphthonius, *Progymn.* 8 (p. 22, 3–4 Rabe).

the person's virtuous deeds,[65] and the importance of Mary's virtues is shown narratively by the amount of space devoted to documenting her virtue, especially her $\sigma\omega\phi\rho\sigma\acute{\nu}\nu\eta$, or self-control. Thus when Mary is six months' pregnant (13:1), the author provides lengthy accounts of her adamant insistence on her self-control and consequent purity in the face of disbelief first from Joseph (13:1–14:8) and then from the high priest (15:4–16:8). To both she insists that she has not had sex with any man (13:8; 15:13), and her insistence is upheld with divine confirmation. Thus Joseph has a dream in which a heavenly messenger informs him that Mary's child is of the holy spirit (14:5–7), and the high priest demands that both Joseph and Mary take the Lord's drink test, after which he publicly exonerates her: 'If the Lord God has not exposed your sin, then neither do I condemn you' (16:7). Mary has, in short, exercised self-control ever since leaving the Temple.

Shortly afterward, Joseph and Mary make the trip to Bethlehem (17:1), and even here Mary and her virtue remain in the foreground. The author expands the canonical accounts by detailing the arrangements Joseph made for Mary's giving birth. He finds a cave to give her privacy (18:1) and then goes off in search of a Hebrew midwife to assist her (18:2; 19:1–12). The midwife arrives too late to be of assistance (19:15–17), but her confession announces a miracle attending the birth of Jesus: 'A virgin has given birth' (19:18). Even a skeptical Salome can only confirm the truth of this confession (19:19–20:4). When the visit of the astrologers puts the infant Jesus at risk (21:1–12), it is Mary, not Joseph, as in the canonical version (see Matt 2:13–14), who protects him by wrapping him in strips of cloth and hiding him in a feeding trough (22:1–4). Courage as well as self-control are among Mary's virtuous deeds.

The story now shifts to Elizabeth and Zechariah, who likewise must protect John from the threat posed by Herod's soldiers (22:5–24:12). This shift to the parents of John has troubled scholars, as we have seen (see above 4.1). And even if they no longer postulate the use of a separate source, as was done formerly, they still have difficulty in seeing these chapters as part of a coherent structure for the entire gospel.[66] Given an encomiastic purpose for the Infancy Gospel of James, however, these chapters create no difficulties, for they also follow the conventions of writing an $\grave{\epsilon}\gamma\kappa\acute{\omega}\mu\iota o\nu$, specifically the instruction calling for the use of $\sigma\acute{\nu}\gamma\kappa\rho\iota\sigma\iota s$, or comparison.[67] Thus the extraordinary courage of Zechariah in the face of Herod's

---

65. See Aphthonius, *Progymn.* 8 (p. 22, 5–6 Rabe).
66. See, e.g., Allen, "Protevangelium," 511, whose outline of the Infancy Gospel of James cannot account for this section.
67. See Aphthonius, *Progymn.* 8 (p. 22, 9–10 Rabe).

threats to learn the whereabouts of his son (23:1–8) and his eventual martyrdom as the price of remaining silent (23:9–24:11) provide a positive comparison which functions to highlight further Mary's own courage in hastening to protect Jesus and her virtuous character generally.

In addition, certain other encomiastic topics—manner of death, subsequent renown, and fame of descendants—deserve brief mention. To be sure, the alleged circumstances of James composing his ἱστορία shortly after the death of Herod in 4 B.C.E. precludes any reference to the manner of Mary's death, but various statements scattered throughout the Infancy Gospel of James clearly attest to her subsequent renown and to the fame of her son. For example, Mary's subsequent renown is anticipated as soon as she is conceived. Anna is told by a messenger of the Lord: 'Your child will be talked about all over the world' (4:1). Other anticipations are voiced by Joachim (6:7), by the high priests (6:9; 7:7; 12:2), by the midwife (19:17), and even by Mary herself, if only incredulously (12:6). Similarly, the fame of her son is predicted, as a heavenly messenger tells both Mary and Joseph that 'Jesus . . . will save his people from their sins' (11:8; 14:6). Indeed, all nature recognizes his significance by stopping momentarily when Mary is giving birth (18:3–11). Finally, the Infancy Gospel of James ends with a doxology: 'Grace will be with all those who fear the Lord. Amen' (25:4), a style that recalls the instruction to conclude an ἐγκώμιον with something rather like a prayer.[68]

It should now be obvious that the Infancy Gospel of James gains in coherence when it is viewed as an ἱστορία which has the structure and purpose of an ἐγκώμιον. Mary's race, ancestors, parents, upbringing, adult pursuits, skills, and virtues; the comparison with Elizabeth and Zechariah to the same threat posed by Herod; and even the scattered anticipations of her subsequent renown and the fame of her son—all these topics are conventional in an ἐγκώμιον. Their use in the Infancy Gospel of James not only gives it a transparent structure and supplies it with recognizable themes and details from beginning to end, but it also strengthens the case for the literary unity of the whole. In addition, if its purpose is not so much to defend Mary as to praise her, then the audience for the Infancy Gospel of James is not so much those outside the church, whether they are Jewish or pagan detractors of Mary as those inside the church, Christians who were familiar with Mary from the canonical accounts but who were eager to learn more about her and why she was chosen to be the mother of the Son of God. For these Christians the Infancy Gospel of James may have answered some attacks on Mary which they had heard, but it certainly presented her much more as a person who was worthy of the highest praise.

---

68. See Aphthonius, *Progymn.* 8 (p. 22, 10–11 Rabe).

5. Literary Borrowings and Innovations

Even if, as argued above, the Infancy Gospel of James is not a mere compilation of three earlier sources but a carefully crafted encomiastic ἱστορία, it does not follow that the author was not dependent on earlier literature, not to mention more general cultural values, conventions, and predispositions. In fact, the literary and cultural borrowings are legion, and a brief survey of them will set the Infancy Gospel of James more firmly in its literary and cultural context.

5.1 The Septuagint

Scholars have recently emphasized the extent to which the author of the Infancy Gospel of James drew on the Septuagint, or Greek translation of the Hebrew Scriptures, for historical analogies, turns of phrase, and information about Jewish life and practices.[69] The Notes to the Translation will identify these borrowings in detail, but a small sample here will establish the overall pattern within which to size up any one borrowing.

Most obvious of the borrowings from the Septuagint are those explicit references to figures of Israelite history who serve as models for the characters in the Infancy Gospel of James. For example, when Joachim and Anna lament their childlessness, they recall the analogous circumstances of Abraham and Sarah (1:8; 2:9; cf. Gen 21:1–7), and Anna's later expression of joy at being able to show her baby to the people echoes a statement of Sarah (6:9; cf. Gen 21:7). Similarly, when Joseph objects to having to receive Mary from the Temple, the high priest persuades him to do so by recalling the fate of Dathan, Abiron, and Kore (9:9; cf. Num 16:1–35). And later, when Joseph returns home from building houses and finds Mary pregnant, he compares himself to Adam, who had found Eve deceived and defiled (13:1–5; cf. Gen 3:1–20), and he even asks Mary the same question as God had Eve: 'Why have you done this?' (13:6; cf. Gen 3:13).

Explicit citations, however, hardly exhaust the borrowings. Throughout the Infancy Gospel of James are turns of phrase that come from the Septuagint. For example, the oft-used oath formula 'As the Lord God lives . . .' (4:2; 6:3; 13:10; 15:13, 15; 19:19) is also a favorite Septuagintal phrase (Jud 8:19; Ruth 3:13; 1 Sam 14:39; etc.), and other clear echoes of Septuagintal phrasing include Anna's lament, 'The Lord God has greatly shamed me' (2:5; cf. Isa 64:1), and Juthine's taunt to Anna, 'The Lord God has made your womb sterile so you won't bear any children for Israel' (2:6; cf. 1 Sam 1:6). Shorter phrases and individual words are also claimed to have come from the Septuagint. Often it is not clear whether the similar

---

69. See esp. van Stempvoort, "Protevangelium," 415–19; Smid, *Commentary*, 9–12; and Cothenet, "Protévangile," 4261–62.

language is a deliberate echo or just a coincidence, but there are enough of them so that a few at the very least must have been deliberate: for example, 'without spot or blemish (4:5; cf. Exod 29:38; Lev 12:6) and 'fruit of his righteousness' (6:12; cf. Prov 11:30; 13:2; Amos 6:12).

At times, moreover, the Septuagint served as a source of information about Jewish life. For example, the author makes use of the Septuagint for specific laws regarding marriage (14:2-4; cf. Deut 22:23-24) and childbirth (5:9; cf. Lev 12:1-8). There are also details about the Temple: the third step of the altar (7:9; cf. Ezek 43:13-17) and the various threads used in making the Temple veil (10:7; cf. Exod 26:31, 36; 35:25). In addition, the episodes involving the widowers' staffs (8:7-8) and the drink test (16:3-5) more or less follow procedures outlined in the Septuagint (Num 17:1-11; 5:11-32). And several narrative details ought not to go unnoticed: Joachim's being 'very rich' (1:1; cf. Sus 4) and aspects of Anna's situation, such as her childlessness but later having a child whom she dedicates to God (2:1-6; 4:1-2; cf. 1 Sam 1:1-11).

5.2 New Testament Writings (outside the canonical Birth Stories)

The Septuagint was not the only literary source used by the author of the Infancy Gospel of James. Not surprisingly, he also made frequent use of early Christian writings. Turns of phrase suggest a familiarity with several New Testament writings. A limited sample includes: 'The great day of the Lord' (1:4; 2:2; cf. Acts 2:20), 'he came down from the Temple of the Lord acquitted' (5:4; cf. Luke 18:14), 'the surrounding territory' (8:9; cf. Luke 4:14), 'cry bitterly' (13:2; 15:13; cf. Matt 26:20), 'handing innocent blood over to a death sentence' (14:3; cf. Matt 27:4; Luke 24:20), 'under God's mighty hand' (15:17; cf. 1 Pet 5:6), 'neither do I condemn you' (16:7; cf. John 8:11), 'unless I insert my finger' (19:19; cf. John 20:25), 'she was instantly healed' (20:11; cf. Luke 8:47), and 'The Lord will receive my spirit' (23:8; cf. Acts 7:59).

Besides these turns of phrase, however, the author of the Infancy Gospel of James takes specific details from these writings and weaves them into his story. For example, at Jesus' death the Temple veil is said to have been split in two (Matt 27:51). This detail may lie behind the author's decision to have Mary help in making the Temple veil (10:1-8), giving it further, if ironic, significance. In addition, the mention of the murder of a certain Zechariah between Temple and altar (Matt 23:35) is the source for the murder of Zechariah, the father of John (23:1-9). The mention of Joseph being a carpenter (Matt 13:55) is taken over (9:1), though now used to keep him and Mary apart (9:12).

5.3 The Canonical Birth Stories

The most profound borrowing, of course, comes from the canonical birth stories of Matt 1-2 and Luke 1-2. That the author of the Infancy Gospel of

James borrowed so much from these stories is not surprising, given the considerable overlap between his story and theirs. But a brief analysis of the extent of the borrowing will further clarify the literary texture of the Infancy Gospel of James.[70]

The borrowing from the canonical birth stories is especially evident in five sections of the Infancy Gospel of James: 1) the annunciation to Mary and her subsequent visit to Elizabeth (11:1–12:7; cf. Luke 1:26–56), 2) Joseph's dilemma over what to do with a pregnant Mary (14:1–8; cf. Matt 1:18–25), 3) Joseph's and Mary's trip to Bethlehem in response to the census by Augustus (17:1–5; cf. Luke 2:1–7), 4) the visit of the astrologers (21:1–12; cf. Matt 2:1–12), and 5) Herod's murder of the infants (22:1–2; cf. Matt 2:16–18).

The closest borrowing occurs when the author of the Infancy Gospel of James retells the visit of the astrologers (21:1–12). He narrates the same events—the astrologers following a star; their interview with Herod; their gifts of gold, pure incense, and myrrh; their departure by another route. Even the wording itself, at times, follows the Matthean source rather closely. Still, there are a few innovations, in particular the arrival of the astrologers initially in Bethlehem, not in Jerusalem (21:1; cf. Matt 2:11), and their visit to the cave to worship Jesus, not to the house (21:10; cf. Matt 2:11).

The retelling of the annunciation to Mary and her visit to Elizabeth (11:1–12:7) is also rather close, in that once again we can find much that agrees with its canonical source. For example, Mary does not know the source of the angel's voice, John jumps for joy in Elizabeth's womb when Mary arrives, and the visit lasts three months. And the wording is often a mere paraphrase, especially in the conversations between Mary and the heavenly messenger (11:2–9; cf. Luke 1:28, 31, 32, 35, 38, 42) and between Mary and Elizabeth (12:3–7; cf. Luke 1:39–56).

When we compare the stories of Joseph's pondering over what to do with Mary, now that she is pregnant, we find more innovation. To be sure, the heavenly messenger's statement to Joseph is repeated almost verbatim (14:5–6; cf. Matt 1:20–21), and Joseph's decision 'I'll divorce her quietly' (14:4) is so thoughtlessly taken from Matthew's story (Matt 1:19) that it becomes problematic in its new context. Nevertheless, the innovations dominate. The story has been considerably expanded with new material at the outset, including a soliloquy by Joseph about Mary's condition (13:1–5) and a confrontation between Joseph and Mary (13:6–10), both of which precede the point at which the Infancy Gospel of James begins to borrow from Matthew (14:1–4). And, of course, the ending is different, too, as

---

70. See further, Michaelis, *Apokryphen Schriften*, 92–95; Cothenet, "Protévangile," 4260–61; and Vorster, "Intertextuality," 264–69.

Joseph does not marry Mary (cf. Matt 1:24), but only renews his commitment to protect her (14:7-8).

The last two sections—the journey to Bethlehem and the murder of the infants—show the author of the Infancy Gospel of James at his innovative best. In fact, the author does little more than allude to the canonical accounts by echoing the beginnings of the canonical stories (17:1; cf. Luke 2:1-4; and 22:1-2; cf. Matt 2:16) before going on to tell of events unknown to Matthew or Luke. Thus in the former case there is the familiar reference to a census and the need for Joseph to travel to Bethlehem to register (17:1; cf. Luke 2:1), but then the author goes off on his own to tell of Joseph's pondering over how to register Mary (17:2-3), of his taking his sons along on the journey (17:5), and of his having to stop before reaching Bethlehem in order for Mary to deliver her child (17:1-10). To these events the author then appends Joseph's search for a midwife (18:2), his vision of the world arrested in movement (18:3-11), his persuading a midwife to help him (19:11), their arriving back too late to be of help (19:12-17), the midwife's confessing that she had witnessed a miracle (19:18), and Salome's skepticism turned into belief (19:19-20:11). Luke's brief report of the trip to Bethlehem is simply overwhelmed by all this new material.

Similarly, in the case of Matthew's story about the murder of the infants, the author of the Infancy Gospel of James starts by telling of Herod's anger at the astrologers' deception and of his plans to murder all infants under two years of age (22:1-2), two points also found in Matthew (2:16). But once again he goes on to tell his own story of how Mary had to protect Jesus by hiding him in a feeding trough (22:3-4), of how Elizabeth fled to the hills with John to escape Herod's soldiers (22:5-9), and of how Zechariah saved his son's life but only with his own (23:1-9).

These innovations do not end, however, with changed or new events. They extend also to characterization. Scholars have long noted these changes, in particular the elevation of minor characters—e.g., Elizabeth and Zechariah—to greater importance, and the creation of new ones as well—e.g., Joachim and Anna.[71] But of particular significance are the changes in the portrayals of Joseph and Mary.[72] For example, Joseph in the Infancy Gospel of James is very different from the Joseph of the canonical accounts. There he is assumed to be of marriageable age and is in fact engaged to Mary (Matt 1:18, 20, 24; Luke 1:27; 2:5) and eventually married (Matt 1:25; cf. Luke 2:41). Here, however, Joseph is an old man and a widower with grown sons and consequently embarrassed to be receiving a young woman from the Temple into his house (9:8). Later in the story he is ashamed to enroll Mary as his wife (17:2-3), later still he denies that she is

71. See, e.g., de Strycker, Protévangile, 354-55; Vielhauer, Geschichte, 672; and Smid, Commentary, passim.
72. See also Vorster, "Intertextuality," 272-73.

his wife (19:9), and he never regards her as anything more than a person deserving his protection (9:7, 11–12; 13:3; 14:8; 16:8; 18:1).

These changes in Joseph's characterization are necessitated by the author's emphasis on Mary's purity, and this emphasis has likewise changed Mary's portrayal in the Infancy Gospel of James. To be sure, she is a virgin in the canonical accounts (Matt 1:23; Luke 1:27), but there the word is used more in its ordinary sense—of a young woman of marriageable age. Here, however, Mary is a virgin in an extraordinary sense—of a young woman of singular purity and of unending duration. That her purity is central to her characterization is evident in the oft-repeated description of her as having been raised in the Temple and fed by a heavenly messenger (8:2; 13:7; 15:6, 11; 19:8). And unlike the canonical accounts in which Jesus is merely Mary's first-born child (Matt 13:55–56), the author of the Infancy Gospel of James asserts that Mary continued to be a virgin after giving birth to Jesus (19:18); Joseph's and Mary's other children are now assigned to a marriage of Joseph's before he received Mary as his ward (9:8).

In sum, it is clear that the author of the Infancy Gospel of James borrowed extensively from the canonical birth stories, but it is just as clear that he did not hesitate to be innovative in retelling those stories. Indeed, the innovations involve rearranged details, new events, and changes in characterization—all of which give the Infancy Gospel of James a familiar yet fresh quality.

5.4 Cultural Borrowings

As extensive as the borrowings from the Septuagint and the canonical gospels are, they are not the only ones. The Infancy Gospel of James also reflects many literary and social conventions from the larger Greco-Roman world. Indeed, the very use of the Septuagint and the gospel stories has rightly been called 'an ecclesiastical Atticism,' or the attempt on the part of Christian writers to parallel the similar use of Homer and other classic texts among Greek writers of the author's day.[73] And we have already drawn attention to the influence of Greek rhetoric and in particular to the use of the encomiastic topics learned in school which account for both the structure and the contents of the Infancy Gospel of James.

But specific parallels between the Infancy Gospel of James and Greco-Roman literature, especially those popular narratives known as Greek romances,[74] will further illustrate the importance of reading this Christian writing within its larger social and intellectual context. Scholars have occasionally noted similarities in style and motifs between it and the romances—for example, Anna's lament (3:2–8) and the numerous laments

---

73. For the phrase "ecclesiastical Atticism," see van Stempvoort, "Protevangelium," 419.
74. On the romances and their significance for early Christian literature, see Hock, "Greek Novel," 127–46, and Pervo, "Early Christian Fiction," 239–54.

in the romances.[75] But the parallels go beyond form, for Daphnis' lament in Longus' *Daphnis and Chloe* also takes place in a garden,[76] and Joseph's very language in his lament over Mary's pregnancy ('What sort of face should I present to the Lord God?') (13:2) matches the language of Clitophon's lament in Achilles Tatius' *Leucippe and Clitophon*.[77] Moreover, the episode of the Lord's drink test to assure the purity of Mary (16:3–6) is similar in function to the water test of Leucippe's purity.[78]

Other parallels show more than similarities in language or action. They also clarify conventions of behavior whose functions are left unsaid in the Infancy Gospel of James and hence are lost on a modern reader. For example, when Mary hears a male voice at the well and then rushes home to her work with the scarlet and purple threads (11:1–4), it is not said why she acts as she does. But in Longus' *Daphnis and Chloe* we learn why, for in this romance we have discussions between the young shepherdess Chloe and her mother Nape in which it becomes clear that, as Chloe nears marriageable age, her mother wants her at home carding wool and whirling the spindle rather than being outside on the hillsides where she might lose her virginity to some young shepherd in return for apples or roses.[79] In other words, Mary rushes back home to her work in order to assume a posture of purity and innocence.[80]

But the real value of comparing the Infancy Gospel of James with the Greek romances is that they put us in touch with the fundamental values that inform both of them and, by implication, their readers, and the most important shared value is the emphasis placed on σωφροσύνη, or sexual purity. As we have seen, the principal theme of the Infancy Gospel of James is Mary's extraordinary purity. That theme is also fundamental to the romances, as is clear, for example, in Xenophon's *Ephesian Tale*. Its heroine Anthia can claim at the end of this romance in which she and her husband Habrocomes had become separated but are finally reunited that, despite numerous threats to her virtue, she had remained pure for him.[81] Purity was expected not only of women but also of men. Thus the self-control that the high priest expected of Joseph when he took Mary into his house (15:14–16) is mirrored in Anthia's husband Habrocomes, who at one point speaks of his self-control by personifying it as his σύντροφος, or slave-companion since childhood.[82] In short, the social value of purity that was dear to Greco-Roman society as a whole and is reflected literarily in the

75. See Smid, *Commentary*, 36.
76. See Longus, *Daphnis and Chloe* 4.28.3.
77. See Achilles Tatius, *Leucippe and Clitophon* 5.11.3.
78. See Achilles Tatius, *Leucippe and Clitophon* 8.3.3; 6.1- 5; 13.1–14.2.
79. See Longus, *Daphnis and Chloe* 3.4.5; 25.2.
80. On this posture of purity, see also the *Greek Anthology*, 6.39, 47, 48, 174, 247, and 285.
81. See Xenophon, *An Ephesian Tale* 5.14.2.
82. See Xenophon, *An Ephesian Tale* 2.1.4.

romances makes plausible the central claim of the Infancy Gospel of James: Mary was chosen to be the mother of the Son of God because of her extraordinary purity.

6. Subsequent Influences

A brief survey of the subsequent influence of the Infancy Gospel of James is in order because its importance for later Christian art and piety, as has been said, 'cannot be overestimated.'[83] This influence is all the more remarkable, given the gospel's non-canonical status and, in the West, its actual rejection in the Gelasian decree.[84] Hence its influence in the West was largely indirect, in that it was mediated by a later reworking of this gospel into another work, the Gospel of Pseudo-Matthew.[85] In the Byzantine East, however, the Infancy Gospel of James did not face official rejection. In fact, by the early fifth century Mary herself was becoming an important figure in eastern Christianity, as Pulcheria, sister of the Emperor Theodosius II, dedicated her life to the Virgin Mary. She built churches to her in Constantinople, retrieved her relics, and made her the center of public religious ceremony. She also achieved official recognition for Mary through the Council of Ephesus, which, in 431, declared Mary to be Theotokos, or Mother of God.[86] Consequently, Mary's exalted status stimulated interest in her life and prompted many to build and dedicate churches to her. In the following centuries, therefore, Mary's life, as presented in the Infancy Gospel of James, became the basis of feasts to honor Mary during which this gospel was read liturgically, such as on September 8, as part of the celebration of the birth of Mary,[87] and again on November 21, to mark the presentation of Mary in the Temple.[88]

The walls of churches likewise were used to honor Mary, as artists turned to the Infancy Gospel of James for events in her life to serve as subjects for frescoes and mosaics. A cycle of over twenty events from Mary's life became subjects for these artistic renderings. J. Lafontaine-Dosogne has surveyed the evidence in churches throughout the Byzantine world and accorded special attention to the virtually complete cycle, wrought in mosaics, at the Chora Monastery in Constantinople.[89] The cycle begins with Joachim's

---

83. The phrase is Quasten's (*Patrology*, 122).
84. For the Gelasian decree, see Schneemelcher, "Introduction," 38–40.
85. On this gospel, see Elliott, *Apocryphal New Testament*, 84–99.
86. On Pulcheria's efforts on behalf of Mary, see further V. Limberis, *Divine Heiress*, esp. 47–61.
87. See further Trombley and Carr, "Birth," *ODB* 1.291.
88. See further Trombley and Carr, "Presentation," *ODB* 3.1715. Daniels (*Manuscript Tradition*, 1.11–13) notes that many MSS have the dates of these feasts—e.g., "For the eighth of September"—written on them, thereby indicating how the MSS were used.
89. For what follows, see Lafontaine-Dosogne, "Life of the Virgin," 4.163–94.

Offerings Rejected and continues with such moments as the Annunciation to Anna, the Birth of the Virgin, the Blessing of Mary by the Priests, the Presentation of Mary in the Temple, the Annuciations at the Well and at Home, and the Trial by Water.

The influence of the Infancy Gospel of James extends even to those paintings and biblical manuscripts that illustrate scenes from the cycle of Jesus' life. These pictures, not to mention illustrated manuscripts of sermons and commentaries on the canonical gospels, often contain details that appear only in the Infancy Gospel of James. For example, manuscript illustrations of the Lukan annunciation (Luke 1:26–38) frequently depict Mary by a well or have her hold a skein of purple wool, details taken from the Infancy Gospel of James (11:1, 4).[90] Likewise, illustrations of the Lukan trip to Bethlehem (Luke 2:1–7) or the Matthean trip to Egypt (Matt 2:13–15) often have Joseph turning back toward Mary, another detail appearing only in the Infancy Gospel of James (17:6, 8).[91] Similarly, illustrations of the Matthean massacre of the infants (Matt 2:16–18) frequently include Elizabeth fleeing to the hills with her son John, again a scene known only from the Infancy Gospel of James (22:5–9).[92] More examples could be cited, but it should already be clear that the Infancy Gospel of James had a profound impact on subsequent Christian art and liturgy. Christians looked to the Infancy Gospel of James for information about Mary, and that information, transferred to the pictorial images of church decorations and manuscript illuminations, decisively shaped Christian imagination and understanding regarding important facets of their faith.

7. The Greek Text

The rejection of the Infancy Gospel of James in the West, combined with its later inclusion in the Latin Pseudo-Matthew, resulted in this writing becoming unknown in Medieval and Renaissance Europe until Postel, following a trip to Byzantium, reintroduced it in Latin dress in 1552.[93] Not long after, in 1564, a Greek edition by M. Neander appeared.[94] The manuscript on which this edition was based has since disappeared, but the edition itself continued to be used for subsequent editions as late as the nineteenth century. Of these editions, that by J. Fabricius in 1703, deserves note, for it introduced the convention of dividing the Infancy Gospel of James into twenty-five chapters.[95]

90. See further Maguire, *Eloquence in Byzantium*, 44–52.
91. See Lafontaine-Dosogne, "Infancy of Christ," 4.197–241, esp. 205 and 227.
92. For details, see Maguire, *Eloquence in Byzantium*, 22- 34.
93. On this and other early editions of the Infancy Gospel of James, see further Daniels, *Manuscript Tradition*, 1.19–29, and de Strycker, *Protévangile*, 3–6.
94. Neander, *Catechesis*, 356–92.
95. Fabricius, *Codex apocryphus*, 1.66–125.

In the nineteenth century scholars initiated a massive search for manuscripts of all ancient literature—first in libraries and eventually in the sands of Egypt. The Infancy Gospel of James was one of the beneficiaries of that search. For example, J. Thilo set aside earlier texts and based his edition, published in 1832, on nine new MSS from Paris and Venice, and depended on the collations of others for some Vatican MSS.[96] His edition, complete with critical and interpretive notes, represented a major advance.[97] But his work was soon overshadowed by that of C. von Tischendorf, who, in 1849, visited various European libraries in search of MSS. His search yielded six more MSS that contained the Infancy Gospel of James, so that, with Thilo's and previous editors' work to build upon, Tischendorf was able to base his text on seventeen MSS; he published the text, complete with critical apparatus and verse numbers to go along with Fabricius' chapter numbers, as part of his *Evangelia Apocrypha* in 1853. A second edition, published in 1876,[98] became the 'textus receptus,' as it were, for translations of the Infancy Gospel of James for almost a century.[99]

In the early twentieth century the sands of Egypt began to yield papyri that contained fragments of the Infancy Gospel of James.[100] But at first these new texts had minimal effect on the established text of the Infancy Gospel of James. This situation changed dramatically, however, in 1958 when M. Testuz published a complete, if also somewhat abbreviated, papyrus text of this gospel.[101] Known as Papyrus Bodmer V, this text was dated to the late third or, better, early fourth century[102] and hence necessitated a reevaluation of the text that had been based on the much later European MSS. In 1961 E. de Strycker published a new critical text of the Infancy Gospel of James,[103] a text based principally on the Bodmer papyrus but also on other papyrus MSS, most notably a fifth (not fourth) century papyrus, known as PSI 1.6, which contains a very fragmentary text of chapters 13–23.[104] De Strycker not only incorporated the MSS known to

---

96. Thilo, *Codex aprocryphus*, 159–273.
97. Daniels, *Manuscript Tradition*, 1.22.
98. Tischendorf, *Evangelia Apocrypha*, 1–50.
99. Note that Elliott's most recent translation of the Infancy Gospel of James still uses Tischendorf's text, though a few significant departures in the Bodmer Papyrus are also noted (see Elliott, *Apocryphal New Testament*, 52, 57–67).
100. On these papyri, see de Strycker, "Handschriften," 578–82. Since de Strycker's study, another papyrus fragment, namely of chap. 25, has been published. See Cockle, "P.Oxy. 3524," 8–12. Cockle (p. 9) mentions two other papyrus fragments awaiting publication. So far as I know, they have not been.
101. See Testuz, *Papyrus Bodmer V*.
102. See de Strycker, "Handschriften," 579–80.
103. See de Strycker, *Protévangile*.
104. Pistelli, *Pubblicazioni*, 9–15. Incidentally, Pistelli (p. 9) dated this papyrus to the fourth century, but two papyrologists have independently revised the dating to the fifth (see de Strycker, "Handschriften," 608 n. 11). Elliott (*Apocryphal New Testament*, 52), however, still gives a fourth century dating.

Tischendorf, but he also used the many versions of this most popular gospel.[105]

Today de Strycker's text remains the standard, if still provisional, edition. The provisional character of this text is admitted by de Strycker himself.[106] He has continued to investigate the Greek MS tradition and raised the number to 140 MSS, which he has divided into five families.[107] This work on the Greek MS tradition has been paralleled by two American scholars, B. Daniels and G. Zervos.[108] Perhaps a definitive edition is not too far off.

In the meantime, however, scholars must continue to use de Strycker's text. Accordingly, the text presented here is based on de Strycker's text, but I have departed from it in a number of ways. First, de Strycker's preference for the page and line numbers of the Bodmer papyrus has been dropped in favor of the traditional chapter numbers (though the verse numbers introduced by Tischendorf have been dropped in favor of a new versification system that allows for more precise notation). Second, I have standardized the spelling of many words in de Strycker's text which follows the spelling of the papyrus. Third, at several places, all marked, I have departed from the reading de Strycker's text, often preferring Tischendorf's reading and sometimes the readings of MSS not favored by either of these two editors. Fourth, the apparatus notes virtually all places where Tischendorf's text and de Strycker's text differ to such an extent that a noticeable difference in translation would result. The two texts differ at over 500 places, and 40% of these would result in differing translations. The reader will thus begin to appreciate the significance of the discovery of the Bodmer papyrus for establishing the text of the Infancy Gospel of James, not to mention coming to an increased appreciation for the fluidity of this text when compared with the canonical gospels. Finally, the papyrus fragment of chap. 25, Oxyrhynchus Papyrus 3524 (6th c.),[109] that came to light after de Strycker published his text will be fully incorporated into the text and apparatus.

---

105. For the expanded textual basis of this new edition, see further de Strycker, *Protévangile*, 30–45.
106. See de Strycker, "Handschriften," 580.
107. See de Strycker, "Handschriften," 588–607.
108. See Daniels, *Manuscript Tradition*, and Zervos, *Prolegomena*.
109. See Cockle, "P. Oxy. 3524," 8–12.

Facing page: Papyrus Bodmer V, an important fourth century c.e. papyrus codex of the Infancy Gospel of James, first published in 1958 by M. Testuz. Shown here is a photograph of the first page of this papyrus codex which contains the title "Birth of Mary, Revelation of James" as well as the opening verses of the gospel (=1.1–5). *Photograph courtesy of the Bibliotheca Bodmeriana, Geneva, Switzerland.*

The Infancy
Gospel
of James

Childless Joachim **1** Ἐν ταῖς ἱστορίαις τῶν δώδεκα φυλῶν τοῦ Ἰσραήλ, ἦν Ἰωακεὶμ πλούσιος σφόδρα, ²καὶ προσέφερε κυρίῳ τὰ δῶρα αὐτοῦ διπλᾶ ³λέγων ἐν ἑαυτῷ· Ἔσται τὸ τῆς περισσείας μου ἅπαντι τῷ λαῷ καὶ τὸ τῆς ἀφέσεως κυρίῳ τῷ θεῷ εἰς ἱλασμὸν ἐμοί.

⁴Ἤγγισεν δὲ ἡ ἡμέρα κυρίου ἡ μεγάλη, καὶ προσέφερον οἱ υἱοὶ Ἰσραὴλ τὰ δῶρα αὐτῶν. ⁵καὶ ἔστη κατενώπιον αὐτοῦ Ῥουβὴλ λέγων· Οὐκ ἔξεστί σοι πρώτῳ ἐνεγκεῖν τὰ δῶρά σου, καθότι σπέρμα οὐκ ἐποίησας ἐν τῷ Ἰσραήλ.

⁶Καὶ ἐλυπήθη Ἰωακεὶμ σφόδρα, καὶ ἀπῆλθεν εἰς τὴν δωδεκάφυλον τοῦ λαοῦ λέγων ἐν ἑαυτῷ· Θεάσομαι τὴν δωδεκάφυλον τοῦ Ἰσραήλ, εἰ ἐγὼ μόνος οὐκ ἐποίησα σπέρμα ἐν τῷ Ἰσραήλ. ⁷καὶ ἠρεύνησε, καὶ εὗρεν πάντας τοὺς δικαίους ὅτι σπέρμα ἐν τῷ Ἰσραὴλ ἀνέστησαν. ⁸καὶ ἐμνήσθη τοῦ πατριάρχου Ἀβραάμ, ὅτι ἐν τῇ ἐσχάτῃ αὐτοῦ ἡμέρᾳ ἔδωκεν αὐτῷ κύριος ὁ θεὸς υἱὸν τὸν Ἰσαάκ.

⁹Καὶ ἐλυπήθη Ἰωακεὶμ σφόδρα καὶ οὐκ ἐφάνη τῇ γυναικὶ αὐτοῦ, ἀλλὰ ἔδωκεν ἑαυτὸν εἰς τὴν ἔρημον καὶ ἔπηξεν τὴν

Title: Γένεσις Μαρίας, Ἀποκάλυψις Ἰακώβ: de Strycker. Γέννησις Μαρίας τῆς ἁγίας Θεοτόκου καὶ ὑπερενδόξου μητρὸς Ἰησοῦ Χριστοῦ: Tischendorf. See further Introduction 2.1.   **1:1.** τοῦ Ἰσραήλ: Tischendorf. de Strycker omits.   **1:2.** κυρίῳ¹: de Strycker. Tischendorf omits. **1:2.** ἐν ἑαυτῷ: de Strycker. Tischendorf omits.   **1:5.** Ῥουβήλ: de Strycker. Ῥουβίμ: Tischendorf.   **1:6.** ἐν ἑαυτῷ: de Strycker. Tischendorf omits.   **1:8.** κύριος ὁ θεός: de Strycker. ὁ θεός: Tischendorf.   **1:9.** ἐλυπήθη: Tischendorf. ἐλυπεῖτο: de Strycker.

1 According to the records of the twelve tribes of Israel, there *Childless Joachim* once was a very rich man named Joachim. ²He always doubled the gifts he offered to the Lord, ³and would say to himself, "One gift, representing my prosperity, will be for all the people; the other, offered for forgiveness, will be my sin-offering to the Lord God."

⁴Now the great day of the Lord was approaching, and the people of Israel were offering their gifts. ⁵And Reubel confronted Joachim and said, "You're not allowed to offer your gifts first because you haven't produced an Israelite child."

⁶And Joachim became very upset and went to the book of the twelve tribes of the people, saying to himself, "I'm going to check the book of the twelve tribes of Israel to see whether I'm the only one in Israel who hasn't produced a child." ⁷And he searched ⟨the records⟩ and found that all the righteous people in Israel did indeed have children. ⁸And he remembered the patriarch Abraham because in his last days the Lord God had given him a son, Isaac.

⁹And so he continued to be very upset and did not see his wife but banished himself to the wilderness and pitched his tent

---

- **1:1–5:4.** The circumstances of Mary's birth revolve around the childlessness of her parents, Joachim and Anna. After being reproached for not having a child, they both decide to confront God in prayer. A messenger from the Lord tells them that their prayers are answered, and Anna is pregnant. She promises to give the child to God, and Joachim celebrates with a banquet.
- **1:1–11.** Joachim, despite his wealth and piety, is an object of reproach because of his childlessness. He learns that he alone among the righteous in Israel has had no offspring and decides to confront God over the matter. He goes to the desert and while there fasts and prays for forty days in hopes of learning why he is childless.
- **1:1.** The name *Joachim* is clearly an Old Testament name (see Neh 12:26; Jud 4:6; Sus 4), but the author was probably thinking especially of Sus 4, since the Joachim mentioned there is also described as *a very rich man.*
- **1:4.** *the great day of the Lord:* This very phrase appears in Joel 2:11, which is then quoted in Acts 2:20, but in both cases the phrase refers to the day of judgment. Here, however, a festival is clearly intended. In fact, the Feast of Tabernacles has been

suggested (cf. John 7:37 where the last day of this feast is called "the great day") (Lowe, "IOYΔAIOI," 65 and n. 36), but the vagueness of the reference precludes any precise determination (de Strycker, *Protévangile*, 65 n. 3; Smid, *Commentary*, 27).
- **1:5.** *Reubel* (or Reuben, according to many MSS) is not a priest, as some MSS add, but probably a farmer and certainly one with many children who publicly reproaches Joachim for his childlessness (Michaelis, *Apokryphen Schriften*, 92). Why Joachim had been offering his gifts *first* is not clear, though it has been suggested that he did so by reason of his wealth and generosity (de Strycker, *Protévangile*, 67 n. 5).
- **1:5.** *you haven't produced an Israelite child:* Childlessness was a matter of great disgrace, since it was often viewed, not as having a natural cause, but as a sign of divine displeasure or punishment (see Gen 16:2; 20:18; Hos 9:14; and esp. 1 Sam 1:5–6).
- **1:6.** The word *book* is not in the Greek but is widely assumed by scholars. Some sort of genealogical register has been suggested (Michaelis, *Apokryphen Schriften*, 92).
- **1:8.** For the story of the birth of *Isaac*, see Gen 21:1–7.

σκηνὴν αὐτοῦ ἐκεῖ. ¹⁰καὶ ἐνήστευσεν τεσσαράκοντα ἡμέρας καὶ νύκτας τεσσαράκοντα, ¹¹λέγων ἐν ἑαυτῷ· Ἰωακείμ· Οὐ καταβήσομαι οὔτε ἐπὶ βρωτὸν οὔτε ἐπὶ ποτόν, ἕως ἐπισκέψηταί με κύριος ὁ θεός μου· καὶ ἔσται μου ἡ εὐχὴ βρώματα καὶ πόματα.

Childless Anna   **2** ῾Η δὲ γυνὴ αὐτοῦ ῎Αννα δύο θρήνους ἐθρήνει καὶ δύο κοπετοὺς ἐκόπτετο λέγουσα· Κόψομαι τὴν χηροσύνην μου καὶ κόψομαι τὴν ἀτεκνίαν μου.

²῎Ηγγισεν δὲ ἡ ἡμέρα κυρίου ἡ μεγάλη. ³καὶ εἶπεν Ἰουθίνη ἡ παιδίσκη αὐτῆς πρὸς αὐτήν· ῞Εως πότε ταπεινοῖς τὴν ψυχήν σου; Ἰδοὺ ἤγγισε ἡ ἡμέρα κυρίου ἡ μεγάλη, καὶ οὐκ ἔξεστί σοι πενθεῖν· ⁴ἀλλὰ λάβε τοῦτο τὸ κεφαλοδέσμιον, ὃ ἔδωκέν μοι ἡ κυρία τοῦ ἔργου, καὶ οὐκ ἔξεστί μοι δήσασθαι αὐτό, καθότι παιδίσκη εἰμὶ σὴ καὶ χαρακτῆρα ἔχει βασιλικόν.

⁵Καὶ εἶπεν ῎Αννα· Ἀπόστηθι ἀπ᾿ ἐμοῦ. καὶ ταῦτα οὐκ ἐποίησα, καὶ κύριος ὁ θεὸς ἐταπείνωσέν με σφόδρα. μήπως τοῦτο πανοῦργος ἔδωκέν σοι, καὶ ἦλθες κοινωνῆσαί με τῇ ἁμαρτίᾳ σου.

⁶Καὶ εἶπεν Ἰουθίνη ἡ παιδίσκη· Τί ἀράσωμαί σε, καθότι οὐκ ἤκουσας τῆς φωνῆς μου; ἀπέκλεισεν κύριος ὁ θεὸς τὴν μήτραν σου, τοῦ μὴ δοῦναί σοι καρπὸν ἐν Ἰσραήλ.

⁷Καὶ ἐλυπήθη ῎Αννα σφόδρα, καὶ περιείλετο τὰ ἱμάτια αὐτῆς τὰ πενθικὰ καὶ ἀπεσμήξατο τὴν κεφαλὴν αὐτῆς καὶ ἐνεδύσατο τὰ ἱμάτια αὐτῆς τὰ νυμφικά, ⁸καὶ περὶ ὥραν ἐνάτην κατέβη εἰς τὸν παράδεισον αὐτῆς τοῦ περιπατῆσαι. καὶ εἶδεν δαφνιδέαν καὶ ἐκάθισεν ὑποκάτω αὐτῆς, ⁹καὶ μετὰ τὸ ἀναπαύσασθαι ἐλιτάνευσεν τὸν δεσπότην λέγουσα· ῾Ο θεὸς τῶν πατέρων μου, εὐλόγησόν με καὶ ἐπάκουσον τῆς δεήσεώς μου, καθὼς εὐλόγησας τὴν μητέρα Σάραν καὶ ἔδωκας αὐτῇ υἱὸν τὸν Ἰσαάκ.

2:3. Ἰουθίνη: de Strycker. Ἰουδίθ: Tischendorf. The name of Anna's slave varies considerably in the mss. For full discussion, see de Strycker, *Protévangile*, 313–15.   **2:3.** πρὸς αὐτήν: de Strycker. Tischendorf omits. **2:4.** σή: de Strycker. Tischendorf omits.   **2:5.** κύριος ὁ θεός: de Strycker. κύριος: Tischendorf.   **2:6.** οὐκ ἤκουσας τῆς φωνῆς μου: de Strycker. Tischendorf omits.   **2:6.** κύριος ὁ θεός: de Strycker. κύριος: Tischendorf. **2:9.** μετὰ τὸ ἀναπαύσασθαι: de Strycker. Tischendorf omits.   **2:9.** πατέρων μου: de Strycker. παρτέρων ἡμῶν: Tischendorf.   **2:9.** τὴν μητέρα Σάραν: de Strycker. τὴν μήτραν Σάρρας: Tischendorf. See further de Strycker, *Protévangile*, 234–35.

there. [10]And Joachim fasted 'forty days and forty nights.' [11]He would say to himself, "I will not go back for food or drink until the Lord my God visits me. Prayer will be my food and drink."

2 Now his wife Anna was mourning and lamenting on two counts: "I lament my widowhood and I lament my childlessness."

Childless Anna

[2]The great day of the Lord approached, however, [3]and Juthine her slave said to her, "How long are you going to humble yourself? Look, the great day of the Lord has arrived, and you're not supposed to mourn. [4]Rather, take this headband which the mistress of the workshop gave to me, but which I'm not allowed to wear because I'm your slave and because it bears a royal insignia."

[5]And Anna said, "Get away from me! I won't take it. The Lord God has greatly shamed me. Maybe a trickster has given you this, and you've come to make me share in your sin."

[6]And Juthine the slave replied, "Should I curse you just because you haven't paid any attention to me? The Lord God has made your womb sterile so you won't bear any children for Israel."

[7]Anna, too, became very upset. She took off her mourning clothes, washed her face, and put on her wedding dress. [8]Then, in the middle of the afternoon, she went down to her garden to take a walk. She spied a laurel tree and sat down under it. [9]After resting, she prayed to the Lord: "O God of my ancestors, bless me and hear my prayer, just as you blessed our mother Sarah and gave her a son, Isaac."

• **1:10.** Fasting in the wilderness for forty days and forty nights is a common biblical theme (e.g., Exod 24:18; 34:28; 1 Kgs 19:8; Matt 4:2).

• **2:1–3:8.** Anna, Joachim's wife, feels abandoned by her husband because of her childlessness and then is reproached for it by her slave Juthine. In response she, too, decides to confront God. She dresses in her wedding clothes and walks about her garden before expressing her lament to God. The author had not included Joachim's actual prayer to God, but he does provide Anna's lament, a poignant expression of her sense of isolation in a world that is otherwise exceedingly fertile and prolific.

• **2:1.** The name *Anna* is, like Joachim, an Old Testament name (see 1 Sam 1:2; Tob 1:20).

• **2:3.** *not supposed to mourn:* Festivals, of course, were a time for rejoicing (Ps 118:24; Jud 8:6).

• **2:4.** *headband . . . mistress of the workshop . . . royal insignia:* Obscure phrases whose meanings are not at all assured.

• **2:5.** *trickster:* Again, the meaning is not clear. Perhaps the word refers to a clever young man with whom Juthine has had an affair (Michaelis, *Apokryphen Schriften*, 74).

• **2:6.** *God has made your womb sterile:* The taunt of sterility, even the wording, recalls the similar situation of Hannah in 1 Sam 1:6.

• **2:8.** *in the middle of the afternoon.* Literally "about the ninth hour" (counting from six a.m.). This time of day is a conventional one for prayer (see Acts 3:1 and Smid, *Commentary*, 34).

• **2:9.** On Sarah's blessing, see Gen 17:16.

Anna laments **3** Καὶ ἠτένισεν "Αννα εἰς οὐρανόν, καὶ εἶδεν καλιὰν στρουθῶν ἐν τῇ δαφνιδέᾳ. ²καὶ εὐθέως ἐποίησεν θρῆνον "Αννα ἐν αὐτῇ λέγουσα·

Οἴμοι, τίς με ἐγέννησεν; ποία δὲ μήτρα ἐξέφυσέν με; ³ὅτι ἐγὼ κατάρα ἐγεννήθην ἐνώπιον τῶν υἱῶν Ἰσραήλ. καὶ ὠνειδίσθην καὶ ἐμυκτήρισαν καὶ ἐξώρισάν με ἐκ ναοῦ κυρίου τοῦ θεοῦ μου.

⁴Οἴμοι, τίνι ὡμοιώθην ἐγώ; οὐχ ὡμοιώθην ἐγὼ τοῖς πετεινοῖς τοῦ οὐρανοῦ, ὅτι καὶ τὰ πετεινὰ τοῦ οὐρανοῦ γόνιμά ἐστιν ἐνώπιόν σου, κύριε.

⁵Οἴμοι, τίνι ὡμοιώθην ἐγώ; οὐχ ὡμοιώθην ἐγὼ τοῖς ἀλόγοις ζώοις, ὅτι καὶ τὰ ἄλογα ζῷα γόνιμά εἰσιν ἐνώπιόν σου, κύριε.

⁶Οἴμοι, τίνι ὡμοιώθην ἐγώ; οὐχ ὡμοιώθην ἐγὼ τοῖς θηρίοις τῆς γῆς, ὅτι καὶ τὰ θηρία τῆς γῆς γόνιμά εἰσιν ἐνώπιόν σου, κύριε.

⁷Οἴμοι, τίνι ὡμοιώθην ἐγώ; οὐχ ὡμοιώθην ἐγὼ τοῖς ὕδασιν τούτοις, ὅτι καὶ τὰ ὕδατα ταῦτα γόνιμά εἰσιν ἐνώπιόν σου, κύριε.

⁸Οἴμοι, τίνι ὡμοιώθην ἐγώ; οὐχ ὡμοιώθην ἐγὼ τῇ γῇ ταύτῃ, ὅτι καὶ ἡ γῆ προσφέρει τοὺς καρποὺς αὐτῆς κατὰ καιρὸν καί σε εὐλογεῖ, κύριε.

Anna's vision **4** Καὶ ἰδοὺ ἄγγελος κυρίου ἐπέστη λέγων· "Αννα "Αννα, ἐπήκουσεν κύριος ὁ θεὸς τῆς δεήσεώς σου. συλλήψει καὶ γεννήσεις καὶ λαληθήσεται τὸ σπέρμα σου ἐν ὅλῃ τῇ οἰκουμένῃ.

²Καὶ εἶπεν "Αννα· Ζῆ κύριος ὁ θεός· ἐὰν γεννήσω εἴτε ἄρσενα εἴτε θήλειαν, προσάξω αὐτὸ δῶρον κυρίῳ τῷ θεῷ μου, καὶ ἔσται λειτουργῶν αὐτῷ πάσας τὰς ἡμέρας τῆς ζωῆς αὐτοῦ.

3:1. "Αννα: de Strycker. Tischendorf omits.   3:2. εὐθέως: de Strycker. Tischendorf omits.   3:2. "Αννα: de Strycker. Tischendorf omits.   3:3. τοῦ θεοῦ μου: de Strycker. Tischendorf omits.   3:5. Οἴμοι, τίνι ὡμοιώθην ἐγώ; οὐχ ὡμοιώθην κτλ.: de Strycker. Tischendorf omits entire verse. 3:7. γόνιμά εἰσιν ἐνώπιόν σου, κύριε: Tischendorf. γαληνιῶντα καὶ σκιρτῶντα, καὶ οἱ ἰχθύες αὐτῶν σε εὐλογοῦσιν, κύριε: de Strycker.   3:8. προσφέρει: Tischendorf. προφέρει: de Strycker.   4:1. ἐπέστη: Tischendorf. ἔστη: de Strycker.   4:2. ὁ θεός: de Strycker. ὁ θεός μου: Tischendorf.

3 And Anna looked up toward the sky and saw a nest of sparrows in the laurel tree. ²And immediately Anna began to lament, saying to herself: "Poor me! Who gave birth to me? What sort of womb bore me? ³For I was born under a curse in the eyes of the people of Israel. And I've been reviled and mocked and banished from the temple of the Lord my God.

⁴"Poor me! What am I like? I am not like the birds of the sky, because even the birds of the sky reproduce in your presence, O Lord.

⁵"Poor me! What am I like? I am not like the domestic animals, because even the domestic animals bear young in your presence, O Lord.

⁶"Poor me! What am I like? I am not like the wild animals of the earth, because even the animals of the earth reproduce in your presence, O Lord.

⁷"Poor me! What am I like? I am not like these waters, because even these waters are productive in your presence, O Lord.

⁸"Poor me! What am I like? I am not like this earth, because even the earth produces its crops in season and blesses you, O Lord."

Anna laments

4 Suddenly a messenger of the Lord appeared to her and said: "Anna, Anna, the Lord God has heard your prayer. You will conceive and give birth, and your child will be talked about all over the world."

²And Anna said, "As the Lord God lives, whether I give birth to a boy or a girl, I'll offer it as a gift to the Lord my God, and it will serve him its whole life."

Anna's vision

• **3:4–8.** Beginning with *Poor me! What am I like?* Anna's lament becomes a repetitive, though powerful, statement of her barrenness in contrast to the fruitfulness of everything around her: birds, domestic animals, animals in the wild, waters, even the earth itself. The MSS differ in the number of stanzas, the order of stanzas, and the wording (see further Smid, *Commentary*, 37–38; Daniels, *Manuscript Tradition*, 1.194–97).

• **4:1–5:4.** The prayers of Joachim and Anna are answered. Anna is told by a heavenly messenger that she will finally have a child and in joy offers the child to God. Joachim is likewise told of Anna's pregnancy. Once reunited and happy, they celebrate with a large feast and, feeling vindicated, await the birth of their child.

• **4:1.** *Suddenly a messenger of the Lord appeared.* These words seem modeled on Luke 2:9; cf. also Acts 12:7.

• **4:1.** *You will conceive and give birth:* These words are natural enough, but they may also be patterned after Luke 1:31.

• **4:1.** *talked about all over the world:* This language recalls similar claims made in Matt 24:14 and 26:13.

• **4:2.** *As the Lord God lives.* This phrase, which is used throughout this gospel for vows and oaths, also appears in the Old Testament (Judg 8:19; Ruth 3:13; 1 Sam 14:39; 25:26; 26:10). For a similar vow made on behalf of an unborn child, namely that of Hannah on behalf of Samuel, see 1 Sam 1:11, 28.

• **4:2.** Since Anna vows service for the child's *whole life*, she is in effect already ensuring

³Καὶ ἰδοὺ ἦλθον ἄγγελοι δύο λέγοντες αὐτῇ· Ἰδοὺ Ἰωακεὶμ ὁ ἀνήρ σου ἔρχεται μετὰ τῶν ποιμνίων αὐτοῦ. ⁴ἄγγελος γὰρ κυρίου κατέβη πρὸς Ἰωακεὶμ λέγων· Ἰωακεὶμ Ἰωακείμ, ἐπήκουσεν κύριος ὁ θεὸς τῆς δεήσεώς σου· κατάβηθι ἐντεῦθεν· ἰδοὺ ἡ γυνή σου Ἄννα ἐν γαστρὶ εἴληφεν.

⁵Καὶ εὐθέως κατέβη Ἰωακεὶμ καὶ ἐκάλεσεν τοὺς ποιμένας λέγων αὐτοῖς· Φέρετέ μοι ὧδε δέκα ἀμνάδας ἀσπίλους καὶ ἀμώμους, καὶ ἔσονται αἱ δέκα ἀμνάδες κυρίῳ τῷ θεῷ· ⁶καὶ φέρετέ μοι δώδεκα μόσχους ἁπαλούς, καὶ ἔσονται οἱ δώδεκα μόσχοι τοῖς ἱερεῦσιν καὶ τῇ γερουσίᾳ· ⁷καὶ ἑκατὸν χιμάρους, καὶ ἔσονται οἱ ἑκατὸν χίμαροι παντὶ τῷ λαῷ.

⁸Καὶ ἰδοὺ ἥκει Ἰωακεὶμ μετὰ τῶν ποιμνίων αὐτοῦ. καὶ ἔστη Ἄννα πρὸς τῇ πύλῃ ⁹καὶ εἶδεν Ἰωακεὶμ ἐρχόμενον μετὰ τῶν ποιμνίων αὐτοῦ καὶ εὐθὺς ἔδραμεν καὶ ἐκρέμασεν αὐτὴν εἰς τὸν τράχηλον αὐτοῦ Ἄννα λέγουσα· Νῦν οἶδα ὅτι κύριος ὁ θεὸς εὐλόγησέν με σφόδρα· ἰδοὺ γὰρ ἡ χήρα οὐκέτι χήρα, καὶ ἡ ἄτεκνος ἰδοὺ ἐν γαστρὶ εἴληφα.

¹⁰Καὶ ἀνεπαύσατο Ἰωακεὶμ τῇ πρώτῃ ἡμέρᾳ ἐν τῷ οἴκῳ αὐτοῦ.

Birth of Mary

5 Τῇ δὲ ἐπαύριον ἔφερεν τὰ δῶρα αὐτοῦ λέγων ἐν ἑαυτῷ· Ἐὰν κύριος ὁ θεὸς ἱλασθῇ μοι, τὸ πέταλον τοῦ ἱερέως φανερόν μοι ποιήσει. ²καὶ προσέφερεν τὰ δῶρα αὐτοῦ Ἰωακεὶμ καὶ προσεῖχε

4:4. εἴληφεν: de Strycker. λήψεται: Tischendorf. On the textual problem here and at 4:9 below and the theological significance of the different tenses, see the corresponding note to the translation and de Strycker, "Handschriften," 581–82.   **4:5.** αἱ δέκα ἀμνάδες: de Strycker. Tischendorf omits.   **4:6.** οἱ δώδεκα μόσχοι: de Strycker. Tischendorf omits.   **4:7.** καὶ ἔσονται οἱ ἑκατὸν χίμαροι: de Strycker. Tischendorf omits.   **4:8.** μετὰ τῶν ποιμνίων αὐτοῦ: de Strycker. Tischendorf omits.   **4:9.** εἴληφα: de Strycker. λήψομαι: Tischendorf.   **5:1.** ποιήσει: Tischendorf. ποιῆσαι: de Strycker.

³And right then two messengers reported to her: "Look, your husband Joachim is coming with his flocks. ⁴You see, a messenger of the Lord had come down to Joachim and said, 'Joachim, Joachim, the Lord God has heard your prayer. Get down from there. Look, your wife Anna is pregnant.'"

⁵And Joachim went down right away and summoned his shepherds with these instructions: "Bring me ten lambs without spot or blemish, and the ten lambs will be for the Lord God. ⁶Also, bring me twelve tender calves, and the twelve calves will be for the priests and the council of elders. ⁷Also, one hundred goats, and the one hundred goats will be for the whole people."

⁸And so Joachim came with his flocks, while Anna stood at the gate. ⁹Then she spotted Joachim approaching with his flocks and rushed out and threw her arms around his neck: "Now I know that the Lord God has blessed me greatly. This widow is no longer a widow, and I, once childless, am now pregnant!"

¹⁰And Joachim rested the first day at home.

5 But on the next day, as he was presenting his gifts, he thought to himself, "If the Lord God has really been merciful to me, the polished disc on the priest's headband will make it clear to me." ²And so Joachim was presenting his gifts and paying

Birth of Mary

---

that Mary will not marry but be a virgin throughout her life (Smid, *Commentary*, 39–40).

• **4:4.** The MSS differ over whether Joachim is told that Anna *is pregnant* (perfect tense) or that she "will be pregnant" (future tense) (see Daniels, *Manuscript Tradition*, 2.134–35), and scholars themselves differ over which reading to accept as original. Those who decide on the future tense base their decision on a sexual connotation to the word *rested* in 4:10 (Smid, *Commentary*, 41). Such a connotation is possible but unlikely, especially given the use of the same word in 15:1, where it definitely has no such meaning. And, given the author's stress on Mary's purity throughout the document, it is probable that he understands Mary to have also been the product of a miraculous conception (de Strycker, *Protévangile*, 81 n. 3; "Handschriften," 581–82).

• **4:5.** *without spot or blemish* recalls the sacrificial stipulations recorded in Exod 29:38 and Lev 12:6.

• **4:5–7.** *ten lambs . . . twelve tender calves . . .*

one hundred goats: The number of animals sacrificed is yet another sign of Joachim's wealth and generosity (cf. 1:1).

• **4:9.** *This widow is no longer a widow . . . .:* Anna's humiliation over becoming a widow and being childless (2:1–6) is now over, and her vindication is expressed with an effective antithesis, a rhetorical figure much beloved at this time.

• **5:1.** *polished disc:* Lit. "leaf," including a leaf of metal, such as of gold. Indeed, this disc or plate, which was part of the high priest's vestments (see Exod 28:1–39), is described as made of gold and suspended from the mitre of the high priest and hanging down on his forehead (see esp. vv 36–38; cf. also 39:30–31). Just how this plate would disclose Joachim's sin is not made clear, either here or in the Exodus description. Perhaps the gold plate acted as a mirror in which Joachim looked for a distorted or non-distorted image of himself. Mirrors, in any case, were often used to obtain divine revelations (see Lucian, *Lover of Lies* 19, and Allen, "Hellenistic Magic").

τῷ πετάλῳ τοῦ ἱερέως ἕως ἐπέβη ἐπὶ τὸ θυσιαστήριον κυρίου,
καὶ οὐκ εἶδεν ἁμαρτίαν ἐν αὐτῷ. ³καὶ εἶπεν Ἰωακείμ· Νῦν οἶδα ὅτι
κύριος ὁ θεὸς ἱλάσθη μοι καὶ ἀφῆκέν μοι πάντα τὰ ἁμαρτήματά
μου. ⁴καὶ κατέβη ἐκ τοῦ ναοῦ κυρίου δεδικαιωμένος, καὶ ἦκει ἐν τῷ
οἴκῳ αὐτοῦ.

⁵Καὶ ἐπληρώθησαν οἱ μῆνες αὐτῆς· τῷ δὲ ἐνάτῳ μηνὶ ἐγέννησεν Ἄννα ⁶καὶ εἶπεν τῇ μαίᾳ· Τί ἐγέννησα;
⁷Καὶ εἶπεν ἡ μαῖα· Θήλειαν.
⁸Καὶ εἶπεν Ἄννα· Ἐμεγαλύνθη ἡ ψυχή μου τὴν ἡμέραν
ταύτην. καὶ ἀνέκλινεν αὐτήν.
⁹Πληρωθεισῶν δὲ τῶν ἡμερῶν ἀπεσμήξατο ἡ Ἄννα τῆς
ἀφέδρου αὐτῆς καὶ ἔδωκε μαστὸν τῇ παιδὶ καὶ ὠνόμασεν τὸ
ὄνομα αὐτῆς Μαρία.

Mary's first birthday

6 Ἡμέρα δὲ καὶ ἡμέρα ἐκραταιοῦτο ἡ παῖς· ²γενομένης δὲ
αὐτῆς ἐξαμήνου ἔστησεν αὐτὴν ἡ μήτηρ αὐτῆς χαμαί, διαπει-
ρᾶσαι εἰ ἵσταται. καὶ ἑπτὰ βήματα περιπατήσασα ἦλθεν εἰς τὸν
κόλπον τῆς μητρὸς αὐτῆς. ³καὶ ἀνήρπασεν αὐτὴν ἡ μήτηρ αὐτῆς
λέγουσα· Ζῇ κύριος ὁ θεός μου, οὐ μὴ περιπατήσῃς ἐν τῇ γῇ
ταύτῃ ἕως σε ἀπάξω ἐν τῷ ναῷ κυρίου.

5:2. ἐν αὐτῷ: various MSS. ἐν ἑαυτῷ: Tischendorf and de Strycker. See
Daniels, *Manuscript Tradition*, 2.187–88; Smid, *Commentary*, 46–47. **5:3.**
κύριος ὁ θεός: de Strycker. κύριος: Tischendorf.   **5:5.** οἱ μῆνες αὐτῆς:
Tischendorf. μῆνες αὐτῇ ὡσεὶ ἕξ: de Strycker.   **5:5.** ἐνάτῳ: Tischendorf.
ἑβδόμῳ: de Strycker. The text is very insecure at this point, as sixth,
seventh, eighth, and ninth months are all attested. For details, see de
Strycker, *Protévangile*, 86 and 87 n. 5.   **5:9.** τῆς ἀφέδρου αὐτῆς: de
Strycker. Tischendorf omits.   **6:2.** τῆς μητρὸς αὐτῆς: de Strycker. αὐτῆς:
Tischendorf.   **6:3.** ἡ μήτηρ αὐτῆς: de Strycker. Tischendorf inadver-
tently omits (cf. de Strycker, *Protévangile*, 90).

attention to the priest's headband until he went up to the altar of the Lord. And he saw no sin in it. ³And Joachim said, "Now I know that the Lord God has been merciful to me and has forgiven me all my sins." ⁴And he came down from the temple of the Lord acquitted and went back home.

⁵And so her pregnancy came to term, and in the ninth month Anna gave birth. ⁶And she said to the midwife, "Is it a boy or a girl?"

⁷And her midwife said, "A girl."

⁸And Anna said, "I have been greatly honored this day." Then the midwife put the child to bed.

⁹When, however, the prescribed days were completed, Anna cleansed herself of the flow of blood. ¹⁰And she offered her breast to the infant and gave her the name Mary.

6 Day by day the infant grew stronger. ²When she was six months old, her mother put her on the ground to see if she could stand. She walked seven steps and went to her mother's arms. ³Then her mother picked her up and said, "As the Lord my God lives, you will never walk on this ground again until I take you into the temple of the Lord."

Mary's first birthday

• **5:4.** This sentence is an unmistakable echo of Luke 18:14. It is also appropriate, for the charge of childlessness against Joachim (1:5) implied that he was not righteous. Joachim is now *acquitted* because he has seen no sin in the plate. Now that both Anna (see above at 4:9) and Joachim are vindicated of all charges made against them, they begin to recede from the narrative, at least as its main characters and altogether after 8:1.

• **5:5–8:2.** The narrative now focuses on Mary, her birth and childhood, though only episodically. After her birth we have brief accounts of incidents when Mary was six months old, one year old, and finally two and three years old.

• **5:5–10.** Anna's pregnancy comes to term. For the birth she is aided by a midwife. Anna then follows the religious prescriptions for purity following the birth and names her child Mary.

• **5:5.** *the ninth month:* The MSS vary widely, saying now sixth, now seventh, now ninth month (see Daniels, *Manuscript Tradition*, 2.194–98). For the ninth month being original, see Smid, *Commentary*, 47–48.

• **5:8.** *the midwife put the child to bed:* The Greek of this sentence is ambiguous and even misleading, as it merely says "she" put the child to bed. The grammatical antecedent would be Anna, but the context requires the midwife, as one copyist actually realized and changed accordingly (Daniels, *Manuscript Tradition*, 2.203–4).

• **5:9.** Childbirth rendered a woman ritually unclean and so prohibited her from touching anything holy or entering the temple. The obligations called for after *the prescribed days* are spelled out in Lev 12:1–8. Such obligations were, in fact, rather widespread (see Cole, "Gender Difference," 110–11).

• **6:1–5.** At six months of age Mary is already taking her first steps, after which Anna transforms her bedroom into a sanctuary to assure the purity of Mary.

• **6:1.** *grew stronger:* The language recalls similar statements made about John the Baptist (Luke 1:80) and Jesus (2:40).

• **6:1–2.** That Mary, when only *six months old*, can stand and even walk *seven steps* is highly unusual. Mary is no ordinary little girl.

• **6:3.** *until I take you into the temple of the Lord:* These words recall the vow Anna had made when she learned that she was pregnant (see 4:2)

⁴Καὶ ἐποίησεν ἁγίασμα ἐν τῷ κοιτῶνι αὐτῆς, καὶ πᾶν κοινὸν καὶ ἀκάθαρτον οὐκ εἴα διέρχεσθαι δι᾽ αὐτῆς. ⁵καὶ ἐκάλεσε τὰς θυγατέρας τῶν Ἑβραίων τὰς ἀμιάντους, καὶ διεπλάνων αὐτήν.

⁶Ἐγένετο δὲ πρῶτος ἐνιαυτὸς τῇ παιδί, καὶ ἐποίησεν Ἰωακεὶμ δοχὴν μεγάλην καὶ ἐκάλεσε τοὺς ἀρχιερεῖς καὶ τοὺς ἱερεῖς καὶ τοὺς γραμματεῖς καὶ τὴν γερουσίαν καὶ ὅλον τὸν λαὸν τοῦ Ἰσραήλ. ⁷καὶ προσήνεγκεν τὴν παῖδα Ἰωακεὶμ τοῖς ἱερεῦσιν, καὶ ηὐλόγησαν αὐτὴν λέγοντες· Ὁ θεὸς τῶν πατέρων ἡμῶν, εὐλόγησον τὴν παῖδα ταύτην καὶ δὸς αὐτῇ ὄνομα ὀνομαστὸν αἰώνιον ἐν πάσαις ταῖς γενεαῖς.

⁸Καὶ εἶπεν πᾶς ὁ λαός· Γένοιτο, ἀμήν.

⁹Καὶ προσήνεγκεν αὐτὴν τοῖς ἀρχιερεῦσιν, καὶ εὐλόγησαν αὐτὴν λέγοντες· Ὁ θεὸς τῶν ὑψωμάτων, ἐπίβλεψον ἐπὶ τὴν παῖδα ταύτην καὶ εὐλόγησον αὐτὴν ἐσχάτην εὐλογίαν ἥτις διαδοχὴν οὐκ ἔχει.

¹⁰Καὶ ἀνήρπασεν αὐτὴν ἡ μήτηρ αὐτῆς ἐν τῷ ἁγιάσματι τοῦ κοιτῶνος καὶ ἔδωκε μαστὸν τῇ παιδί. ¹¹καὶ ἐποίησεν ᾆσμα κυρίῳ τῷ θεῷ Ἄννα λέγουσα· Ἄισω ᾠδὴν ἁγίαν κυρίῳ τῷ θεῷ μου, ὅτι ἐπεσκέψατό με καὶ ἀφεῖλεν ἀπ᾽ ἐμοῦ ὀνειδισμὸν τῶν ἐχθρῶν μου· ¹²καὶ ἔδωκέν μοι κύριος ὁ θεός μου καρπὸν δικαιοσύνης αὐτοῦ

6:4. πᾶν: Tischendorf. de Strycker omits.   6:6. τοὺς ἀρχιερεῖς καὶ: de Strycker. Tischendorf omits.   6:9. προσήνεγκεν: Tischendorf. προσ- ήνεγκον: de Strycker.   6:11. ἁγίαν: de Strycker. Tischendorf omits. 6:12. κύριος ὁ θεός μου: de Strycker. κύριος: Tischendorf.

⁴And so she turned her bedroom into a sanctuary and did not permit anything profane or unclean to pass the child's lips. ⁵She sent for the undefiled daughters of the Hebrews, and they kept her amused.

⁶Now the child had her first birthday, and Joachim gave a great banquet and invited the high priests, priests, scholars, council of elders, and all the people of Israel. ⁷Joachim presented the child to the priests, and they blessed her: "God of our fathers, bless this child and give her a name which will be on the lips of future generations forever."

⁸And everyone said, "So be it. Amen."

⁹He presented her to the high priests, and they blessed her: "Most high God, look on this child and bless her with the ultimate blessing, one which cannot be surpassed."

¹⁰Her mother then took her up to the sanctuary—the bedroom—and gave her breast to the child. ¹¹And Anna composed a song for the Lord God: "I will sing a sacred song to the Lord my God because he has visited me and taken away the disgrace attributed to me by my enemies. ¹²The Lord my God

---

• **6:4.** The language of *profane or unclean* again recalls Exod 29:38 and Lev 12:6. Anna is insuring that Mary remains pure.

• **6:4.** The translation *the child's lips* is an interpretation of the pronoun "it." Translators often understand the "it" to mean the bedroom. But the gender of the pronoun, which is feminine, makes such a rendering problematic. Rather, as de Strycker (*Protévangile*, 91 n. 3) argues, Anna is closely monitoring Mary's diet (cf. Mark 7:2; Acts 10:14; 11:8).

• **6:5.** *the undefiled daughters of the Hebrews* likewise assure the purity of Mary's human contacts. Just who they are supposed to be, however, is less clear. To be sure, Judith is described as "a daughter of the Hebrews" (Jud 10:12), but there is no evidence of a group of undefiled daughters, as the author imagines. Scholars suppose that the author is thinking of a contemporary group of Christian virgins which he has anachronistically assumed to have a counterpart in Mary's day (de Strycker, *Protévangile*, 91 n. 4). The point, though, is to underscore that Mary's first years were spent in the purest seclusion of her mother's bedroom.

• **6:5.** The words *they kept her amused* render

a single Greek word (διεπλάνων), a verb whose meaning is regularly "cause to wander, mislead, or deceive." Such a meaning is out of the question here, which explains why some MSS have a different but similarly spelled word (διακονεῖν="to serve, wait on") and why one scholar proposed another similar but more appropriate word (διαπλύνειν="to wash") (Daniels, *Manuscript Tradition*, 2.226–27). Other scholars, however, claim that "to amuse" is one late meaning of the word διαπλανᾶν and so understand it as I have translated it (de Strycker, *Protévangile*, 303; Smid, *Commentary*, 51).

• **6:6–14.** On Mary's first birthday Joachim celebrates with a great banquet, during which Mary is blessed by priests and high priests and Anna can finally affirm that she, too, is fruitful.

• **6:6.** *gave a great banquet:* The language recalls that of Luke 5:29 and 14:16. That so many are invited again attests to Joachim's wealth and high social status.

• **6:11–13.** Anna's song of vindication reverses the tone of despair that characterized her earlier lament to God in the garden (see 3:2–8).

μονοούσιον πολυπλάσιον ἐνώπιον αὐτοῦ. ¹³τίς ἀγγελεῖ τοῖς υἱοῖς ῾Ρουβὴλ ὅτι Ἄννα θηλάζει; ἀκούσατε ἀκούσατε, αἱ δώδεκα φυλαὶ τοῦ Ἰσραήλ, ὅτι Ἄννα θηλάζει.

¹⁴Καὶ ἀνέπαυσεν αὐτὴν ἐν τῷ κοιτῶνι τοῦ ἁγιάσματος, καὶ ἐξῆλθεν καὶ διηκόνει αὐτοῖς. ¹⁵τελεσθέντος δὲ τοῦ δείπνου κατέβησαν εὐφραινόμενοι καὶ ἐδόξασαν τὸν θεὸν Ἰσραήλ.

Mary at the temple

7 Τῇ δὲ παιδὶ προσετίθεντο οἱ μῆνες αὐτῆς. ἐγένετο δὲ διετὴς ἡ παῖς, καὶ εἶπεν Ἰωακείμ· Ἀνάξωμεν αὐτὴν ἐν ναῷ κυρίου ὅπως ἀποδῶμεν τὴν ἐπαγγελίαν ἣν ἐπηγγειλάμεθα, μήπως ἀποστείλῃ ὁ δεσπότης ἐφ᾿ ἡμᾶς καὶ ἀπρόσδεκτον ἔσται τὸ δῶρον ἡμῶν.

²Καὶ εἶπεν Ἄννα· Ἀναμείνωμεν τὸ τρίτον ἔτος, ὅπως μὴ ζητήσῃ πατέρα ἢ μητέρα.

³Καὶ εἶπεν Ἰωακείμ· Ἀναμείνωμεν.

⁴Ἐγένετο δὲ τριετὴς ἡ παῖς, καὶ εἶπεν Ἰωακείμ· Καλέσωμεν τὰς θυγατέρας τῶν Ἑβραίων τὰς ἀμιάντους, ⁵καὶ λαβέτωσαν ἀνὰ λαμπάδα, καὶ ἔστωσαν καιόμεναι, ἵνα μὴ στραφῇ ἡ παῖς εἰς τὰ ὀπίσω καὶ αἰχμαλωτισθήσεται ἡ καρδία αὐτῆς ἐκ ναοῦ κυρίου. ⁶καὶ ἐποίησαν οὕτως ἕως ἀνέβησαν ἐν ναῷ κυρίου.

⁷Καὶ ἐδέξατο αὐτὴν ὁ ἱερεύς, καὶ φιλήσας αὐτὴν εὐλόγησεν καὶ εἶπεν· Ἐμεγάλυνεν κύριος ὁ θεὸς τὸ ὄνομά σου ἐν πάσαις ταῖς γενεαῖς· ⁸ἐπὶ σοὶ ἐπ᾿ ἐσχάτων τῶν ἡμερῶν φανερώσει κύριος τὸ λύτρον τοῖς υἱοῖς Ἰσραήλ.

⁹Καὶ ἐκάθισεν αὐτὴν ἐπὶ τρίτου βαθμοῦ τοῦ θυσιαστηρίου, καὶ ἔβαλλε κύριος ὁ θεὸς χάριν ἐπ᾿ αὐτήν, ¹⁰καὶ κατεχόρευε τοῖς ποσὶν αὐτῆς, καὶ ἠγάπησεν αὐτὴν πᾶς οἶκος Ἰσραήλ.

6:12. πολυπλάσιον: de Strycker. πολυπλούσιον: Tischendorf. 6:13. ῾Ρουβήλ: de Strycker. ῾Ρουβίμ: Tischendorf. 7:4. Καλέσωμεν: de Strycker. καλέσατε: Tischendorf. 7:5. ἡ παῖς: Tischendorf. de Strycker omits. 7:7. κύριος ὁ θεός: de Strycker. κύριος: Tischendorf.

has given me the fruit of his righteousness, single yet manifold before him. ¹³Who will announce to the sons of Reubel that Anna has a child at her breast? 'Listen, listen, you twelve tribes of Israel: Anna has a child at her breast!'"

¹⁴Anna made her rest in the bedroom—the sanctuary—and then went out and began serving her guests. ¹⁵When the banquet was over, they left in good spirits and praised the God of Israel.

Mary at
the temple

7 Many months passed, but when the child reached two years of age, Joachim said, "Let's take her up to the temple of the Lord, so that we can keep the promise we made, or else the Lord will be angry with us and our gift will be unacceptable."

²And Anna said, "Let's wait until she is three, so she won't miss her father or mother."

³And Joachim agreed: "Let's wait."

⁴When the child turned three years of age, Joachim said, "Let's send for the undefiled Hebrew daughters. ⁵Let them each take a lamp and light it, so the child won't turn back and have her heart captivated by things outside the Lord's temple." ⁶And this is what they did until the time they ascended to the Lord's temple.

⁷The priest welcomed her, kissed her, and blessed her: "The Lord God has exalted your name among all generations. ⁸In you the Lord will disclose his redemption to the people of Israel during the last days."

⁹And he sat her down on the third step of the altar, and the Lord showered favor on her. ¹⁰And she danced, and the whole house of Israel loved her.

- **6:12.** *fruit of his righteousness.* The phrase recalls Prov 11:30; 13:2; Amos 6:12; Jas 3:18.
- **6:12.** *single yet manifold:* A most obscure phrase. For full, if indecisive, discussion, see de Strycker (*Protévangile*, 301–2).
- **6:13.** *Who will announce to the sons of Reubel that Anna has a child at her breast?:* This sentence is clearly modeled on the similar situation of Sarah in Gen 21:7.
- **7:1–8:2.** Mary's parents must carry through on the vow Anna made regarding their child (see 4:2). Joachim brings up the vow when Mary is two, but Anna persuades him to wait until she is three. At that time she is taken to the temple, accompanied by unde-filed Hebrew daughters with lamps to keep her from looking back. Mary arrives at the temple and is welcomed there.
- **7:1.** For *the promise* to offer their child to the Lord, see above 4:2.
- **7:2.** *Let's wait:* Anna's reluctance parallels that of Hannah, who likewise sought a delay in handing her child over to the temple (1 Sam 1:22).
- **7:9.** *third step of the altar.* The author may have in mind the description of the altar in Ezek 43:13–17, where steps are assumed. Ordinarily only priests could approach the altar.
- **7:10.** That Mary *danced* may indicate that she has gladly accepted her new home.

Mary at twelve　**8** Καὶ κατέβησαν οἱ γονεῖς αὐτῆς θαυμάζοντες καὶ ἐπαινοῦντες καὶ δοξάζοντες τὸν δεσπότην θεὸν ὅτι οὐκ ἀπεστράφη ἡ παῖς ἐπ᾽ αὐτούς. ²ἦν δὲ Μαρία ἐν ναῷ κυρίου ὡσεὶ περιστερὰ νεμομένη καὶ ἐλάμβανε τροφὴν ἐκ χειρὸς ἀγγέλου.

³Γενομένης δὲ αὐτῆς δωδεκαετοῦς, συμβούλιον ἐγένετο τῶν ἱερέων λεγόντων· Ἰδοὺ Μαρία γέγονεν δωδεκαετὴς ἐν τῷ ναῷ κυρίου· ⁴τί οὖν αὐτὴν ποιήσωμεν, μήπως μιάνῃ τὸ ἁγίασμα κυρίου τοῦ θεοῦ ἡμῶν; ⁵καὶ εἶπον τῷ ἀρχιερεῖ· Σὺ ἕστηκας ἐπὶ τὸ θυσιαστήριον κυρίου. εἴσελθε καὶ πρόσευξαι περὶ αὐτῆς· καὶ ὃ ἐὰν φανερώσῃ σοι κύριος ὁ θεός, τοῦτο ποιήσομεν.

⁶Καὶ εἰσῆλθεν ὁ ἀρχιερεὺς λαβὼν τὸν δωδεκακώδωνα εἰς τὰ ἅγια τῶν ἁγίων καὶ ηὔξατο περὶ αὐτῆς. ⁷καὶ ἰδοὺ ἄγγελος κυρίου ἐπέστη λέγων· Ζαχαρία Ζαχαρία, ἔξελθε καὶ ἐκκλησίασον τοὺς χηρεύοντας τοῦ λαοῦ, καὶ ἐνεγκάτωσαν ἀνὰ ῥάβδον, ⁸καὶ ᾧ ἐὰν ἐπιδείξῃ κύριος ὁ θεὸς σημεῖον, τούτῳ ἔσται γυνή. ⁹ἐξῆλθον δὲ οἱ κήρυκες καθ᾽ ὅλης τῆς περιχώρου τῆς Ἰουδαίας, καὶ ἤχησεν ἡ σάλπιγξ κυρίου, καὶ ἰδοὺ ἔδραμον ἅπαντες.

8:1. ἐπαινοῦντες καὶ δοξάζοντες: de Strycker. αἰνοῦντες: Tischendorf. **8:1.** ἡ παῖς: Tischendorf. de Strycker omits. **8:1.** ἐπ᾽ αὐτούς: de Strycker. εἰς τὰ ὀπίσω: Tischendorf. **8:4.** κυρίου τοῦ θεοῦ ἡμῶν: de Strycker. κυρίου: Tischendorf. **8:5.** τῷ ἀρχιερεῖ: Tischendorf. αὐτῷ οἱ ἱερεῖς: de Strycker. **8:5.** κύριος ὁ θεός: de Strycker. κύριος: Tischendorf. **8:6.** ὁ ἀρχιερεύς: Tischendorf. ὁ ἱερεύς: de Strycker. **8:7.** ἐπέστη: Tischendorf. ἔστη: de Strycker. **8:8.** κύριος ὁ θεός: de Strycker. κύριος: Tischendorf. **8:9.** ἡ σάλπιγξ: Tischendorf. σάλπιγξ: de Strycker.

8 Her parents left for home marveling and praising and   *Mary at twelve*
glorifying the Lord God because the child did not look back at
them. ²And Mary lived in the temple of the Lord. She was fed
there like a dove, receiving her food from the hand of a heavenly
messenger.

³When she turned twelve, however, there was a meeting of
the priests . "Look," they said, "Mary has turned twelve in the
temple of the Lord. ⁴What should we do with her so she won't
pollute the sanctuary of the Lord our God?" ⁵And they said to
the high priest, "You stand at the altar of the Lord. Enter and
pray about her, and we'll do whatever the Lord God discloses to
you."

⁶And so the high priest took the vestment with the twelve
bells, entered the Holy of Holies, and began to pray about her.
⁷And suddenly a messenger of the Lord appeared: "Zechariah,
Zechariah, go out and assemble the widowers of the people and
have them each bring a staff. ⁸She will become the wife of the
one to whom the Lord God shows a sign." ⁹And so heralds
covered the surrounding territory of Judea. The trumpet of the
Lord sounded and all the widowers came running.

• **8:2.** The *dove* is associated with Mary here and in 9:6. Its association may underscore Mary's purity (cf. Matt 10:16). Certainly her being fed *from the hand of a heavenly messenger* underscores her continuing purity.

• **8:3–9:12.** Mary's years in the temple come to an end when she turns twelve. The priests must decide what to do with her. The high priest receives a revelation in which he is instructed to summon all the widowers in Israel. Among them is Joseph, whose staff displays a sign that designates him as the one to receive Mary. His objections are brushed aside and he takes her to his house.

• **8:3–9.** When Mary turns twelve the priests prevail upon the high priest Zechariah to take their concern about Mary to God himself. The high priest enters the Holy of Holies and prays, after which a messenger from the Lord instructs him to summon all the widowers. Each is to bring his staff.

• **8:3–4.** At age *twelve* Mary poses a threat to the temple's purity, since menstruation would render her and hence the temple unclean (see Lev 15:19–33 and more broadly Cole, "Gender Difference," 111).

• **8:6.** The word "vestment" in the phrase *the vestment with the twelve bells* is not in the Greek and has been supplied for sense (Smid, *Commentary*, 67–68). *Bells* are mentioned as part of the hem decoration of the high priest's robe (Exod 28:33; 39:25–26; cf. Sir 45:8–13).

• **8:7.** That *each brings a staff* is remininiscent of several stories in which staffs become instruments of divine will. See, e.g., Num 17:1–9; Hos 4:12.

• **8:8.** *She will become the wife:* This heavenly message assumes that Mary is to be married to one of the widowers. The high priest will soon reinterpret this message (see 9:7).

• **8:9.** *the surrounding territory:* This phrase may be an echo of Mark 1:28. If so, then it is the only one to this gospel. It may, however, be an echo of Luke 4:14.

• **8:9.** This *trumpet of the Lord* is otherwise unknown.

9 Ἰωσὴφ δὲ ῥίψας τὸ σκέπαρνον ἐξῆλθεν καὶ αὐτὸς εἰς συνάντησιν αὐτῶν· ²καὶ συναχθέντες ὁμοῦ ἀπῆλθον πρὸς τὸν ἀρχιερέα, λαβόντες τὰς ῥάβδους. ³λαβὼν δὲ ἁπάντων τὰς ῥάβδους εἰσῆλθεν εἰς τὸ ἱερὸν καὶ ηὔξατο. ⁴τελέσας δὲ τὴν εὐχὴν ἔλαβε τὰς ῥάβδους καὶ ἐξῆλθεν καὶ ἔδωκεν αὐτοῖς· ⁵καὶ σημεῖον οὐκ ἦν ἐν αὐταῖς. τὴν δὲ ἐσχάτην ῥάβδον ἔλαβε ὁ Ἰωσήφ· ⁶καὶ ἰδοὺ περιστερὰ ἐξῆλθεν ἀπὸ τῆς ῥάβδου καὶ ἐπεστάθη ἐπὶ τὴν κεφαλὴν τοῦ Ἰωσήφ. ⁷καὶ εἶπεν ὁ ἀρχιερεύς· Ἰωσὴφ Ἰωσήφ, σὺ κεκλήρωσαι τὴν παρθένον κυρίου παραλαβεῖν εἰς τήρησιν σεαυτῷ.

⁸Καὶ ἀντεῖπεν ὁ Ἰωσὴφ λέγων· Υἱοὺς ἔχω καὶ πρεσβύτης εἰμί· αὕτη δὲ νεᾶνις· μήπως ἔσομαι περίγελος τοῖς υἱοῖς Ἰσραήλ.

⁹Καὶ εἶπεν ὁ ἀρχιερεύς· Ἰωσήφ, φοβήθητι κύριον τὸν θεόν σου, καὶ μνήσθητι ὅσα ἐποίησεν ὁ θεὸς Δαθὰν καὶ Ἀβιρὼν καὶ Κορέ, πῶς ἐδιχάσθη ἡ γῆ καὶ κατεπόθησαν ἅπαντες διὰ τὴν ἀντιλογίαν αὐτῶν. ¹⁰καὶ νῦν φοβήθητι, Ἰωσήφ, μήπως ἔσται ταῦτα ἐν τῷ οἴκῳ σου.

¹¹Καὶ φοβηθεὶς Ἰωσὴφ παρέλαβεν αὐτὴν εἰς τήρησιν ἑαυτῷ. ¹²καὶ εἶπεν αὐτῇ· Μαρία, παρέλαβόν σε ἐκ ναοῦ κυρίου. καὶ νῦν καταλείπω σε ἐν τῷ οἴκῳ μου. ἀπέρχομαι γὰρ οἰκοδομῆσαι τὰς οἰκοδομάς, καὶ ἥξω πρὸς σέ· κύριός σε διαφυλάξει.

9:1. καὶ αὐτός: de Strycker. Tischendorf omits.   9:2. ὁμοῦ: de Strycker. Tischendorf omits.   9:2. τὸν ἀρχιερέα: Tischendorf. τὸν ἱερέα: de Strycker.   9:3. λαβὼν δὲ ἁπάντων τὰς ῥάβδους εἰσῆλθεν: Tischendorf. δεξάμενος δὲ ὁ ἱερεὺς τὰς ῥάβδους ἀπ᾽ αὐτῶν εἰσῆλθεν: de Strycker. 9:6. ἐπεστάθη: de Strycker. ἐπετάσθη: Tischendorf. See further de Strycker, "Handschriften," 584.   9:7. ὁ ἀρχιερεύς: various mss. ὁ ἱερεύς: Tischendorf and de Strycker.   9:7. Ἰωσὴφ Ἰωσήφ: de Strycker. Tischendorf omits.   9:9. ὁ ἀρχιερεύς: various mss. ὁ ἱερεύς: Tischendorf and de Strycker.   9:12. καὶ εἶπεν αὐτῇ· Μαρία: de Strycker. καὶ εἶπεν Ἰωσὴφ τῇ Μαριάμ· Ἰδού: Tischendorf.

9 And Joseph, too, threw down his carpenter's axe and left for the meeting. [2]When they had all gathered, they went to the high priest with their staffs. [3]After the high priest had collected everyone's staff, he entered the temple and began to pray. [4]When he had finished his prayer, he took the staffs and went out and began to give them back to each man. [5]But there was no sign on any of them. Joseph got the last staff. [6]Suddenly a dove came out of this staff and perched on Joseph's head. [7]"Joseph, Joseph," the high priest said, "you've been chosen by lot to take the virgin of the Lord into your care and protection."

Joseph accepts Mary

[8]But Joseph objected: "I already have sons and I'm an old man; she's only a young woman. I'm afraid that I'll become the butt of jokes among the people of Israel."

[9]And the high priest responded, "Joseph, fear the Lord your God and remember what God did to Dathan, Abiron, and Kore: the earth was split open and they were all swallowed up because of their objection. [10]So now, Joseph, you ought to take heed so that the same thing won't happen to your family."

[11]And so out of fear Joseph took her into his care and protection. [12]He said to her, "Mary, I've gotten you from the temple of the Lord, but now I'm leaving you at home. I'm going away to build houses, but I'll come back to you. The Lord will protect you."

- **9:1–12.** The priests carry out their task of finding a home for Mary. The widowers who are assembled turn in their staffs. When they are returned, Joseph's staff displays a sign in which a dove flies out of it and perches on Joseph's head. He is thereby designated to receive Mary. His objections are countered, and he returns home with Mary but does not stay there long, as he is off to build buildings, trusting the Lord to protect her.
- **9:1.** *Joseph* is introduced at this point into the story. But it is surprising–at least to those familiar with the stories in Matthew and Luke–that he is included among the widowers summoned. In fact, Joseph will be characterized quite differently throughout this gospel from what is said about him in Matthew and Luke. The changes are due to the author's stress on the purity of Mary (see Introduction 5.3).
- **9:7.** This is the first time Mary is identified as a virgin—indeed, *a virgin of the Lord.* Since the high priest says it, it becomes an interpretation of the heavenly messenger's order, which referred to Mary as someone's future "wife" (8:8). That possibility has now changed. She is simply given to Joseph as his ward; he becomes her guardian and is obligated to give her his *care and protection.*
- **9:8.** *I already have sons and I'm an old man:* Other changes in Joseph's characterization include assigning the brothers (and sisters) (see Mark 6:3; Matt 13:55–56; and Meier, "Brothers and Sisters," 1–28) to a previous marriage of Joseph and making him much older than is assumed in the canonical accounts where Joseph is naturally understood to be of marriageable age (see Matt 1:18–19; Luke 2:5). Here, however, he is so old as to be embarrassed by the association with a *young woman.*
- **9:9.** For the story of *Dathan, Abiron, and Kore,* see Num 16:1–35, esp. 31–32.
- **9:11.** *took her:* The language recalls Matt 1:24, but with one significant difference. The pronoun "her" replaces Matthew's "his wife," which is now inappropriate.
- **9:12.** *The Lord will protect you:* In his absence Joseph calls on God to take over his newly-assumed responsibility for the care and protection of Mary. This absence functions, of course, to avoid any hint that Joseph could have been intimate with Mary.

*Virgins &
temple veil*

10 Ἐγένετο δὲ συμβούλιον τῶν ἱερέων λεγόντων· Ποιήσωμεν καταπέτασμα τῷ ναῷ κυρίου.

²Καὶ εἶπεν ὁ ἀρχιερεύς· Καλέσατέ μοι τὰς παρθένους τὰς ἀμιάντους ἀπὸ τῆς φυλῆς τοῦ Δαυίδ. ³καὶ ἀπῆλθον οἱ ὑπηρέται καὶ ἐξεζήτησαν καὶ εὗρον ἑπτὰ παρθένους. ⁴καὶ ἐμνήσθη ὁ ἀρχιερεὺς τῆς παιδὸς Μαρίας ὅτι ἦν τῆς φυλῆς τοῦ Δαυὶδ καὶ ἀμίαντος τῷ θεῷ. ⁵καὶ ἀπῆλθον οἱ ὑπηρέται καὶ ἤγαγον αὐτήν.

⁶Καὶ εἰσήγαγον αὐτὰς ἐν τῷ ναῷ κυρίου· ⁷καὶ εἶπεν ὁ ἀρχιερεύς· Λάχετέ μοι ὧδε, τίς νήσει τὸν χρυσὸν καὶ τὸ ἀμίαντον καὶ τὴν βύσσον καὶ τὸ σιρικὸν καὶ τὸ ὑακίνθινον καὶ τὸ κόκκινον καὶ τὴν ἀληθινὴν πορφύραν.

⁸Καὶ ἔλαχε τὴν Μαρίαν ἡ ἀληθινὴ πορφύρα καὶ τὸ κόκκινον. καὶ λαβοῦσα ἀπῄει ἐν τῷ οἴκῳ αὐτῆς. ⁹τῷ δὲ καιρῷ ἐκείνῳ Ζαχαρίας ἐσίγησεν, καὶ ἐγένετο ἀντὶ αὐτοῦ Σαμουήλ, μέχρι ὅτε ἐλάλησεν Ζαχαρίας. Μαρία δὲ λαβοῦσα τὸ κόκκινον ἔκλωθεν.

Mary's vision

11 Καὶ ἔλαβεν τὴν κάλπιν καὶ ἐξῆλθεν γεμίσαι ὕδωρ· ²καὶ ἰδοὺ φωνὴ λέγουσα αὐτῇ· Χαῖρε, κεχαριτωμένη· ὁ κύριος μετὰ σοῦ· εὐλογημένη σὺ ἐν γυναιξίν. ³καὶ περιεβλέπετο τὰ δεξιὰ καὶ

10:2. ὁ ἀρχιερεύς: various MSS. ὁ ἱερεύς: Tischendorf and de Strycker. 10:3. παρθένους: Tischendorf. de Strycker omits.   10:4. ὁ ἀρχιερεύς: various MSS. ὁ ἱερεύς: Tischendorf and de Strycker.   10:7. ὁ ἀρχιερεύς: various MSS. ὁ ἱερεύς: Tischendorf and de Strycker.   11:3. περιεβλέπετο: Tischendorf. περιέβλεπεν: de Strycker.

10 Meanwhile, there was a council of the priests, who agreed: "Let's make a veil for the temple of the Lord."

²And the high priest said, "Summon the true virgins from the tribe of David." ³And so the temple assistants left and searched everywhere and found seven. ⁴And the high priest then remembered the girl Mary, that she, too, was from the tribe of David and was pure in God's eyes. ⁵And so the temple assistants went out and got her.

⁶And they took the maidens into the temple of the Lord. ⁷And the high priest said, "Cast lots for me to decide who'll spin which threads for the veil: the gold, the white, the linen, the silk, the violet, the scarlet, and the true purple."

⁸And the true purple and scarlet threads fell to Mary. And she took them and returned home. ⁹Now it was at this time that Zechariah became mute, and Samuel took his place until Zechariah regained his speech. ¹⁰Meanwhile, Mary had taken up the scarlet thread and was spinning it.

11 And she took her water jar and went out to fill it with water. ²Suddenly there was a voice saying to her, "Greetings, favored one! The Lord is with you. Blessed are you among women." ³Mary began looking around, both right and left, to see

---

• **10:1–12:9.** While Joseph is away Mary occupies herself by helping to make a new veil for the temple. During this time she is visited by a heavenly messenger, who announces that she has found favor with the Lord and will bear a son of God. After finishing her task on the veil Mary then visits her relative Elizabeth, herself pregnant with the future John the Baptist.

• **10:1–10.** Mary is selected as a virgin from the tribe of David who is to help in the weaving of a temple veil. She and seven others are assigned the various colors, Mary being given scarlet and true purple.

• **10:1.** On the *veil*, which is presumably the one that protects the Holy of Holies, see Exod 26:31, 36; 35:25; 36:35; 2 Chr 3:14 and Smid, *Commentary*, 76–77.

• **10:2.** *true virgins from the tribe of David:* There may have been a convention of having virgin weavers make the temple veil (see Manns, *Essais*, 106–9), but the evidence suggests 80 women, not eight (10:3–4), and in any case there was no tribe of David.

• **10:4.** *the girl Mary:* The author again denies that Mary is Joseph's "wife." In addition, the claim of Davidic descent for Mary contrasts with the canonical accounts, in which Mary is related to Elizabeth, a daughter of Aaron (Luke 1:5, 36). It is Joseph, however, who is assigned Davidic descent (Matt 1:20; Luke 2:4).

• **10:9.** *Now it was at this time:* The author is clearly, if awkwardly, trying to place his narrative within the framework of the canonical accounts (see Luke 1:20–22, 64).

• **11:1–9.** While out to get water Mary hears a voice addressing her which frightens her and sends her back home and specifically to her spinning. But she is addressed again and told that she is to bear a son of the Most High. She assents, as is appropriate for a slave of the Lord.

• **11:2.** *Greetings, favored one! The Lord is with you:* This part of the message is taken from Gabriel's greeting in Luke 1:28, but the next part, *Blessed are you among women,* comes from Elizabeth's greeting, taken from Luke 1:42.

τὰ ἀριστερὰ Μαρία πόθεν αὕτη εἴη ἡ φωνή. ⁴καὶ ἔντρομος γενομένη εἰσῄει εἰς τὸν οἶκον αὐτῆς καὶ ἀναπαύσασα τὴν κάλπιν ἔλαβεν τὴν πορφύραν καὶ ἐκάθισεν ἐπὶ τοῦ θρόνου καὶ εἷλκεν αὐτήν.

⁵Καὶ ἰδοὺ ἔστη ἄγγελος ἐνώπιον αὐτῆς λέγων· Μὴ φοβοῦ, Μαρία· εὗρες γὰρ χάριν ἐνώπιον τοῦ πάντων δεσπότου. συλλήψει ἐκ λόγου αὐτοῦ.

⁶Ἡ δὲ ἀκούσασα Μαρία διεκρίθη ἐν ἑαυτῇ λέγουσα· Εἰ ἐγὼ συλλήψομαι ἀπὸ κυρίου θεοῦ ζῶντος, καὶ γεννήσω ὡς πᾶσα γυνὴ γεννᾷ; ⁷Καὶ εἶπεν ὁ ἄγγελος κυρίου· Οὐχ οὕτως, Μαρία· δύναμις γὰρ θεοῦ ἐπισκιάσει σοι· διὸ καὶ τὸ γεννώμενον ἅγιον κληθήσεται υἱὸς ὑψίστου. ⁸καὶ καλέσεις τὸ ὄνομα αὐτοῦ Ἰησοῦν· αὐτὸς γὰρ σώσει τὸν λαὸν αὐτοῦ ἐκ τῶν ἁμαρτιῶν αὐτῶν.

⁹Καὶ εἶπε Μαρία· Ἰδοὺ ἡ δούλη κυρίου κατενώπιον αὐτοῦ· γένοιτό μοι κατὰ τὸ ῥῆμά σου.

Mary & Elizabeth 12 Καὶ ἐποίησεν τὴν πορφύραν καὶ τὸ κόκκινον, καὶ ἀνήνεγκεν τῷ ἀρχιερεῖ. ²καὶ λαβὼν ὁ ἀρχιερεὺς εὐλόγησεν αὐτὴν καὶ εἶπεν· Μαρία, ἐμεγάλυνεν κύριος ὁ θεὸς τὸ ὄνομά σου, καὶ ἔσῃ εὐλογημένη ἐν πάσαις ταῖς γενεαῖς τῆς γῆς.

³Χαρὰν δὲ λαβοῦσα Μαρία ἀπῄει πρὸς τὴν συγγενίδα αὐτῆς Ἐλισάβεδ. ⁴καὶ ἔκρουσεν πρὸς τὴν θύραν, καὶ ἀκούσασα ἡ Ἐλισάβεδ ἔρριψεν τὸ κόκκινον καὶ ἔδραμεν πρὸς τὴν θύραν καὶ ἤνοιξεν αὐτῇ ⁵καὶ εὐλόγησεν αὐτὴν καὶ εἶπεν· Πόθεν μοι τοῦτο

11:3. Μαρία: de Strycker. Tischendorf omits.   **11:4.** αὐτήν: Tischendorf. τὴν πορφύραν: de Strycker.   **11:5.** ἄγγελος: de Strycker. ἄγγελος κυρίου: Tischendorf.   **11:6.** Μαρία: de Strycker. Tischendorf omits.   **11:6.** Εἰ ἐγὼ συλλήψομαι ἀπὸ κυρίου θεοῦ ζῶντος, καὶ γεννήσω ὡς πᾶσα γυνὴ γεννᾷ: Tischendorf. Ἐγὼ συλλήψομαι ἀπὸ κυρίου θεοῦ ζῶντος ὡς πᾶσα γυνὴ γεννᾷ: de Strycker.   **11:7.** Καὶ εἶπεν ὁ ἄγγελος κυρίου: Tischendorf. Καὶ ἰδοὺ ἄγγελος ἔστη λέγων αὐτῇ: de Strycker.   **11:7.** θεοῦ: de Strycker. κυρίου: Tischendorf.   **12:1.** ἀρχιερεῖ: various MSS. ἱερεῖ: Tischendorf and de Strycker.   **12:2.** λαβών: de Strycker. Tischendorf omits (not noted by de Strycker).   **12:2.** ἀρχιερεύς: various MSS. ἱερεύς: Tischendorf and de Strycker.   **12:5.** εὐλόγησεν: de Strycker. ἰδοῦσα τὴν Μαριὰμ εὐλόγησεν: Tischendorf.

where the voice was coming from. ⁴She became terrified and
went home. After putting the water jar down and taking up the
purple thread, she sat down on her chair and began to spin.

⁵A heavenly messenger suddenly stood before her: "Don't be
afraid, Mary. You see, you've found favor in the sight of the
Lord of all. You will conceive by means of his word."

⁶But as she listened, Mary was doubtful and said, "If I actually
conceive by the Lord, the living God, will I also give birth the
way women usually do?"

⁷And the messenger of the Lord replied, "No, Mary, because
the power of God will overshadow you. Therefore, the child to
be born will be called holy, son of the Most High. ⁸And you will
name him Jesus—the name means 'he will save his people from
their sins.'"

⁹And Mary said, "Here I am, the Lord's slave before him. I
pray that all you've told me comes true."

12 And she finished ⟨spinning⟩ the purple and the scarlet   *Mary & Elizabeth*
thread and took her work up to the high priest. ²The high priest
accepted them and praised her and said, "Mary, the Lord God
has extolled your name and so you will be blessed by all the
generations of the earth."

³Mary rejoiced and left to visit her relative Elizabeth. ⁴She
knocked at the door. Elizabeth heard her, tossed aside the
scarlet thread, ran to the door, and opened it for her. ⁵And she

---

• **11:4.** That Mary *went home* and then is depicted as *taking up the purple thread* shows that Mary is behaving properly. Going outside puts a girl in danger, even if the well is regarded as not as public well but as one in her garden, as the story of the attempt on Susannah shows (see Sus 15–27). In any case, she returns home and specifically to her spinning, the traditional role for the virtuous woman (see Introduction 5.4).
• **11:5.** What the messenger says is a condensed paraphrase of Luke 1:30–33.
• **11:6.** Mary is likewise *doubtful* in Luke 1:34.
• **11:7.** Again, what the messenger says is a slight paraphrase of Luke 1:35.
• **11:8.** This entire verse is taken word for word from Matt 1:21, but here it is addressed to Mary, not to Joseph. She is instructed to name him Jesus.
• **11:9.** Mary's response follows closely that in Luke 1:38.
• **12:1–9.** After completing her assignment for the temple veil Mary visits her relative Elizabeth and stays for three months. When

she returns home, her pregnancy causes her to go into hiding.
• **12:2.** The high priest's words recall those of Luke 1:46, 48, though with some striking changes, such as their being said to Mary, not by her, and their reversing the subject and object, so that it is Mary, not the Lord, who is exalted.
• **12:3.** *Elizabeth* is not introduced by the author, who presumably supposes that his readers will already know her from Luke's gospel as the wife of Zechariah and mother of John the Baptist (see esp. Luke 1:5, 57, 60). The following incident (12:3–7) is based on Mary's visit to Elizabeth in Luke 1:39–56.
• **12:4.** *the scarlet thread:* These words have the overwhelming support of the MSS and are preferred by both Tischendorf and de Strycker. They are nonetheless problematic, in that they seemingly place Elizabeth, who is married, among the virgins who were given the task of preparing the threads for the temple veil (see above 10:1–3). One copyist sensed the problem and proposed

ἵνα ἡ μήτηρ τοῦ κυρίου μου ἔλθῃ πρὸς ἐμέ; ἰδοὺ γὰρ τὸ ἐν ἐμοὶ ἐσκίρτησεν καὶ εὐλόγησέν σε.

⁶Ἡ δὲ Μαρία ἐπελάθετο τῶν μυστηρίων ὧν ἐλάλησεν Γαβριὴλ ὁ ἄγγελος. καὶ ἠτένισεν εἰς τὸν οὐρανὸν καὶ εἶπεν· Τίς εἰμι ἐγώ, κύριε, ὅτι πᾶσαι αἱ γενεαὶ τῆς γῆς μακαριοῦσίν με;

⁷Καὶ ἐποίησεν τρεῖς μῆνας πρὸς τὴν Ἐλισάβεδ. ⁸καὶ ἡμέρᾳ ἀφ᾽ ἡμέρας ἡ γαστὴρ αὐτῆς ὠγκοῦτο. καὶ φοβηθεῖσα ἡ Μαρία ἦλθεν ἐν τῷ οἴκῳ αὐτῆς καὶ ἔκρυπτεν αὐτὴν ἀπὸ τῶν υἱῶν Ἰσραήλ. ⁹ἦν δὲ ἐτῶν δέκα ἓξ ὅτε ταῦτα τὰ μυστήρια ἐγένετο αὐτῇ.

Joseph accuses Mary

13 Καὶ ἐγένετο αὐτῇ ἕκτος μήν, καὶ ἰδοὺ ἦλθεν Ἰωσὴφ ἀπὸ τῶν οἰκοδομῶν αὐτοῦ καὶ εἰσῆλθεν ἐν τῷ οἴκῳ καὶ εὗρεν αὐτὴν ὠγκωμένην. ²καὶ ἔτυψεν τὸ πρόσωπον αὐτοῦ καὶ ἔρριψεν αὐτὸν χαμαὶ ἐπὶ τὸν σάκκον καὶ ἔκλαυσεν πικρῶς λέγων· Ποίῳ προσώπῳ ἀτενίσω πρὸς κύριον τὸν θεόν; ³τί ἄρα εὔξωμαι περὶ αὐτῆς ὅτι παρθένον παρέλαβον αὐτὴν ἐκ ναοῦ κυρίου τοῦ θεοῦ καὶ οὐκ ἐφύλαξα αὐτήν; ⁴τίς ὁ θηρεύσας με; τίς τὸ πονηρὸν τοῦτο ἐποίησεν ἐν τῷ οἴκῳ μου; τίς ἠχμαλώτευσε τὴν παρθένον ἀπ᾽ ἐμοῦ καὶ ἐμίανεν αὐτήν; ⁵μήτι ἐν ἐμοὶ ἀνεκεφαλαιώθη ἡ ἱστορία τοῦ Ἀδάμ; ὥσπερ γὰρ Ἀδὰμ ἦν ἐν τῇ ὥρᾳ τῆς δοξολογίας

12:6. ἄγγελος: de Strycker. ἀρχάγγελος: Tischendorf.　　**12:6.** Τίς εἰμι ἐγώ, κύριε, ὅτι: Tischendorf. Τίς εἰμι ἐγὼ ὅτι ἰδού: de Strycker.　　**12:6.** αἱ γενεαί: Tischendorf. αἱ γυναῖκες: de Strycker.　　**13:2.** τὸν θεόν: de Strycker. τὸν θεόν μου: Tischendorf.　　**13:3.** περὶ αὐτῆς: de Strycker. περὶ τῆς κόρης ταύτης: Tischendorf.　　**13:3.** αὐτήν: Tischendorf. de Strycker omits.　　**13:3.** τοῦ θεοῦ: de Strycker. τοῦ θεοῦ μου: Tischendorf.　　**13:4.** τίς ἠχμαλώτευσε τὴν παρθένον ἀπ᾽ ἐμοῦ: de Strycker. Tischendorf omits.　　**13:4.** αὐτήν: de Strycker. τὴν παρθένον: Tischendorf.

blessed her and said, "Who am I that the mother of my Lord should visit me? You see, the baby inside me has jumped for joy and blessed you."

⁶But Mary forgot the mysteries which the heavenly messenger Gabriel had spoken, and she looked up to the sky and said, "Who am I, Lord, that every generation on earth will congratulate me?"

⁷She spent three months with Elizabeth. ⁸Day by day her womb kept swelling. And so Mary became frightened, returned home, and hid from the people of Israel. ⁹She was just sixteen years old when these mysterious things happened to her.

13 She was in her sixth month when one day Joseph came home from his building projects, entered his house, and found her pregnant. ²He struck himself in the face, threw himself to the ground on sackcloth, and began to cry bitterly: "What sort of face should I present to the Lord God? ³What prayer can I say on her behalf since I received her as a virgin from the temple of the Lord God and didn't protect her? ⁴Who has set this trap for me? Who has done this evil deed in my house? Who has lured this virgin away from me and violated her? ⁵The story of Adam has been repeated in my case, hasn't it? For just as Adam was

Joseph accuses Mary

"what was in her hands" instead (Smid, *Commentary*, 89). At any rate, like Mary, Elizabeth is depicted as working virtuously at the loom.

• **12:5.** Elizabeth's words are a loose paraphrase of what she says in Luke 1:43–44.

• **12:6.** The heavenly messenger is only now identified as *Gabriel*, whose name comes from Luke 1:26. Mary's response is patterned after Luke 1:48.

• **12:7.** Mary's stay of *three months* comes from Luke 1:56.

• **12:8.** *hid:* This motif also comes from Luke 1:24, though there said of Elizabeth.

• **12:9.** *sixteen years old:* The MSS differ considerably regarding the age of Mary. The majority read "sixteen," but twelve, fourteen, fifteen, and seventeen are also attested (Smid, *Commentary*, 92). Twelve, or perhaps fourteen, is the most logical, if the charge against an absent Joseph is to be plausible (see below 15:3–18). It has been supposed that the author simply forgot what he had said about Mary's age at 8:3 (de Strycker, *Protévangile*, 411).

• **13:1–16:8.** Joseph returns home from his building to find Mary pregnant. He suspects the worst, reproaches himself, and then

confronts Mary. A visitor likewise sees Mary's pregnancy and brings the matter to the high priest. Joseph and Mary are questioned and tested and then exonerated.

• **13:1–14:8.** Joseph's return home initiates a crisis. He reproaches himself for not protecting her and then demands an explanation from Mary. She insists on her innocence, which prompts Joseph to ponder what to do with her. He decides to "divorce" her (see note on 14:4), but does not carry through with this decision because a messenger from Lord tells him in a dream of the divine origin of Mary's pregnancy. He then decides to protect her.

• **13:1.** By the *sixth month* Mary's pregnancy is clearly visible.

• **13:3.** *I received her as a virgin from the temple of the Lord and didn't protect her:* Although Joseph had handed over responsibility of Mary to the Lord when he went to build buildings (see 9:12), he now acknowleges responsibility and blames himself for her condition.

• **13:5.** *The story of Adam:* The incident summarized here comes, of course, from Gen 3:1–20.

αὐτοῦ καὶ ἦλθεν ὁ ὄφις καὶ εὗρεν τὴν Εὔαν μόνην καὶ ἐξηπάτησεν αὐτὴν καὶ ἐμίανεν αὐτήν, οὕτως κἀμοὶ συνέβη.

⁶Καὶ ἀνέστη Ἰωσὴφ ἀπὸ τοῦ σάκκου καὶ ἐκάλεσεν αὐτὴν καὶ εἶπεν αὐτῇ· Μεμελημένη θεῷ, τί τοῦτο ἐποίησας; ⁷ἐπελάθου κυρίου τοῦ θεοῦ σου; τί ἐταπείνωσας τὴν ψυχήν σου, ἡ ἀνατραφεῖσα εἰς τὰ ἅγια τῶν ἁγίων καὶ τροφὴν λαμβάνουσα ἐκ χειρὸς ἀγγέλου; ⁸Ἡ δὲ ἔκλαυσεν πικρῶς λέγουσα ὅτι καθαρά εἰμι ἐγὼ καὶ ἄνδρα οὐ γινώσκω.

⁹Καὶ εἶπεν αὐτῇ Ἰωσήφ· Πόθεν οὖν τοῦτό ἐστιν ἐν τῇ γαστρί σου; ¹⁰Ἡ δὲ εἶπεν· Ζῇ κύριος ὁ θεός μου καθότι οὐ γινώσκω πόθεν ἐστὶν ἐν ἐμοί.

Joseph's vision   **14** Καὶ ἐφοβήθη ὁ Ἰωσὴφ σφόδρα καὶ ἠρέμησεν ἐξ αὐτῆς, διαλογιζόμενος αὐτὴν τί ποιήσει. ²καὶ εἶπεν Ἰωσὴφ ἐν ἑαυτῷ· Ἐὰν αὐτῆς κρύψω τὸ ἁμάρτημα, εὑρεθήσομαι μαχόμενος τῷ νόμῳ κυρίου· ³καὶ ἐὰν αὐτὴν φανερώσω τοῖς υἱοῖς Ἰσραήλ, φοβοῦμαι μήπως ἀγγελικόν ἐστιν τὸ ἐν αὐτῇ, καὶ εὑρεθήσομαι παραδιδοὺς ἀθῷον αἷμα εἰς κρίμα θανάτου. ⁴τί οὖν αὐτὴν ποιήσω; λάθρα αὐτὴν ἀπολύσω ἀπ᾽ ἐμοῦ.

⁵Καὶ κατέλαβεν αὐτὸν νύξ. καὶ ἰδοὺ ἄγγελος κυρίου φαίνεται αὐτῷ κατ᾽ ὄνειρον λέγων· Μὴ φοβηθῇς τὴν παῖδα ταύτην· τὸ γὰρ ἐν αὐτῇ ὂν ἐκ πνεύματός ἐστιν ἁγίου· ⁶τέξεται δέ σοι υἱὸν καὶ

13:5. καὶ ἐμίανεν αὐτήν: de Strycker. Tischendorf omits.   **13:6.** αὐτήν: de Strycker. τὴν Μαριάμ: Tischendorf.   **13:8.** ὅτι: Tischendorf. καθότι: de Strycker.   **14:2.** ἐν ἑαυτῷ: various mss. Tischendorf and de Strycker omit.

praying when the serpent came and found Eve alone, deceived her, and corrupted her, so the same thing has happened to me."

⁶So Joseph got up from the sackcloth and summoned Mary and said to her, "God has taken a special interest in you—how could you have done this? ⁷Have you forgotten the Lord your God? Why have you brought shame on yourself, you who were raised in the Holy of Holies and fed by a heavenly messenger?"

⁸But she began to cry bitter tears: "I'm innocent. I haven't had sex with any man."

⁹And Joseph said to her, "Then where did the child you're carrying come from?"

¹⁰And she replied, "As the Lord my God lives, I don't know where it came from."

14 And Joseph became very frightened and no longer spoke with her as he pondered what he was going to do with her. ²And Joseph said to himself, "If I try to cover up her sin, I'll end up going against the law of the Lord. ³And if I disclose her condition to the people of Israel, I'm afraid that the child inside her might be heaven-sent and I'll end up handing innocent blood over to a death sentence. ⁴So what should I do with her? ⟨I know,⟩ I'll divorce her quietly."

Joseph's vision

⁵But when night came a messenger of the Lord suddenly appeared to him in a dream and said: "Don't be afraid of this girl, because the child in her is the holy spirit's doing. ⁶She will

---

- **13:6.** *how could you have done this?:* This is the very question that God puts to Eve (Gen 3:13).
- **13:8.** *I haven't had sex with any man:* This portion of Mary's answer comes from Luke 1:34.
- **14:1.** *no longer spoke with her:* This translation is very tentative. The verb ἠρεμεῖν usually means "to be quiet, still, unmoved," as indeed it is used in the only other occurrence in this gospel (18:4). This meaning does not fit here, however, and hence translators vary greatly. For fuller discussions, see de Strycker, *Protévangile*, 304–5; Smid, *Commentary*, 99.
- **14:3.** The phrase *handing over innocent blood* also appears in Matt 27:4, while *to a death sentence* is found in Luke 24:20. For the former phrase, see also Deut 27:25; for the latter, Deut 21:22.
- **14:4.** *I'll divorce her quietly:* This sentence is problematic. One problem is that it could be read as a question, as some scholars take it: "Should I divorce her?" It really depends

on whether Joseph is understood to be undecided over what to do with Mary or whether his little soliloquy has led to a decision. The story would be more effective if the following appearance of the messenger of the Lord (14:5–8) involves a Joseph who has already made up his mind. But a larger problem is the reference to divorce, which is surely inappropriate in this context, as Mary is only his ward, not his wife. The sentence, of course, is based on Matt 1:19, and it seems that the author has taken it over without thinking about the changed circumstances in his own narrative. Or perhaps the word translated "divorce" should be rendered more generally as "release" or "dismiss," as is often done. In this case Joseph is simply saying, "I'll get rid of her."

- **14:6.** This entire verse is taken directly from Matt 1:21 and addressed, as there, to Joseph. Contrast the use of this verse, addressed to Mary, at 11:8.

καλέσεις τὸ ὄνομα αὐτοῦ Ἰησοῦν· αὐτὸς γὰρ σώσει τὸν λαὸν αὐτοῦ ἐκ τῶν ἁμαρτημάτων αὐτῶν. ⁷καὶ ἀνέστη Ἰωσὴφ ἀπὸ τοῦ ὕπνου καὶ ἐδόξασεν τὸν θεὸν τοῦ Ἰσραὴλ τὸν δόντα αὐτῷ τὴν χάριν ταύτην. ⁸καὶ ἐφύλασσε τὴν παῖδα.

Mary & Joseph accused

15 ⁹Ἦλθεν δὲ Ἄννας ὁ γραμματεὺς πρὸς αὐτὸν καὶ εἶπεν αὐτῷ· Ἰωσήφ, διὰ τί οὐκ ἐφάνης τῇ συνόδῳ ἡμῶν;

²Καὶ εἶπεν αὐτῷ· Ὅτι ἔκαμον ἐκ τῆς ὁδοῦ καὶ ἀνεπαυσάμην τὴν μίαν ἡμέραν.

³Καὶ ἐστράφη Ἄννας καὶ εἶδεν τὴν Μαρίαν ὠγκωμένην.

⁴Καὶ ἀπῄει δρομαῖος πρὸς τὸν ἀρχιερέα καὶ εἶπεν αὐτῷ· Ἰδοὺ Ἰωσήφ, ᾧ σὺ μαρτυρεῖς, ἠνόμησεν σφόδρα.

⁵Καὶ εἶπεν ὁ ἀρχιερεύς· Τί τοῦτο;

⁶Καὶ εἶπεν· Τὴν παρθένον ἣν Ἰωσὴφ παρέλαβεν ἐκ ναοῦ κυρίου, ἐμίανεν αὐτὴν καὶ ἔκλεψεν τοὺς γάμους αὐτῆς καὶ οὐκ ἐφανέρωσεν τοῖς υἱοῖς Ἰσραήλ.

⁷Καὶ εἶπεν αὐτῷ ὁ ἀρχιερεύς· Ἰωσὴφ ταῦτα ἐποίησεν;

⁸Καὶ εἶπεν αὐτῷ· Ἀπόστειλον ὑπηρέτας καὶ εὑρήσεις τὴν παρθένον ὠγκωμένην.

⁹Καὶ ἀπῆλθον οἱ ὑπηρέται καὶ εὗρον αὐτὴν καθὼς εἶπεν καὶ ἀπήγαγον αὐτὴν ἅμα τῷ Ἰωσὴφ εἰς τὸ κριτήριον.

¹⁰Καὶ εἶπεν αὐτῇ ὁ ἀρχιερεύς· Μαρία, τί τοῦτο ἐποίησας; τί ἐταπείνωσας τὴν ψυχήν σου; ¹¹ἐπελάθου κυρίου τοῦ θεοῦ σου, ἡ ἀνατραφεῖσα εἰς τὰ ἅγια τῶν ἁγίων καὶ λαβοῦσα τροφὴν ἐκ χειρὸς ἀγγέλων; ¹²σὺ ἡ ἀκούσασα τῶν ὕμνων αὐτῶν καὶ χορεύσασα ἐνώπιον αὐτῶν, τί τοῦτο ἐποίησας;

¹³Ἡ δὲ ἔκλαυσε πικρῶς λέγουσα· Ζῇ κύριος ὁ θεὸς καθότι καθαρά εἰμι ἐνώπιον αὐτοῦ καὶ ἄνδρα οὐ γινώσκω.

14:7. χάριν ταύτην: Tischendorf. χάριν αὐτοῦ: de Strycker.   **14:8.** τὴν παῖδα: de Strycker. αὐτήν: Tischendorf.   **15.1.** Ἰωσήφ: de Strycker. Tischendorf omits.   **15:2.** αὐτῷ: de Strycker. αὐτῷ Ἰωσήφ: Tischendorf.   **15:3.** Ἄννας: de Strycker. Tischendorf omits.   **15:4.** ἀρχιερέα: various MSS. ἱερέα: Tischendorf and de Strycker.   **15:4.** Ἰδού: de Strycker. Tischendorf omits.   **15:5.** ἀρχιερεύς: de Strycker. ἱερεύς: Tischendorf.   **15:6.** Ἰωσήφ: de Strycker. Tischendorf omits.   **15:7.** εἶπεν αὐτῷ ὁ ἀρχιερεύς: de Strycker. ἀποκριθεὶς ὁ ἱερεὺς εἶπεν: Tischendorf.   **15:8.** εἶπεν αὐτῷ: de Strycker. εἶπεν Ἄννας ὁ γραμματεύς: Tischendorf.   **15:9.** αὐτήν¹: de Strycker. Tischendorf omits.   **15:9.** ἅμα τῷ Ἰωσὴφ εἰς τὸ κριτήριον: Tischendorf. εἰς τὸ ἱερόν, καὶ ἔστη εἰς τὸ κριτήριον: de Strycker.   **15:10.** εἶπεν αὐτῇ ὁ ἀρχιερεύς: de Strycker. εἶπεν ὁ ἱερεύς: Tischendorf.   **15:11.** ἀγγέλων: de Strycker. ἀγγέλου: Tischendorf.   **15:12.** αὐτῶν: de Strycker. Tischendorf omits. **15:12.** αὐτῶν²: de Strycker. αὐτοῦ: Tischendorf.   **15:13.** θεός: de Strycker. θεός μου: Tischendorf.

have a son and you will name him Jesus—the name means 'he will save his people from their sins.'" [7]And Joseph got up from his sleep and praised the God of Israel, who had given him this favor. [8]And so he began to protect the girl.

15 Then Annas the scholar came to him and said to him, "Joseph, why haven't you attended our assembly?"

Mary & Joseph accused

[2]And he replied to him, "Because I was worn out from the trip and rested my first day home."

[3]Then Annas turned and saw that Mary was pregnant.

[4]He left in a hurry for the high priest and said to him, "You remember Joseph, don't you—the man you yourself vouched for? Well, he has committed a serious offense."

[5]And the high priest asked, "In what way?"

[6]"Joseph has violated the virgin he received from the temple of the Lord," he replied. "He had his way with her and hasn't disclosed his action to the people of Israel."

[7]And the high priest asked him, "Has Joseph really done this?"

[8]And he replied, "Send temple assistants and you'll find the virgin pregnant."

[9]And so the temple assistants went and found her just as Annas had reported, and then they brought her, along with Joseph, to the court.

[10]"Mary, why have you done this?" the high priest asked her. "Why have you humiliated yourself? [11]Have you forgotten the Lord your God, you who were raised in the Holy of the Holies and were fed by heavenly messengers? [12]You of all people, who heard their hymns and danced for them—why have you done this?"

[13]And she wept bitterly: "As the Lord God lives, I stand innocent before him. Believe me, I've not had sex with any man."

- **14:8.** *began to protect the girl:* Mary had been given into the care and protection of Joseph by the priests (9:7), but he, after receiving her, had handed over this responsibility to the Lord (9:12). Only now, after confronting Mary's pregnancy and his apparent failure to protect her (13:2–3), does Joseph personally accept his role as guardian.
- **15:1–16:8.** An apparently innocent visit by Annas the scholar to Joseph's house leads to Mary's pregnancy becoming known generally and to Joseph's and Mary's appearance in court. Interrogation and testing, however, end in public vindication.
- **15:1.** *Annas the scholar:* The author may

have taken the name Annas from Luke 3:2; cf. also John 18:13 and InfThom 3:1.
- **15:6.** *had his way with her and hasn't disclosed his action:* Implicit in this accusation is the assumption that Joseph could have treated Mary as his wife, if only he had notified the people of Israel. Such an assumption is strange. To be sure, the original instruction from the messenger of the Lord specifically intended marriage for Mary (8:8). But the high priest himself immediately restricted Joseph's role to that of a guardian (9:7).
- **15:13.** *I've not had sex with any man:* As at 13:8, this part of Mary's assertion of her innocence is taken from Luke 1:34.

¹⁴Καὶ εἶπεν ὁ ἀρχιερεύς· Ἰωσήφ, τί τοῦτο ἐποίησας;
¹⁵Εἶπεν δὲ Ἰωσήφ· Ζῆ κύριος καθότι καθαρός εἰμι ἐγὼ ἐξ αὐτῆς.

¹⁶Καὶ εἶπεν ὁ ἀρχιερεύς· Μὴ ψευδομαρτύρει, ἀλλὰ λέγε τὰ ἀληθῆ· ἔκλεψας τοὺς γάμους σου καὶ οὐκ ἐφανέρωσας τοῖς υἱοῖς Ἰσραήλ, ¹⁷καὶ οὐκ ἔκλινας τὴν κεφαλήν σου ὑπὸ τὴν κραταιὰν χεῖρα ὅπως εὐλογηθῇ τὸ σπέρμα σου.
¹⁸ Καὶ Ἰωσὴφ ἐσίγησεν.

The drink test

16 Καὶ εἶπεν ὁ ἀρχιερεύς· Ἀπόδος τὴν παρθένον ἣν παρέλαβες ἐκ ναοῦ κυρίου.
²Καὶ περιδάκρυτος γενόμενος ὁ Ἰωσήφ. . . .
³Καὶ εἶπεν ὁ ἀρχιερεύς· Ποτιῶ ὑμᾶς τὸ ὕδωρ τῆς ἐλέγξεως κυρίου, καὶ φανερώσει τὸ ἁμάρτημα ὑμῶν ἐν ὀφθαλμοῖς ὑμῶν.

⁴Καὶ λαβὼν ὁ ἀρχιερεὺς ἐπότισεν τὸν Ἰωσὴφ καὶ ἔπεμψεν αὐτὸν εἰς τὴν ἔρημον, καὶ ἦλθεν ὁλόκληρος. ⁵καὶ ἐπότισεν καὶ τὴν παῖδα καὶ ἔπεμψεν αὐτὴν εἰς τὴν ἐρεμίαν, καὶ κατέβη ὁλόκληρος. ⁶Καὶ ἐθαύμασεν πᾶς ὁ λαὸς ὅτι οὐκ ἐφάνη ἡ ἁμαρτία αὐτῶν. ⁷καὶ εἶπεν ὁ ἀρχιερεύς· Εἰ κύριος ὁ θεὸς οὐκ ἐφανέρωσεν τὸ ἁμάρτημα ὑμῶν, οὐδὲ ἐγὼ κρίνω ὑμᾶς. καὶ ἀπέλυσεν αὐτούς. ⁸καὶ παρέλαβεν Ἰωσὴφ τὴν Μαριὰμ καὶ ἀπῆει ἐν τῷ οἴκῳ αὐτοῦ χαίρων καὶ δοξάζων τὸν θεὸν Ἰσραήλ.

On the way to Bethlehem

17 Κέλευσις δὲ ἐγένετο ἀπὸ Αὐγούστου τοῦ βασιλέως ἀπογράψασθαι ὅσοι εἰσὶν ἐν Βηθλέεμ τῆς Ἰουδαίας. ²καὶ εἶπεν

15:14. ὁ ἀρχιερεύς· Ἰωσήφ: de Strycker. ὁ ἱερεύς πρὸς Ἰωσήφ: Tischendorf.   **15:15.** Ζῆ κύριος: Tischendorf. Ζῆ κύριος ὁ θεός μου καὶ ζῇ ὁ Χριστὸς αὐτοῦ καὶ ὁ τῆς ἀληθείας αὐτοῦ μάρτυς: de Strycker. On de Strycker's proposed trinitarian formula, see de Strycker, *Protévangile*, 137 n. 7. For criticism, see Smid, *Commentary*, 109–10.   **15:16.** ἀρχιερεύς: de Strycker. ἱερεύς: Tischendorf.   **15:16.** γάμους σου: de Strycker. γάμους αὐτῆς: Tischendorf.   **16:1.** ἀρχιερεύς: de Strycker. ἱερεύς: Tischendorf.   **16:2.** Ἰωσήφ . . . : de Strycker suspects a lacuna here (see *Protévangile*, 138).   **16:3.** ἀρχιερεύς: de Strycker. ἱερεύς: Tischendorf.   **16:3.** τὸ ἁμάρτημα: de Strycker. τὰ ἁμαρτήματα: Tischendorf. **16:4.** ἀρχιερεύς: de Strycker. ἱερεύς: Tischendorf.   **16:4.** τὴν ἔρημον: de Strycker. τὴν ὀρεινήν: Tischendorf.   **16:5.** τὴν παῖδα: de Strycker. τὴν Μαριάμ: Tischendorf.   **16:5.** τὴν ἐρεμίαν: de Strycker. τὴν ὀρεινήν: Tischendorf.   **16:6.** ἡ ἁμαρτία αὐτῶν: de Strycker. ἁμαρτία ἐν αὐτοῖς: Tischendorf.   **16:7.** ἀρχιερεύς: de Strycker. ἱερεύς: Tischendorf. **16:7.** τὸ ἁμάρτημα: de Strycker. τὰ ἁμαρτήματα: Tischendorf.   **16:8.** Μαριάμ: Tischendorf. Μαριάμμην: de Strycker.   **17:1.** ὅσοι εἰσίν ἐν Βηθλέεμ: de Strycker. πάντας τοὺς ἐν Βηθλεέμ: Tischendorf.

¹⁴And the high priest said, "Joseph, why have you done this?"

¹⁵And Joseph said, "As the Lord lives, I am innocent where she is concerned."

¹⁶And the high priest said, "Don't perjure yourself, but tell the truth. You've had your way with her and haven't disclosed this action to the people of Israel. ¹⁷And you haven't humbled yourself under God's mighty hand, so that your offspring might be blessed."

¹⁸But Joseph was silent.

16 Then the high priest said, "Return the virgin you re-   *The drink test*
ceived from the temple of the Lord."

²And Joseph, bursting into tears. . . .

³And the high priest said, "I'm going to give you the Lord's drink test, and it will disclose your sin clearly to both of you."

⁴And the high priest took the water and made Joseph drink it and sent him into the wilderness, but he returned unharmed. ⁵And he made the girl drink it, too, and sent her into the wilderness. She also came back unharmed. ⁶And everybody was surprised because their sin had not been revealed. ⁷And so the high priest said, "If the Lord God has not exposed your sin, then neither do I condemn you." And he dismissed them. ⁸Joseph took Mary and returned home celebrating and praising the God of Israel.

17 Now an order came from the Emperor Augustus that   *On the way*
everybody in Bethlehem of Judea be enrolled in the census.   *to Bethlehem*

• **15:16.** *Don't perjure yourself:* The high priest is warning Joseph by citing one of the ten commandments (Exod 20:16; Deut 5:20; cf. Matt 19:18; Mark 10:19; Luke 18:20).

• **15:17.** *humbled yourself under God's mighty hand:* The phraseology comes from 1 Pet 5:6.

• **16:3.** *the Lord's drink test:* The author seems to have in mind something like the ritual of the water of bitterness for unfaithful wives outlined in Num 5:11–31. The procedures here, however, are rather different, in particular the application of the test to the man (see Elliott, *Apocryphal New Testament,* 51, and, more generally, Vorster, "Intertextuality," 274). For another similar test, see also Achilles Tatius, *Leucippe and Clitophon,* 8.3.3; 6.1–15; 13.1–14.2.

• **16:7.** *then neither do I condemn you:* With these words, which recall John 8:11, the high priest publicly exonerates Joseph and Mary and implicitly assents to the claim

that the child to be born is of the holy spirit (11:5, 7; cf. 14:3).

• **17:1–24:14.** The remainder of the Infancy Gospel of James more or less parallels the canonical accounts which tell of the birth of Jesus (Luke 2:1–20; Matt 2:1–23). The author obviously depends on these accounts but does not hesitate to elaborate upon them, adding material and changing details throughout, as will be indicated in the following notes.

• **17:1–18:2.** The author opens his story of Jesus' birth, as does Luke, with a reference to the enrollment order of Augustus (Luke 2:1), but, unlike Luke, adds a scene in which Joseph ponders how he will enroll Mary. The trip to Bethlehem is narrated much more fully but ends before arriving there as Mary asks to stop outside Bethlehem to give birth to her child. Joseph finds a cave for her and goes off in search of a midwife.

• **17:1.** *everybody in Bethlehem of Judea be*

Ἰωσήφ· Ἐγὼ ἀπογράψομαι τοὺς υἱούς μου· ταύτην δὲ τὴν παῖδα τί ποιήσω; πῶς αὐτὴν ἀπογράψομαι; ³γυναῖκα ἐμήν; ἐπαισχύνομαι. ἀλλὰ θυγατέρα; οἴδασιν οἱ υἱοὶ Ἰσραὴλ ὅτι οὐκ ἔστιν θυγάτηρ μου. ⁴αὕτη ἡ ἡμέρα κυρίου ποιήσει ὡς βούλεται

⁵Καὶ ἔστρωσεν τὴν ὄνον καὶ ἐκάθισεν αὐτὴν καὶ εἷλκεν ὁ υἱὸς αὐτοῦ καὶ ἠκολούθει Σαμουήλ. ⁶καὶ ἤγγισαν ἐπὶ μίλιον τρίτον, καὶ ἐστράφη Ἰωσὴφ καὶ εἶδεν αὐτὴν στυγνήν. ⁷καὶ εἶπεν ἐν ἑαυτῷ· Ἴσως τὸ ἐν αὐτῇ χειμάζει αὐτήν. ⁸καὶ πάλιν ἐστράφη Ἰωσὴφ καὶ εἶδεν αὐτὴν γελῶσαν καὶ εἶπεν αὐτῇ· Μαρία, τί ἐστίν σοι τοῦτο, ὅτι τὸ πρόσωπόν σου βλέπω ποτὲ μὲν γελῶντα ποτὲ δὲ στυγνάζον;

⁹Καὶ εἶπεν αὐτῷ· Ἰωσήφ, ὅτι δύο λαοὺς βλέπω ἐν τοῖς ὀφθαλμοῖς μου, ἕνα κλαίοντα καὶ κοπτόμενον καὶ ἕνα χαίροντα καὶ ἀγαλλιῶντα.

¹⁰Καὶ ἦλθον ἀνὰ μέσον τῆς ὁδοῦ, καὶ εἶπεν αὐτῷ Μαριάμ· Ἰωσήφ, κατάγαγέ με ἀπὸ τῆς ὄνου, ὅτι τὸ ἐν ἐμοὶ ἐπείγει με προελθεῖν.

¹¹Καὶ κατήγαγεν αὐτὴν ἀπὸ τῆς ὄνου καὶ εἶπεν αὐτῇ· Ποῦ σε ἀπάξω καὶ σκεπάσω σου τὴν ἀσχημοσύνην, ὅτι ὁ τόπος ἔρημός ἐστιν;

17:4. βούλεται: de Strycker. βούλεται κύριος: Tischendorf.   17:5. Σαμουήλ: de Strycker. Ἰωσήφ: Tischendorf.   17:7. καὶ εἶπεν ἐν ἑαυτῷ: Tischendorf. καὶ ἔλεγεν: de Strycker.   17:8. Μαρία: Tischendorf. Μαριάμμη: de Strycker.   17:9. καὶ εἶπεν αὐτῷ· Ἰωσήφ: de Strycker. καὶ εἶπε Μαριὰμ τῷ Ἰωσήφ: Tischendorf.   17:10. Μαριάμ: Tischendorf. Μαριάμμη: de Strycker.   17:10. Ἰωσήφ: de Strycker. Tischendorf omits.   17:10. τῆς ὄνου: Tischendorf. τοῦ ὄνου: de Strycker.   17:11. ἀπὸ τῆς ὄνου: Tischendorf. ἐκεῖ: de Strycker.

²And Joseph wondered, "I'll enroll my sons, but what am I going to do with this girl? How will I enroll her? ³As my wife? I'm ashamed to do that. As my daughter? The people of Israel know she's not my daughter. ⁴How this is to be decided depends on the Lord."

⁵And so he saddled his donkey and had her get on it. His son led it and Samuel brought up the rear. ⁶As they neared the three mile marker, Joseph turned around and saw that she was sulking. ⁷And he said to himself, "Perhaps the baby she is carrying is causing her discomfort." ⁸Joseph turned around again and saw her laughing and said to her, "Mary, what's going on with you? One minute I see you laughing and the next minute you're sulking."

⁹And she replied, "Joseph, it's because I imagine two peoples in front of me, one weeping and mourning and the other celebrating and jumping for joy."

¹⁰Halfway through the trip Mary said to him, "Joseph, help me down from the donkey—the child inside me is about to be born."

¹¹And he helped her down and said to her, "Where will I take you to give you some privacy, since this place is out in the open?"

---

enrolled: Augustus' enrollment order comes from Luke 2:1, but there it involves the whole world, while here it is restricted to Bethlehem.

• **17:2.** *my sons:* Joseph's sons by a previous marriage (see 9:8). It is striking that the author does not refer here also to daughters mentioned in Mark 6:3; Matt 13:56.

• **17:4.** *How this is to be decided depends on the Lord:* Lit. "This day of the Lord will do as the Lord wishes." The "day of the Lord" has been understood as merely Joseph's way of expressing a general trust in providence, as in 9:12: "The Lord will protect you" (Smid, *Commentary*, 119).

• **17:5.** *His son:* Unidentified by name, but it might be an indirect reference to the author himself, i.e., to James (see 25:1 and Smid, *Commentary*, 120). If so, then the author claims to be an eyewitness of the all-important virgin birth to follow (see esp. 18:1, where Joseph's sons, including James, are stationed outside the cave where Jesus is to be born).

• **17:5.** *Samuel* is only one of the many names in the MSS at this point. We also find James, Simon, and even Joseph (see de Strycker, *Protévangile*, 143 n. 7). Tischen-

dorf preferred Joseph, but that cannot be right, as Joseph is clearly imagined as walking ahead of Mary (see vv. 6 and 8). Incidentally, James and Simon are included among the brothers of Jesus named in Mark 6:3 and Matt 13:55, but there is no Samuel.

• **17:6.** *three mile marker:* The author, who otherwise is vague, silent, or even confused about matters of geography, is unusually precise here. The marker is apparently assumed to be three miles from Bethlehem (Smid, *Commentary*, 120).

• **17:9.** *two peoples:* Mary's answer is, perhaps deliberately, enigmatic. The idea of two peoples seems to come from Gen 25:23, but the weeping and celebrating likely derives from Luke 2:34, where Simeon says that Jesus will cause the fall and rising of many in Israel. In any case, the two peoples may refer to Jews and non-Jews or, more likely, to believers and non-believers (see van Stempvoort, "Protevangelium," 421–22).

• **17:11.** *out in the open:* Lit. "the barren, or non-productive, land" which extended beyond the countryside of fields, vineyards, and pastures. The author is departing significantly from the canonical accounts, which have Jesus born in Bethlehem itself.

18 Καὶ εὗρεν ἐκεῖ σπήλαιον καὶ εἰσήγαγεν αὐτὴν καὶ παρέστησεν αὐτῇ τοὺς υἱοὺς αὐτοῦ ²καὶ ἐξῆλθεν ζητῆσαι μαῖαν Ἑβραίαν ἐν χώρᾳ Βηθλεέμ.

³Ἐγὼ δὲ Ἰωσὴφ περιεπάτουν καὶ οὐ περιεπάτουν. ⁴καὶ ἀνέβλεψα εἰς τὸν πόλον τοῦ οὐρανοῦ καὶ εἶδον αὐτὸν ἑστῶτα, καὶ εἰς τὸν ἀέρα καὶ εἶδον αὐτὸν ἔκθαμβον καὶ τὰ πετεινὰ τοῦ οὐρανοῦ ἠρεμοῦντα. ⁵καὶ ἐπέβλεψα ἐπὶ τὴν γῆν καὶ εἶδον σκάφην κειμένην καὶ ἐργάτας ἀνακειμένους, καὶ ἦσαν αἱ χεῖρες αὐτῶν ἐν τῇ σκάφῃ. ⁶καὶ οἱ μασώμενοι οὐκ ἐμασῶντο καὶ οἱ αἴροντες οὐκ ἀνέφερον καὶ οἱ προσφέροντες τῷ στόματι αὐτῶν οὐ προσέφερον, ⁷ἀλλὰ πάντων ἦν τὰ πρόσωπα ἄνω βλέποντα· ⁸Καὶ εἶδον ἐλαυνόμενα πρόβατα, καὶ τὰ πρόβατα ἐστήκει· ⁹καὶ ἐπῆρεν ὁ ποιμὴν τὴν χεῖρα αὐτοῦ τοῦ πατάξαι αὐτά, καὶ ἡ χεὶρ αὐτοῦ ἔστη ἄνω· ¹⁰καὶ ἐπέβλεψα ἐπὶ τὸν χείμαρρον τοῦ ποταμοῦ καὶ εἶδον ἐρίφους καὶ τὰ στόματα αὐτῶν ἐπικείμενα τῷ ὕδατι καὶ μὴ πίνοντα. ¹¹καὶ πάντα θήξει ὑπὸ τοῦ δρόμου αὐτῶν ἀπηλαύνετο.

18:3–11. From this point until 21:10, the Bodmer papyrus differs considerably from most other MSS, omitting portions and drastically reducing others. Most significant is the omission of the vision of Joseph (18:3–11), which is the case for two other MSS as well, but the vision, despite the early dating of the Bodmer papyrus, is clearly orginal (see de Strycker, *Protévangile*, 377–92; Bovon, "Suspension of Time," 394–95). **18:4.** εἰς τὸν πόλον τοῦ οὐρανοῦ: de Strycker. εἰς τὸν ἀέρα: Tischendorf. **18:4.** αὐτὸν ἑστῶτα: de Strycker. τὸν ἀέρα ἔκθαμβον: Tischendorf. **18:4.** καὶ εἰς τὸν ἀέρα καὶ εἶδον αὐτὸν ἔκθαμβον: de Strycker. καὶ ἀνέβλεψα εἰς τὸν πόλον τοῦ οὐρανοῦ, καὶ εἶδον αὐτὸν ἑστῶτα: Tischendorf. **18:5.** ἦσαν: de Strycker. Tischendorf omits. **18:8.** εἶδον ἐλαυνόμενα πρόβατα: de Strycker. ἰδοὺ πρόβατα ἐλαυνόμενα ἦν: Tischendorf. **18:9.** αὐτά: de Strycker. αὐτὰ ἐν τῇ ῥάβδῳ: Tischendorf. **18:10.** ἐρίφους καί: de Strycker. Tischendorf omits. **18:10.** στόματα αὐτῶν: de Strycker. στόματα τῶν ἐρίφων: Tischendorf. **18:10.** τῷ ὕδατι: de Strycker. Tischendorf omits.

18 He found a cave nearby and took her inside. He stationed his sons to guard her ²and went to look for a Hebrew midwife in the country around Bethlehem.

³"Now I, Joseph, was walking along and yet not going anywhere. ⁴I looked up at the vault of the sky and saw it standing still, and then at the clouds and saw them paused in amazement, and at the birds of the sky suspended in midair. ⁵As I looked on the earth, I saw a bowl lying there and workers reclining around it with their hands in the bowl; ⁶some were chewing and yet did not chew; some were picking up something to eat and yet did not pick it up; and some were putting food in their mouths and yet did not do so. ⁷Instead, they were all looking upward.

⁸"I saw sheep being driven along and yet the sheep stood still; ⁹the shepherd was lifting his hand to strike them, and yet his hand remained raised. ¹⁰And I observed the current of the river and saw goats with their mouths in the water and yet they were not drinking. ¹¹Then all of a sudden everything and everybody went on with what they had been doing.

• **18:1.** *cave:* Another departure from the canonical accounts, where Jesus is born in the stable of an inn (Luke 2: 7) or in Joseph's and Mary's house (Matt 2:11). On the cave imagery, see Smid, *Commentary,* 125–26.

• **18:2.** *The country around Bethlehem:* Joseph heads toward the cultivated and hence the inhabited countryside near Bethlehem in search of a midwife.

• **18:3–11.** While searching for a midwife Joseph has a vision in which he sees all about him suspended in time, frozen in the activity they were engaged in. Joseph's description is carefully organized, beginning with what he saw in the vault of heaven and then, ever lower, in the air and finally to men and animals on earth.

• **18:3.** *Now I, Joseph:* Beginning here (and extending through 19:10), the narrative shifts to the first person. Previously scholars have attributed this abrupt shift to the use of a specific source, but such shifts are widely attested (see, e.g., the shift to "we" in Acts 16:10–17; 20:5–15; etc.) and seem to have been a means for the author to enliven and authenticate the vision. In any case, the temporary suspension of all activity, which is coincident with birth in the

cave, is intended to show that all of nature takes note of the birth of Jesus, just as will happen at his crucifixion when darkness, earthquakes, and the tearing of the temple curtain mark his death (see Matt 27:45, 51).

• **18:3.** *not going anywhere:* Joseph himself is frozen in mid-stride, as it were, so that he is participating in the suspension of time he is going to describe. Only his head or perhaps only his eyes move to take in what is happening all around him. On this vision, see Smid, *Commentary,* 128–30; Bovon, "Suspension of Time," 394–403.

• **18:4.** *paused in amazement:* This phrase renders one word in the Greek (ἔκθαμβος), whose usage in this context is not at all clear. For an attempt at interpretation, see Bovon ("Suspension of Time," 403).

• **18:5.** *workers reclining:* These workers out in the fields, coupled with the shepherd in 18:9, have prompted some to suggest that the author has built this scene on Luke 2:8, where shepherds were watching over their flocks by night (Bovon, "Suspension of Time," 403).

• **18:6–7.** *some were chewing:* The workers are caught in various stages of eating when, like Joseph, they look upward.

A child is born **19** Καὶ εἶδον γυναῖκα καταβαίνουσαν ἀπὸ τῆς ὀρεινῆς, καὶ εἶπέν μοι· Ἄνθρωπε, ποῦ πορεύῃ;

²Καὶ εἶπον· Μαῖαν ζητῶ Ἑβραίαν.

³Καὶ ἀποκριθεῖσα εἶπέν μοι· Ἐξ Ἰσραὴλ εἶ;

⁴Καὶ εἶπον αὐτῇ· Ναί.

⁵Ἡ δὲ εἶπεν· Καὶ τίς ἐστιν ἡ γεννῶσα ἐν τῷ σπηλαίῳ;

⁶Καὶ εἶπον ἐγώ· Ἡ μεμνηστευμένη μοι.

⁷Καὶ εἶπέ μοι· Οὐκ ἔστι σου γυνή;

⁸Καὶ εἶπον αὐτῇ· Μαρία ἐστίν, ἡ ἀνατραφεῖσα ἐν ναῷ κυρίου. καὶ ἐκληρωσάμην αὐτὴν γυναῖκα, ⁹καὶ οὐκ ἔστιν μου γυνή, ἀλλὰ σύλλημμα ἔχει ἐκ πνεύματος ἁγίου.

¹⁰Καὶ εἶπεν ἡ μαῖα· Τοῦτο ἀληθές;

¹¹Καὶ εἶπεν αὐτῇ Ἰωσήφ· Δεῦρο καὶ ἴδε.

¹²Καὶ ἀπῄει ἡ μαῖα μετ᾽ αὐτοῦ. ¹³καὶ ἔστησαν ἐν τῷ τόπῳ τοῦ σπηλαίου. καὶ ἦν νεφέλη σκοτεινὴ ἐπισκιάζουσα τὸ σπήλαιον. ¹⁴καὶ εἶπεν ἡ μαῖα· Ἐμεγαλύνθη ἡ ψυχή μου σήμερον, ὅτι εἶδον οἱ ὀφθαλμοί μου παράδοξα σήμερον, ὅτι σωτηρία τῷ Ἰσραὴλ γεγένηται.

¹⁵Καὶ παραχρῆμα ἡ νεφέλη ὑπεστέλλετο τοῦ σπηλαίου, καὶ ἐφάνη φῶς μέγα ἐν τῷ σπηλαίῳ ὥστε τοὺς ὀφθαλμοὺς μὴ φέρειν. ¹⁶Καὶ πρὸς ὀλίγον τὸ φῶς ἐκεῖνο ὑπεστέλλετο, ἕως ἐφάνη βρέφος· καὶ ἦλθεν καὶ ἔλαβε μαστὸν ἐκ τῆς μητρὸς αὐτοῦ Μαρίας.

¹⁷Καὶ ἀνεβόησεν ἡ μαῖα καὶ εἶπεν· Ὡς μεγάλη μοι ἡ σήμερον ἡμέρα, ὅτι εἶδον τὸ καινὸν θέαμα τοῦτο.

¹⁸Καὶ ἐξῆλθεν ἐκ τοῦ σπηλαίου ἡ μαῖα, καὶ ἀπήντησεν ἡ μαῖα τῇ Σαλώμῃ. καὶ εἶπεν αὐτῇ· Σαλώμη Σαλώμη, καινόν σοι θέαμα ἔχω ἐξηγήσασθαι· παρθένος ἐγέννησεν ἃ οὐ χωρεῖ ἡ φύσις αὐτῆς.

19:1–11. The Bodmer papyrus has sharply curtailed the conversation between Joseph and the midwife (19:1–11). The papyrus merely says: Καὶ εὑρὼν ἤνεγκεν ἀπὸ ὀρεινῆς καταβαίνουσαν. καὶ εἶπεν Ἰωσὴφ τῇ μαίᾳ ὅτι Μαρία ἐστὶν ἡ μεμνηστευμένη μοι, ἀλλὰ σύλλημμα ἔχει ἐκ πνεύματος ἁγίου, ἀνατραφεῖσα ἐν ναῷ κυρίου. **19:10.** εἶπεν: de Strycker. εἶπεν αὐτῷ: Tischendorf. **19:12–19.** The Bodmer papyrus no longer abbreviates but now follows the traditional text regarding Joseph's and the midwife's trip back to the cave and their seeing Mary with her newborn infant (19:12–19). **19:12.** ἡ μαῖα: Tischendorf. de Strycker omits. **19:13.** ἦν: de Strycker. ἰδού: Tischendorf. **19:13.** σκοτεινή: de Strycker. φωτεινή: Tischendorf. **19:14.** σήμερον²: de Strycker. Tischendorf omits. **19:17.** ὡς: de Strycker. Tischendorf omits. **19:17.** ἡμέρα: de Strycker. ἡμέρα αὕτη: Tischendorf. **19:18.** ἡ μαῖα τῇ Σαλώμῃ: various MSS. αὐτῇ Σαλώμη: Tischendorf and de Strycker.

19 "Then I saw a woman coming down from the hill country, and she asked, 'Where are you going, sir?' *A child is born*

²"I replied, 'I am looking for a Hebrew midwife.'

³"She inquired, 'Are you an Israelite?'

⁴"I told her, 'Yes.'

⁵"And she said, 'And who's the one having a baby in the cave?'

⁶"I replied, 'My fiancée.'

⁷"And she continued, 'She isn't your wife?'

⁸"I said to her, 'She is Mary, who was raised in the temple of the Lord; I obtained her by lot as my wife. ⁹But she's not really my wife; she's pregnant by the holy spirit.'

¹⁰"The midwife said, 'Really?' "

¹¹Joseph responded, "Come and see."

¹²And the midwife went with him. ¹³As they stood in front of the cave, a dark cloud overshadowed it. ¹⁴The midwife said, "I've really been privileged, because today my eyes have seen a miracle in that salvation has come to Israel."

¹⁵Suddenly the cloud withdrew from the cave and an intense light appeared inside the cave, so that their eyes could not bear to look. ¹⁶And a little later that light receded until an infant became visible; he took the breast of his mother Mary.

¹⁷Then the midwife shouted: "What a great day this is for me because I've seen this new miracle!"

¹⁸And the midwife left the cave and met Salome and said to her, "Salome, Salome, let me tell you about a new marvel: a virgin has given birth, and you know that's impossible!"

• **19:1–17.** Joseph finds a midwife and persuades her to go to the cave, but their arrival is too late, as Mary has already given birth. After a dark cloud dissipates and an intense light fades, they see Mary with the infant Jesus. There is nothing parallel in the canonical accounts to this scene.

• **19:11.** *Joseph responded:* The third person narrative resumes here.

• **19:13.** *dark cloud:* The MSS differ over whether the cloud is dark or bright. The Bodmer papyrus reads "dark cloud," which may be based on the dark cloud of Exod 19:16–18 (so de Strycker, *Protévangile,* 155 n. 4). Most MSS, however, have "bright cloud" (see Daniels, *Manuscript Tradition,* 2.769), which might go back to Exod 16:10 (so Smid, *Commentary,* 134–38).

• **19:14.** *I've been really privileged . . . :* The midwife's response is reminiscent of Luke 2:30, 32, though there these words are on the lips of Simeon.

• **19:15.** The *intense light* hides the actual birth from view, but it is also a sign of the miraculous. Interestingly, many MSS read, not *their eyes,* but "our eyes," which would mean that James as well as the other sons who had been standing guard (see 18:1) are also understood to be witnessing the miraculous birth.

• **19:16.** *took the breast of his mother:* The midwife has nothing to do, either for Mary or for the infant. Contrast Anna who did not nurse Mary until after the prescribed days (see 5:9–10). Mary's immediate feeding of Jesus may emphasize her exceptional purity.

• **19:18–20:12.** Salome visits the cave and, after some initial doubt, confirms the midwife's paradoxical claim–a virgin has given birth. There is nothing parallel in the canonical accounts to this scene. Indeed,

¹⁹Καὶ εἶπεν Σαλώμη· Ζῇ κύριος ὁ θεός μου, ἐὰν μὴ βαλῶ τὸν δάκτυλόν μου καὶ ἐρευνήσω τὴν φύσιν αὐτῆς, οὐ μὴ πιστεύσω ὅτι παρθένος ἐγέννησεν.

Salome's folly **20** Καὶ εἰσῆλθεν ἡ μαῖα καὶ εἶπεν· Μαρία, σχημάτισον σεαυτήν· οὐ γὰρ μικρὸς ἀγὼν πρόκειται περὶ σοῦ. ²Καὶ ἡ Μαρία ἀκούσασα ταῦτα ἐσχημάτισεν αὐτήν. καὶ ἔβαλε Σαλώμη τὸν δάκτυλον αὐτῆς εἰς τὴν φύσιν αὐτῆς. ³καὶ ἀνηλάλαξεν Σαλώμη καὶ εἶπεν· Οὐαὶ τῇ ἀνομίᾳ μου καὶ τῇ ἀπιστίᾳ μου, ὅτι ἐξεπείρασα θεὸν ζῶντα. ⁴καὶ ἰδοὺ ἡ χείρ μου πυρὶ ἀποπίπτει ἀπ᾽ ἐμοῦ.

⁵Καὶ ἔκλινεν τὰ γόνατα πρὸς τὸν δεσπότην Σαλώμη λέγουσα· Ὁ θεὸς τῶν πατέρων μου, μνήσθητί μου ὅτι σπέρμα εἰμὶ Ἀβραὰμ καὶ Ἰσαὰκ καὶ Ἰακώβ· ⁶μὴ παραδειγματίσῃς με τοῖς υἱοῖς Ἰσραήλ, ἀλλὰ ἀπόδος με τοῖς πένησιν· ⁷σὺ γὰρ οἶδας, δέσποτα, ὅτι ἐπὶ τῷ σῷ ὀνόματι τὰς θεραπείας ἐπετέλουν καὶ τὸν μισθόν μου παρὰ σοῦ ἐλάμβανον.

⁸Καὶ ἰδοὺ ἄγγελος κυρίου ἐπέστη λέγων πρὸς αὐτήν· Σαλώμη Σαλώμη, ἐπήκουσεν ὁ πάντων δεσπότης τῆς δεήσεώς σου. ⁹προσένεγκε τὴν χεῖρά σου τῷ παιδίῳ καὶ βάστασον αὐτό, καὶ ἔσται σοι σωτηρία καὶ χαρά.

¹⁰Καὶ προσῆλθε Σαλώμη τῷ παιδίῳ καὶ ἐβάστασεν αὐτὸ λέγουσα· Προσκυνήσω αὐτῷ, ὅτι οὗτος ἐγεννήθη βασιλεὺς τῷ Ἰσραήλ. ¹¹καὶ παραχρῆμα ἰάθη Σαλώμη καὶ ἐξῆλθεν ἐκ τοῦ σπηλαίου δεδικαιωμένη.

¹²Καὶ ἰδοὺ φωνὴ λέγουσα· Σαλώμη Σαλώμη, μὴ ἀναγγείλῃς ὅσα εἶδες παράδοξα ἕως ἔλθῃ ὁ παῖς εἰς Ἱεροσάλημα.

19:19. παρθένος: Tischendorf. ἡ παρθένος: de Strycker. **20:1–7.** Once again the Bodmer papyrus severely abbreviates the traditional text, this time regarding Salome's examination of Mary, her punishment, prayer, and subsequent salvation (20:1–7). The papyrus merely says: Καὶ εἰσῆλθεν καὶ ἐσχημάτισεν αὐτήν. καὶ ἠρεύνησε ἡ Σαλώμη τὴν φύσιν αὐτῆς. καὶ ἀνηλάλαξεν Σαλώμη ὅτι ἐξεπείρασεν θεὸν ζῶντα· Καὶ ἰδοὺ ἡ χείρ μου πυρὶ ἀποπίπτει ἀπ᾽ ἐμοῦ. καὶ προσηύξατο πρὸς κύριον, καὶ ἰάθη ἡ μαῖα ἐν τῇ ὥρᾳ ἐκείνῃ. Καὶ ἰδοὺ ἄγγελος κυρίου ἔστη πρὸς Σαλώμην λέγων· Εἰσηκούσθη ἡ δέησίς σου ἐνώπιον κυρίου τοῦ θεοῦ. προσελθοῦσα ἅψαι τοῦ παιδίου καὶ αὐτὸς ἔσται σοι ἡ σωτηρία. καὶ ἐποίησεν οὕτω καὶ ἰάθη Σαλώμη καθὼς προσεκύνησεν, καὶ ἐξῆλθεν ἐκ τοῦ σπηλαίου. **20:1.** εἶπεν· Μαρία: de Strycker. εἶπε τῇ Μαριάμ: Tischendorf. **20:2.** καὶ ἡ Μαρία ἀκούσασα ταῦτα ἐσχημάτισεν αὐτήν: de Strycker. Tischendorf omits. **20:3.** Σαλώμη: de Strycker. Tischendorf omits. **20:5.** Σαλώμη: de Strycker. Tischendorf omits. **20:8–12.** The Bodmer papyrus picks up the traditional text at this point through the remainder of the chapter. **20:8.** ἐπέστη: Tischendorf. ἔστη: de Strycker. **20:8.** ἐπήκουσεν ὁ πάντων δεσπότης τῆς δεήσεώς σου: de Strycker. ἐπήκουσεν σου κύριος: Tischendorf. **20:10.** καὶ προσῆλθε: Tischendorf. λαβοῦσα δὲ χαρὰν προσῆλθε: de Strycker. **20:10.** τῷ παιδίῳ: de Strycker. Tischendorf omits. **20:10.** οὗτος ἐγεννήθη βασιλεὺς τῷ Ἰσραήλ: de Strycker. βασιλεὺς ἐγεννήθη μέγας τῷ Ἰσραήλ: Tischendorf.

¹⁹And Salome replied, "As the Lord my God lives, unless I insert my finger and examine her, I will never believe that a virgin has given birth."

20 The midwife entered and said, "Mary, position yourself for an examination. You are facing a serious test."   *Salome's folly*

²And so Mary, when she heard these instructions, positioned herself, and Salome inserted her finger into Mary. ³And then Salome cried aloud and said, "I'll be damned because of my transgression and my disbelief; I have put the living God on trial. ⁴Look! My hand is disappearing! It's being consumed by flames!"

⁵Then Salome fell on her knees in the presence of the Lord, with these words: "God of my ancestors, remember me because I am a descendant of Abraham, Isaac, and Jacob. ⁶Do not make an example of me for the people of Israel, but give me a place among the poor again. ⁷You yourself know, Lord, that I've been healing people in your name and have been receiving my payment from you."

⁸And suddenly a messenger of the Lord appeared, saying to her, "Salome, Salome, the Lord of all has heard your prayer. ⁹Hold out your hand to the child and pick him up, and then you'll have salvation and joy."

¹⁰Salome approached the child and picked him up with these words: "I'll worship him because he's been born to be king of Israel." ¹¹And Salome was instantly healed and left the cave vindicated.

¹²Then a voice said abruptly, "Salome, Salome, don't report the marvels you've seen until the child goes to Jerusalem."

---

while those accounts claim that a virgin has conceived, they do not go on, as here, to affirm that a virgin has also given birth.

• **19:18.** The name *Salome* may have been taken from Mark 15:41. If so, it is unlikely that the author assumes identity of person, too. Others derive the name from Semele, the mother of Dionysos (Benko, *Virgin Goddess*, 201).

• **19:19.** *unless I insert my finger:* This phrase recalls John 20:25. Indeed, Salome is portrayed here very much like "doubting" Thomas, that is, being sceptical at first but then believing (see John 20:24–29).

• **20:1.** *Serious test.* Lit. "ordeal." Just as the high priest tested Mary to verify that she had not had sex with any man (see 15:10–13; 16:5), so now Salome must examine her to confirm that a virgin has really given birth.

• **20:3.** *put the living God on trial:* See Deut 6:16, which is cited by Jesus (Matt 4:7).

• **20:6.** *make an example:* This motif comes from Matt 1:19, though there said of Mary.

• **20:6.** *Give me a place among the poor:* The MSS vary widely at this point. Some have "Restore me to my parents," while others have "restore my hand" or "restore my full health" (Daniels, *Manuscript Tradition*, 2.817–22).

• **20:11.** *instantly healed:* For the author Jesus' ability to heal began immediately after birth. That Salome leaves the cave *vindicated* recalls, as with Joachim in 5:4, the language of Luke 18:14.

• **20:12.** *until the child goes to Jerusalem:* The author presumably has in mind the trip narrated in Luke 2:22–39 (de Strycker, *Protévangile*, 167 n. 13).

21 Καὶ ἰδοὺ Ἰωσὴφ ἡτοιμάσθη τοῦ ἐξελθεῖν ἐν τῇ Ἰουδαίᾳ, καὶ θόρυβος ἐγένετο μέγας ἐν Βηθλεὲμ τῆς Ἰουδαίας· ²ἦλθον γὰρ μάγοι λέγοντες· Ποῦ ἐστιν ὁ τεχθεὶς βασιλεὺς τῶν Ἰουδαίων; εἴδομεν γὰρ τὸν ἀστέρα αὐτοῦ ἐν τῇ ἀνατολῇ καὶ ἤλθομεν προσκυνῆσαι αὐτῷ.

³Καὶ ἀκούσας ὁ Ἡρώδης ἐταράχθη καὶ ἔπεμψεν ὑπηρέτας πρὸς τοὺς μάγους· ⁴καὶ μετεπέμψατο καὶ τοὺς ἀρχιερεῖς καὶ ἀνέκρινεν αὐτοὺς ἐν τῷ πραιτωρίῳ λέγων αὐτοῖς· Πῶς γέγραπται περὶ τοῦ Χριστοῦ; ποῦ γεννᾶται; ⁵Λέγουσιν αὐτῷ· Ἐν Βηθλεὲμ τῆς Ἰουδαίας· οὕτως γὰρ γέγραπται. ⁶Καὶ ἀπέλυσεν αὐτούς.

⁷Καὶ ἀνέκρινεν τοὺς μάγους λέγων αὐτοῖς· Τί εἴδετε σημεῖον ἐπὶ τὸν γεννηθέντα βασιλέα;

⁸Καὶ εἶπον οἱ μάγοι· Εἴδομεν ἀστέρα παμμεγέθη λάμψαντα ἐν τοῖς ἄστροις τούτοις καὶ ἀμβλύναντα αὐτούς, ὥστε τοὺς ἀστέρας μὴ φαίνεσθαι· καὶ οὕτως ἔγνωμεν ὅτι βασιλεὺς ἐγεννήθη τῷ Ἰσραήλ, καὶ ἤλθομεν προσκυνῆσαι αὐτῷ.

⁹Καὶ εἶπεν αὐτοῖς Ἡρώδης· Ὑπάγετε καὶ ζητήσατε, καὶ ἐὰν εὕρητε ἀπαγγείλατέ μοι, ὅπως κἀγὼ ἐλθὼν προσκυνήσω αὐτῷ.

¹⁰Καὶ ἐξῆλθον οἱ μάγοι. καὶ ἰδοὺ ὃν εἶδον ἀστέρα ἐν τῇ ἀνατολῇ προῆγεν αὐτοὺς ἕως εἰσῆλθον ἐν τῷ σπηλαίῳ, καὶ ἔστη ἐπὶ τὴν κεφαλὴν τοῦ παιδίου. ¹¹καὶ ἰδόντες αὐτὸν οἱ μάγοι ἑστῶτα μετὰ τῆς μητρὸς αὐτοῦ Μαρίας, ἐξέβαλον ἀπὸ τῆς πήρας αὐτῶν δῶρα χρυσὸν καὶ λίβανον καὶ σμύρναν.

21:2. τεχθεὶς: Tischendorf. de Strycker omits.   21:3–10. Again, the Bodmer papyrus has abbreviated considerably the traditional text of Herod's reaction to the visit of the astrologers (21.1–12). The papyrus, after following the traditional text at the start, continues as follows: Καὶ ἀκούσας ὁ Ἡρώδης ἐταράχθη καὶ ἔπεμψεν ὑπηρέτας καὶ μετεπέμψατο αὐτοὺς καὶ διεσάφησαν αὐτῷ περὶ τοῦ ἀστέρος. καὶ ἰδοὺ εἶδον ἀστέρας ἐν τῇ ἀνατολῇ καὶ προῆγον αὐτοὺς ἕως εἰσῆλθον ἐν τῷ σπηλαίῳ καὶ ἔστη ἐπὶ τὴν κεφαλὴν τοῦ παιδίου.   21:4. ἐν τῷ πραιτωρίῳ: de Strycker. Tischendorf omits.   21:10. τοῦ παιδίου: de Strycker. τοῦ σπηλαίου: Tischendorf.   21:11–12. The Bodmer papyrus takes up the traditional text at this point.   21:11. καὶ ἰδόντες αὐτὸν οἱ μάγοι ἑστῶτα: de Strycker. καὶ εἶδον οἱ μάγοι τὸ παιδίον: Tischendorf.   21:11. δῶρα: de Strycker. Tischendorf omits.

21 Joseph was about ready to depart for Judea, but a great   *Visit of*
uproar was about to take place in Bethlehem in Judea. ²It all   *the astrologers*
started when astrologers came inquiring, "Where is the newborn
king of the Judeans? We're here because we saw his star in the
East and have come to pay him homage."

³When Herod heard about their visit, he was terrified and sent
agents to the astrologers. ⁴He also sent for the high priests and
questioned them in his palace: "What has been written about the
Anointed? Where is he supposed to be born?"

⁵They said to him, "In Bethlehem, Judea, that's what the
scriptures say." ⁶And he dismissed them.

⁷Then he questioned the astrologers: "What sign have you
seen regarding the one who has been born king?"

⁸And the astrologers said, "We saw a star of exceptional
brilliance in the sky, and it so dimmed the other stars that they
disappeared. Consequently, we know that a king was born for
Israel. And we have come to pay him homage."

⁹Herod instructed them: "Go and begin your search, and if
you find him, report back to me, so I can also go and pay him
homage."

¹⁰The astrologers departed. And there it was: the star they had
seen in the East led them on until they came to the cave; then
the star stopped directly above the head of the child. ¹¹After the
astrologers saw him with his mother Mary, they took gifts out of
their pouches—gold, pure incense, and myrrh.

• **21:1–12.** The arrival of the astrologers has
its canonical source in Matt 2:1–16. The
author stays rather close to his source,
though there are some departures, especially regarding the description of the star
in v 8.

• **21:1.** *About ready:* Presumably the author is
referring to Joseph's having now enrolled
his family and so is ready to leave, but this
motive for the trip comes from his Lukan
source, which may have been forgotten now
that he is following, really paraphrasing, his
Matthean source.

• **21:1.** *for Judea:* Once again the author
seems confused on matters of geography.
Since Bethlehem is in Judea, which the
author says in the next clause, it is difficult
to see how departing "for" Judea makes any
sense. Either he meant "for Jerusalem," as
was indicated just before in 20:12, or he
meant "out of" Judea, that is, back to
Nazareth, as some MSS actually read (de
Strycker, *Protévangile*, 167).

• **21:1–2.** *great uproar was about to take place
in Bethlehem in Judea:* In Matt 2:1 the
astrologers arrive in Jerusalem, but here
they come to Bethlehem.

• **21:2.** The astrologers' question is identical
to that in Matt 2:2.

• **21:5.** *what the scriptures say:* It is striking
that the author does not actually quote Mic
5:1, as is done at Matt 2:6.

• **21:7.** Herod's question concerning *what
sign* the astrologers had seen differs from
that in Matt 2:7 where Herod asked about
the time of the star's appearance. Here,
however, he asks about the star itself, which
leads to its fuller description in v. 8.

• **21:9.** Herod's instructions are very close to
those in Matt 2:8.

• **21:10–11.** The visit of the astrologers
remains largely a paraphrase of Matt 2:9–
11, though not without some changes.
Thus, the astrologers follow the star, as in
Matt 2:9, but now to the *cave*, not to the
"house" (Matt 2:11). Likewise, the three

¹²Καὶ χρηματισθέντες ὑπὸ τοῦ ἀγγέλου μὴ εἰσελθεῖν εἰς τὴν
Ἰουδαίαν, διὰ ἄλλης ὁδοῦ ἀνεχώρησαν εἰς τὴν χώραν αὐτῶν.

22 Τότε Ἡρώδης ἰδὼν ὅτι ἐνεπαίχθη ὑπὸ τῶν μάγων
ὀργισθεὶς ²ἔπεμψεν αὐτοῦ τοὺς φονευτὰς λέγων αὐτοῖς ἀνελεῖν
πάντα τὰ βρέφη ἀπὸ διετίας καὶ κάτω.
³Καὶ ἀκούσασα ἡ Μαρία ὅτι τὰ βρέφη ἀναιρεῖται, ⁴φοβηθεῖσα
ἔλαβεν τὸν παῖδα καὶ ἐσπαργάνωσεν αὐτὸν καὶ ἔβαλεν ἐν φάτνῃ
βοῶν.
⁵Ἡ δὲ Ἐλισάβεδ ἀκούσασα ὅτι Ἰωάννης ζητεῖται, λαβοῦσα
αὐτὸν ἀνέβη ἐν τῇ ὀρεινῇ· ⁶καὶ περιεβλέπετο ποῦ αὐτὸν ἀπο-
κρύψῃ, καὶ οὐκ ἦν τόπος ἀπόκρυφος. ⁷τότε στενάξασα ἡ
Ἐλισάβεδ φωνῇ μεγάλῃ λέγει· Ὄρος θεοῦ, δέξαι με μητέρα
μετὰ τέκνου. Οὐ γὰρ ἐδύνατο ἡ Ἐλισάβεδ ἀναβῆναι διὰ τὴν
δειλίαν. ⁸καὶ παραχρῆμα ἐδιχάσθη τὸ ὄρος καὶ ἐδέξατο αὐτήν. καὶ
ἦν τὸ ὄρος ἐκεῖνο διαφαῖνον αὐτῇ φῶς· ἄγγελος γὰρ κυρίου ἦν
μετ᾽ αὐτῶν διαφυλάσσων αὐτούς.

23 Ὁ δὲ Ἡρώδης ἐζήτει τὸν Ἰωάννην, ²καὶ ἀπέστειλεν
ὑπηρέτας ἐν τῷ θυσιαστηρίῳ πρὸς Ζαχαρίαν λέγων αὐτῷ· Ποῦ
ἀπέκρυψας τὸν υἱόν σου;

Slaughter of
the infants

Murder of
Zechariah

22:1. τότε Ἡρώδης ἰδὼν ὅτι: de Strycker. γνοὺς δὲ Ἡρώδης ὅτι:
Tischendorf.   **22:2.** αὐτοῦ τοὺς φονευτάς: de Strycker. φονευτάς:
Tischendorf.   **22:2.** αὐτοῖς ἀνελεῖν πάντα τὰ βρέφη ἀπὸ διετίας καὶ
κάτω: de Strycker. αὐτοῖς· Τὰ βρέφη ἀπὸ διετοῦς καὶ κατωτέρω
ἀποκτείνατε: Tischendorf.   **22:5.** λαβοῦσα: Tischendorf. λαβομένη: de
Strycker.   **22:7.** φωνῇ μεγάλῃ: Tischendorf. de Strycker omits.   **22:7.**
οὐ γὰρ ἐδύνατο ἡ Ἐλισάβεδ ἀναβῆναι διὰ τὴν δειλίαν: de Strycker.
Tischendorf omits.   **22:8.** τὸ ὄρος ἐκεῖνο: de Strycker. Tischendorf
omits.   **22:8.** αὐτῇ: de Strycker. αὐτοῖς: Tischendorf.   **23:1.** ἐν τῷ
θυσιαστηρίῳ: de Strycker. Tischendorf omits.   **23:1.** αὐτῷ: de Strycker.
Tischendorf omits.

¹²Since they had been advised by the heavenly messenger not to go into Judea, they returned to their country by another route.

22 When Herod realized he had been duped by the astrologers, he flew into a rage ²and dispatched his executioners with instructions to kill all the infants two years old and younger.

³When Mary heard that the infants were being killed, she was frightened ⁴and took her child, wrapped him in strips of cloth, and put him in a feeding trough used by cattle.

⁵As for Elizabeth, when she heard that they were looking for John, she took him and went up into the hill country. ⁶She kept searching for a place to hide him, but there was none to be had. ⁷Then she groaned and said out loud, "Mountain of God, please take in a mother with her child." You see, Elizabeth was unable to keep on climbing because her nerve failed her. ⁸But suddenly the mountain was split open and let them in. This mountain allowed the light to shine through to her, ⁹since a messenger of the Lord was with them for protection.

Slaughter of the infants

23 Herod, though, kept looking for John ²and sent his agents to Zechariah serving at the altar with this message for him: "Where have you hidden your son?"

Murder of Zechariah

---

gifts are the same, but now they are taken from *their pouches*, not from "their treasures" (Matt 2:11). The first change is easily explained, the second is not.

• **21:11.** *with his mother:* Literally, "standing with his mother," perhaps another change from the canonical account: the newly-born Jesus already standing (Smid, *Commentary*, 150). But the verb translated "standing" may on occasion not mean much more than that he was present with his mother (see de Strycker, *Protévangile*, 173).

• **21:12.** The departure of the astrologers *by another route* is simply a paraphrase of Matt 2:12.

• **22:1–24:14.** Herod's orders to kill all infants two years old and younger is simply stated in the canonical account (see Matt 2:16–18). Here, however, the author expands the statement into a dramatic narrative involving Mary, Elizabeth, and Zechariah.

• **22:1–9.** Mary and Elizabeth react to the threat of Herod's soldiers in differing, though successful, ways.

• **22:4.** *wrapped him up in strips of cloth and put him in a feeding trough:* These narrative details are familiar from Luke 2:7, but there they describe the birth. Here they are

Mary's way of protecting Jesus from Herod's soldiers. The author has taken an independent course in this respect, for in Luke Jesus was never in danger as an infant and in Matthew his parents avoided it by their flight to Egypt (see Matt 2:13–15). Indeed, the change was too abrupt for some copyists, as a few MSS drop Mary's hiding Jesus in a feeding trough and have Mary, Joseph, and Jesus instead depart for Egypt, thus making the story conform to the canonical account, in content, if not in wording (Smid, *Commentary*, 152–53).

• **22:7.** *because her nerve failed her:* Lit. "on account of timidity." This reason is only poorly attested in the MSS (Daniels, *Manuscript Tradition*, 2.930–31), and it may be secondary (Smid, *Commentary*, 155–56), since the reason for Elizabeth's inability to go farther is obvious, if implicit, namely, weariness.

• **22:8.** *This mountain allowed the light to shine through to her:* A most tentative translation, as the Greek is opaque and probably corrupt (see de Strycker, *Protévangile*, 177).

• **23:1–9.** Zechariah, John's father, fares worse than Elizabeth and Mary and their

³ Ὁ δὲ ἀπεκρίνατο λέγων αὐτοῖς· Ἐγὼ λειτουργὸς ὑπάρχω θεοῦ καὶ προσεδρεύω τῷ ναῷ αὐτοῦ. Τί γινώσκω ποῦ ἐστιν ὁ υἱός μου;

⁴Καὶ ἀπῆλθον οἱ ὑπηρέται αὐτοῦ καὶ ἀνήγγειλαν αὐτῷ πάντα ταῦτα. καὶ ὀργισθεὶς ὁ Ἡρώδης εἶπεν· Ὁ υἱὸς αὐτοῦ μέλλει βασιλεύειν τοῦ Ἰσραήλ;

⁵Καὶ ἔπεμψεν πάλιν τοὺς ὑπηρέτας λέγων αὐτῷ· Εἰπέ μοι τὰ ἀληθῆ· ποῦ ἐστιν ὁ υἱός σου; οἶδας ὅτι τὸ αἷμά σου ὑπὸ τὴν χεῖρά μού ἐστιν;

⁶Καὶ ἀπῆλθον οἱ ὑπηρέται καὶ ἀνήγγειλαν αὐτῷ ταῦτα.

⁷Καὶ ἀποκριθεὶς εἶπεν Ζαχαρίας· Μάρτυς εἰμὶ τοῦ θεοῦ. ἔχε μου τὸ αἷμα· ⁸τὸ δὲ πνεῦμά μου ὁ δεσπότης δέξεται, ὅτι ἀθῷον αἷμα ἐκχεῖς εἰς τὰ πρόθυρα τοῦ ναοῦ κυρίου.

⁹Καὶ περὶ τὸ διάφαυμα ἐφονεύθη Ζαχαρίας, καὶ οὐκ ᾔδεισαν οἱ υἱοὶ Ἰσραὴλ ὅτι ἐφονεύθη.

Zechariah mourned

24 Ἀλλὰ τὴν ὥραν τοῦ ἀσπασμοῦ ἀπῆλθον οἱ ἱερεῖς, καὶ οὐκ ἀπήντησεν αὐτοῖς κατὰ τὸ ἔθος ἡ εὐλογία τοῦ Ζαχαρίου. ²καὶ ἔστησαν οἱ ἱερεῖς προσδοκῶντες τὸν Ζαχαρίαν τοῦ ἀσπάσασθαι αὐτὸν ἐν εὐχῇ καὶ δοξάσαι τὸν ὕψιστον θεόν.

³Χρονίσαντος δὲ αὐτοῦ ἐφοβήθησαν πάντες. ⁴τολμήσας δέ τις ἐξ αὐτῶν εἰσῆλθεν εἰς τὸ ἁγίασμα καὶ εἶδεν παρὰ τὸ θυσιαστήριον κυρίου αἷμα πεπηγὸς ⁵καὶ φωνὴ λέγουσα· Ζαχαρίας πεφόνευται, καὶ οὐκ ἐξαλειφθήσεται τὸ αἷμα αὐτοῦ ἕως ἔλθῃ ὁ ἔκδικος.

⁶Καὶ ἀκούσας τῶν λόγων τούτων ἐφοβήθη καὶ ἐξῆλθεν καὶ ἀνήγγειλεν τοῖς ἱερεῦσιν ἃ εἶδεν καὶ ἤκουσεν. ⁷καὶ τολμήσαντες

23:3. αὐτοῦ: de Strycker. κυρίου: Tischendorf.   **23:3.** τί γινώσκω: de Strycker. οὐκ οἶδα: Tischendorf.   **23:4.** αὐτῷ: de Strycker. τῷ Ἡρώδῃ: Tischendorf.   **23:5.** καὶ ἔπεμψεν πάλιν τοὺς ὑπηρέτας λέγων αὐτῷ: de Strycker. Tischendorf omits.   **23:5.** μοι: de Strycker. Tischendorf omits. **23:7.** ἀποκριθείς: de Strycker. Tischendorf omits.   **23:7.** Ζαχαρίας: Tischendorf. de Strycker omits.   **23:7.** ἔχε: de Strycker. εἰ ἐκχέεις: Tischendorf.   **23:9.** ὅτι: Tischendorf. πῶς: de Strycker. **24:2.** θεόν: de Strycker. Tischendorf omits.   **24:4.** εἰς τὸ ἁγίασμα: de Strycker. Tischendorf omits.   **24:4.** κυρίου: de Strycker. Tischendorf omits. **24:5.** φωνὴ λέγουσα: various mss. φωνὴν λέγουσαν: Tischendorf and de Strycker.   **24:6.** τῶν λόγων τούτων: de Strycker. τὸν λόγον: Tischendorf.   **24:6.** ἃ εἶδεν καὶ ἤκουσεν: de Strycker. Tischendorf omits.

³But he answered them, "I am a minister of God, attending to his temple. How should I know where my son is?"

⁴So the agents left and reported all this to Herod, who became angry and said, "Is his son going to rule over Israel?"

⁵And he sent his agents back with this message for him: "Tell me the truth. Where is your son? Don't you know that I have your life in my power?"

⁶And the agents went and reported this message to him.

⁷Zechariah answered, "I am a martyr for God. Take my life. ⁸The Lord, though, will receive my spirit because you are shedding innocent blood at the entrance to the temple of the Lord."

⁹And so at daybreak Zechariah was murdered, but the people of Israel did not know that he had been murdered.

24 At the hour of formal greetings the priests departed, but Zechariah did not meet and bless them as was customary. ²And so the priests waited around for Zechariah, to greet him with prayer and to praise the Most High God.

Zechariah mourned

³But when he did not show up, they all became fearful. ⁴One of them, however, summoned up his courage, entered the sanctuary, and saw dried blood next to the Lord's altar. ⁵And a voice said, "Zechariah has been murdered! His blood will not be cleaned up until his avenger appears."

⁶When he heard this utterance he was afraid and went out and reported to the priests what he had seen and heard. ⁷And they

---

sons, as he is murdered at the altar for his refusal to divulge the whereabouts of his son. His murder is not a part of the canonical accounts, although the idea for this story may well have been prompted by a notice in Matt 23:35, where a certain Zechariah is said to have been murdered near the altar. Our author seems to have identified these two Zechariahs and so composed an account of his death based on this notice.

- **23:2.** *at the altar:* Zechariah's service at the altar indicates that he is characterized as the high priest, although in Luke 1:5 he is merely a priest. Zechariah's service had ended when he became mute, and Samuel was to have taken his place until he regained his speech (see 10:9). That has apparently happened, and Zechariah is back at the altar (Luke 1:11; cf. Exod 30:1–10).

- **23:4.** It is possible to understand Herod's reply as a statement: "His son is going to rule over Israel."

- **23:5.** *In my power:* Lit. "under my hand." For the idiom, see 1 Sam 21:4.

- **24:1–14.** The priests and people learn of

Zechariah's murder and respond with mourning for three days before casting lots for his replacement. This episode is also not found in the canonical accounts, although the opening scene in which *the priests waited around for Zechariah* (v 2) is taken from Luke 1:21.

- **24:1.** *the priests departed:* The text is secure at this point, but the meaning hardly fits. The priests are clearly assumed to have gone *to* the temple for the greeting after the morning sacrifice, but it is not at all clear where they were departing from—from their homes?—as is assumed in the translation, or from elsewhere in the temple area? See further Smid, *Commentary*, 161–62.

- **24:5.** *his avenger:* It is not immediately obvious who this avenger is. Some have suggested the Emperor Titus who destroyed the temple in 70 C.E., but Zechariah's murder is hardly avenged by destroying the temple. Consequently, others have pointed to Christ himself, given the context of the reference to Zechariah's death in Matt 23:35–36 (Smid, *Commentary*, 164).

εἰσῆλθον καὶ εἶδον τὸ γεγονός. ⁸καὶ τὰ φατνώματα τοῦ ναοῦ ὠλόλυξαν, καὶ αὐτοὶ περιεσχίσαντο ἐπάνωθεν ἕως κάτω. ⁹καὶ τὸ πτῶμα αὐτοῦ οὐχ εὗρον, ἀλλ᾽ εὗρον τὸ αἷμα αὐτοῦ λίθον γεγενημένον. ¹⁰καὶ φοβηθέντες ἐξῆλθον καὶ ἀνήγγειλαν τῷ λαῷ ὅτι Ζαχαρίας πεφόνευται. ¹¹καὶ ἤκουσαν πᾶσαι αἱ φυλαὶ τοῦ λαοῦ καὶ ἐπένθησαν αὐτὸν καὶ ἐκόψαντο τρεῖς ἡμέρας καὶ τρεῖς νύκτας.

¹²Μετὰ δὲ τὰς τρεῖς ἡμέρας ἐβουλεύσαντο οἱ ἱερεῖς τίνα ἀναστήσουσιν εἰς τὸν τόπον τοῦ Ζαχαρίου. ¹³καὶ ἀνέβη ὁ κλῆρος ἐπὶ Συμεών· οὗτος γὰρ ἦν ὁ χρηματισθεὶς ὑπὸ τοῦ ἁγίου πνεύματος μὴ ἰδεῖν θάνατον ἕως ἂν τὸν Χριστὸν ἐν σαρκὶ ἴδῃ.

Author   **25** Ἐγὼ δὲ Ἰάκωβος ὁ γράψας τὴν ἱστορίαν ταύτην ἐν Ἱερουσαλὴμ θορύβου γενομένου, ὅτε ἐτελεύτησεν Ἡρώδης, ²συνέστειλα ἐμαυτὸν ἐν τῇ ἐρήμῳ ἕως κατέπαυσεν ὁ θόρυβος ἐν Ἱερουσαλήμ, ³δοξάζων τὸν δεσπότην θεὸν τὸν δόντα μοι τὴν σοφίαν τοῦ γράψαι τὴν ἱστορίαν ταύτην.

⁴Καὶ ἔσται ἡ χάρις μετὰ πάντων τῶν φοβουμένων τὸν κύριον. Ἀμήν.

Γένεσις Μαρίας

Ἀποκάλυψις Ἰακώβ

Εἰρήνη τῷ γράψαντι καὶ τῷ ἀναγινώσκοντι.

24:9. πτῶμα: de Strycker. σῶμα: Tischendorf. **24:10.** τῷ λαῷ: Tischendorf. de Strycker omits. **24:12.** τίνα ἀναστήσουσιν εἰς τὸν τόπον τοῦ Ζαχαρίου: de Strycker. τίνα ἀντ᾽ αὐτοῦ στήσουσιν: Tischendorf. **25:1.** ὁ γράψας: Tischendorf and de Strycker. ἔγραψα: POxy 3524. **25:1.** Ἱερουσαλήμ: Tischendorf and POxy 3524. Ἱεροσαλύμοις: de Strycker. **25:1.** Ἡρώδης: Tischendorf and de Strycker. ὁ Ἡρώδης: POxy 3524. **25:2.** συνέστειλα ἐμαυτὸν ἐν τῇ ἐρήμῳ: Tischendorf. συνέστελλον ἑαυτὸν ἐν τῇ ἐρήμῳ: de Strycker. POxy 3524 omits. **25:2.** ἕως: Tischendorf and de Strycker. ἕως οὗ: POxy 3524. **25:2.** κατέπαυσεν: Tischendorf and POxy 3524. παύηται: de Strycker. **25:2.** ἐν Ἱερουσαλή: Tischendorf and POxy 3524. Ἱερουσαλήμ: de Strycker. **25:3.** δοξάζων: Tischendorf and POxy 3524. δοξάσω δέ: de Strycker. **25:3.** τὸν δεσπότην θεόν: Tischendorf. τὸν δεσπότην: de Strycker. τὸν θεόν: POxy 3524. **25:3.** τὴν σοφίαν: de Strycker and POxy 3524. τὴν δωρεὰν καὶ τὴν σοφίαν: Tischendorf. **25:3.** ταύτην: Tischendorf and de Strycker. POxy 3524 omits. **25:4.** καὶ ἔσται ἡ χάρις μετὰ πάντων τῶν φοβουμένων τὸν κύριον. Ἀμήν: de Strycker. ἔσται δὲ ἡ χάρις μετὰ τῶν φοβουμένων τὸν κύριον ἡμῶν Ἰησοῦν Χριστόν, ᾧ ἡ δόξα εἰς τοὺς αἰῶνας τῶν αἰώνων, ἀμήν: Tischendorf. POxy 3524 omits. **25:4.** Γένεσις Μαρίας, Ἀποκάλυψις Ἰακώβ: de Strycker. Γένεσις Μαρίας: POxy 3524, which breaks off after Μαρίας . . . . Tischendorf omits. **25:4.** εἰρήνη τῷ γράψαντι καὶ τῷ ἀναγινώσκοντι: de Strycker. Tischendorf omits.

summoned up their courage, entered, and saw what had happened. [8]The panels of the temple cried out, and the priests ripped their robes from top to bottom. [9]They didn't find a corpse, but they did find his blood, now turned to stone. [10]They were afraid and went out and reported to the people that Zechariah had been murdered. [11]When all the tribes of the people heard this, they began to mourn; and they beat their breasts for three days and three nights.

[12]After three days, however, the priests deliberated about whom they should appoint to the position of Zechariah. [13]The lot fell to Simeon. [14]This man, you see, is the one who was informed by the holy spirit that he would not see death until he laid eyes on the Anointed in the flesh.

25
Now I, James, am the one who wrote this account at the time when an uproar arose in Jerusalem at the death of Herod. [2]I took myself off to the wilderness until the uproar in Jerusalem died down. [3]There I praised the Lord God, who gave me the wisdom to write this account.

Author

[4]Grace will be with all those who fear the Lord. Amen.
Birth of Mary
Revelation of James
Peace to the writer and the reader.

• **24:8.** *The panels of the temple cried out, and the priests ripped their robes:* The response to the murder of Zechariah is immediate. The priests and even the temple itself express their horror, as do the people when they are told (see v. 11). That the temple panels should also cry out is an understandable exaggeration, but the phraseology may derive from Amos 8:3.

• **24:9.** *They didn't find a corpse:* Presumably the murderers had carried away his body and buried it in an unmarked grave (Smid, *Commentary*, 165).

• **24:13–14.** *Simeon:* The name Simeon and the following prophecy come from Luke 2:25–26.

• **25:1–4.** Having finished his account, the author appends a first-person narrative telling of the dangerous circumstances in which he wrote.

• **25:1.** *Now I, James:* The narrative is once again, as at 18:3, written in the first person, though now it is the author himself who speaks. *James* is presumably the elder stepbrother of Jesus (see Mark 6:3), hence an eye-witness of the very events he narrated, at least since the time Mary had been taken

by Joseph from the temple (9:11). On the matter of authorship, see the Introduction 3.2.

• **25:1.** *in Jerusalem:* There is a slight change in the punctuation here. Both Tischendorf and de Strycker place a comma after these words in the Greek and so connect them to what precedes, with the result that James composes his account in Jerusalem. But it seems more likely that Jerusalem is the site of the disturbance and that James had to flee to the wilderness in order to write his account.

• **25:1.** By *Herod* the author probably means Herod the Great, whose death was in 4 B.C.E., though Herod Agrippa, the grandson of Herod the Great, who died in 44 C.E., cannot be ruled out, especially since he persecuted the Jerusalem church and even killed another James, the brother of John, the son of Zebedee (see Acts 12:1–2). Nevertheless, since the death of Herod the Great is mentioned in Matt 2:19, the author probably has this Herod in mind, too. If so, then the author is claiming a date right around 4 B.C.E. for his work. On the matter of dating, see the Introduction 3.3.

Bookshelf of Basic Works

1. Texts, Translations, and Study Tools

(For complete listing, see Elliott, *Apocryphal New Testament*, 52–56.)

Cockle, W. (ed.), "P. Oxy. 3524: Protevangelium of James 25:1," in *The Oxyrhynchus Papyri*, Vol. 50; A. K. Bowman *et al.* (eds.); London: Egypt Exploration Society, 1983, 8–12.

Cullmann, O. (tr.), "The Protevangelium of James," in *New Testament Apocrypha. Vol. 1. Gospels and Related Writings*. W. Schneemelcher (ed.); R. McL. Wilson (tr.); Louisville, KY: Westminster-John Knox Press, 1991, 421–38.

Daniels, B., *The Greek Manuscript Tradition of the Protevangelium Jacobi*. 2 vols.; Dissertation, Duke University, 1956.

—— (tr.), "The Gospel of James," in *Documents for the Study of the Gospels*. D. Cartlidge and D. Dungan (eds.); Cleveland: William Collins Publishers, 1980, 107–17.

Elliott, J. K., *Apocryphal New Testament: A Collection of Apocryphal Christian Literature in an English Translation*. Oxford: Clarendon Press, 1993.

Fabricius, J. (ed.), *Codex apocryphus Novi Testamenti*. 2 vols.; Hamburg: Schiller, 1703, 1.66–125.

Fuchs, A., *Konkordanz zum Protevangelium des Jakobus*. SNTU B3; Linz: Plöchl, 1978.

Hock, R. (tr.), "The Infancy Gospel of James," in *The Complete Gospels*. R. Miller (ed.); Santa Rosa, CA: Polebridge Press, rev. 1994, 383–96.

Michaelis, W. (tr.), *Die Apokryphen Schriften zum Neuen Testament*. Bremen: Carl Schunemann, 2nd ed. 1958, 62–95.

Neander, M. (ed.), *Catechesis Martini Lutheri parva graeco-latina*. Basel: Ioannis Oporinum, 1564, 356–92.

Pistelli, E. (ed.), "PSI 1.6: Protevangelium Jacobi," in *Pubblicazioni della Societa Italiana per la recerca dei Papiri greci e latini in Egitto. Papiri Greci e Latini*, vol. 1. Florence: Enrico Ariani, 1912, 9–15.

Smid, H., *Protevangelium Jacobi: A Commentary*. Apocrypha Novi Testamenti 1; Assen: van Gorcum, 1965.

de Strycker, É., "Die griechischen Handschriften des Protevangeliums Iacobi" in *Griechische Kodikologie und Textüberlieferung*. D. Harlfinger (ed.); Darmstadt: Wissenschaftliche Buchgesellschaft, 1980, 577–612.

—————— (ed. and tr.), *La Forme la plus ancienne du Protévangile de Jacques* SHG 33; Brussels: Société des Bollandistes, 1961.

Testuz, M. (ed. and tr.), *Papyrus Bodmer V: Nativité de Marie*. Cologne-Geneva: Bibliotheca Bodmeriana, 1958.

Thilo, J. (ed.), *Codex apocryphus Novi Testamenti*. Leipzig: Vogel, 1832, 159–273.

Tischendorf, C. (ed.), *Evangelia Apocrypha*. Leipzig: Avenarius and Mendelssohn, 2nd ed., 1876, 1–50.

Zervos, G., *Prolegomena to a Critical Edition of the Genesis Marias (Protevangelium Jacobi): The Greek Manuscripts*. Dissertation, Duke University, 1986.

2. Specialized Studies on the Infancy Gospel of James

Allen, J., "The Protevangelium of James as an 'Historia': The Insufficiency of the 'Infancy Gospel' Category," in *Society of Biblical Literature Seminar Papers*. E. Lovering (ed.); Atlanta: Scholars Press, 1991, 508–17.

—————— , "The Protevangelium of James and Hellenistic Magic: The Evidence of 5:1," a paper presented at the Society of Biblical Literature Central States Annual Meeting, Springfield, MO, April 1992.

Bovon, F., "The Suspension of Time in Chapter 18 of Protevangelium Jacobi," in *The Future of Early Christianity: Essays in Honor of Helmut Koester*. B. Pearson (ed.); Minneapolis: Fortress Press, 1991, 393–405.

Carr, A. and A. Kazhdan, "Protoevangelion of James," *ODB* (1991) 3.1744–45.

Cothenet, E., "Le Protévangile de Jacques: origine, genre et signification d'un premier midrash chrétien sur la Nativité de Marie," *ANRW* 2.25.6 (1988) 4252–69.

Lafontaine-Dosogne, J., "Iconography of the Cycle of the Life of the Virgin," in *The Kariye Djami. Volume 4: Studies in the Art of the Kariye Djami and Its Intellectual Background*. P. Underwood (ed.); London: Routledge & Kegan Paul, 1975, 163–94.

Lowe, M. "IOYDAIOI of the Apocrypha: A Fresh Approach to the Gospels of James, Pseudo-Thomas, Peter and Nicodemus," *Nov T* 23 (1981) 56–90.

van Stempvoort, P., "The Protevangelium Jacobi, the Sources of its Theme and Style and their Bearing on its Date," in *Studia Evangelica III*. F. Cross (ed.); TU 88; Berlin: Akademie Verlag, 1964, 410–26.

de Strycker, E., "Le Protévangile de Jacques: Problèmes critiques et exégétiques," in *Studia Evangelica III*. F. Cross (ed.); TU 88; Berlin: Akademie Verlag, 1964, 339–59.

Vorster, W. S., "The Annunciation of the Birth of Jesus in the Protevangelium of James," in *A South African Perspective on the New Testament*. J. Petzer and P. Hartin (eds.); Leiden: E.J. Brill, 1986, 33–53.

—————— , "The Protevangelium of James and Intertextuality," in *Text and Testimony: Essays on New Testament and Apocryphal Literature in Honour of A.F.J. Klijn*. T. Baarda *et al.* (eds.); Kampen: J.H. Kok, 1988, 262–75.

Zervos, G., "Dating the Protevangelium of James: The Justin Martyr Connection," in *Society of Biblical Literature 1994 Seminar Papers*. E. Lovering (ed.); Atlanta: Scholars Press, 1994, 415–34.

3. Related Studies

Benko, S., *The Virgin Goddess: Studies in the Pagan & Christian Roots of Mariology*. SHR 59; Leiden: E.J. Brill, 1993.

Berendts, A., *Studien über Zacharias-Apokryphen und Zacharias-Legenden*. Leipzig: Deichert, 1895.

Bonner, S., *Education in Ancient Rome: From the Elder Cato to the Younger Pliny*. Berkeley: University of California Press, 1977.

Bouwsma, W. J., *Concordia Mundi: The Career and Thought of Guillaume Postel*. Cambridge, MA: Harvard University Press, 1957.

Brown, R., *The Birth of the Messiah: A Commentary on the Infancy Narratives in the Gospels of Matthew and Luke*. New York: Doubleday, 2nd updated ed. 1993.

Cohen, J., *The Origin and Evolution of the Moses Nativity Story*. SHR 58; Leiden: E.J. Brill, 1993.

Cole, S. G., "*Gynaiki ou Themis*: Gender Difference in the Greek *Leges Sacrae*," *Helios* 19 (1992) 104–22.

Georgiadou, A. and D. Larmour, "Lucian and Historiography: 'De Historia Conscribenda' and 'Verae Historiae,'" *ANRW* 2.34.2 (1993) 1448–1509.

von Harnack, A., *Die Chronologie der altchristlichen Literatur bis Eusebius*. 2 vols.; Leipzig: J.C. Hinrichs, 1897–1904.

Hilgenfeld, A., *Kritische Untersuchungen über die Evangelien Justins, der clementinischen Homilien und Marcions*. Halle: C.A. Schwetschke, 1850.

Hock, R., "The Greek Novel," in *Greco-Roman Literature and the New Testament*. D. Aune (ed.); SBLSBS 21; Atlanta, GA: Scholars Press, 1988, 127–46.

Hoffmann, R., *Jesus Outside the Gospels*. New York: Prometheus Books, 1984.

————— (tr.), *Celsus, On the True Doctrine: A Discourse against the Christians*. New York: Oxford University Press, 1987.

Hunger, H., *Die Hochsprachliche profane Literatur der Byzantiner*. 2 vols.; Munich: C.H. Beck, 1978.

Kennedy, G., *Greek Rhetoric under Christian Emperors*. Princeton: Princeton University Press, 1983.

Koester, H., "Überlieferung und Geschichte der frühchristlichen Evangelienliteratur," *ANRW* 2.25.2 (1984) 1463–1542.

Lafontaine-Dosogne, J., "The Iconography of the Cycle of the Infancy of Christ," in *The Kariye Djami. Volume 4: Studies in the Art of the Kariye Djami and Its Intellectual Background*. P. Underwood (ed.); London: Routledge & Kegan Paul, 1975, 197–241.

Limberis, V., *Divine Heiress: The Virgin Mary and the Creation of Chrisian Constantinople*. New York: Routledge, 1994.

Maguire, H., *Art and Eloquence in Byzantium*. Princeton: Princeton University Press, 1981.

Manns, F., *Essais sur le Judéo-Christianisme*. SBFA 12; Jerusalem: Franciscan Printing Press, 1977.

Massaux, E., *The Influence of the Gospel of Saint Matthew on Christian Literature before Saint Irenaeus*. 2 vols.; N. Belval and S. Hecht (trs.); NGS 5; Atlanta: Mercer University Press, 1990.

Meier, J. P., "The Brothers and Sisters of Jesus in Ecumenical Perspective," *CBQ* 54 (1992) 1–28.

Pervo, R., "Early Christian Fiction," in *Greek Fiction: The Greek Novel in Context*. J.R. Morgan and R. Stoneman (eds.); New York: Routledge, 1994, 239–54.

Pratscher, W., *Der Herrenbruder Jakobus und die Jakobustradition*. FRLANT 139; Göttingen: Vandenhoeck & Ruprecht, 1987.

Quasten, J., *Patrology: The Beginnings of Patristic Literature*. Westminster, MD: Newman Press, 1950.

Schaberg, J., *The Illegitimacy of Jesus: A Feminist Theological Interpretation of the Infancy Narratives*. San Francisco: Harper & Row, 1987.

Schneemelcher, W., "General Introduction," in *New Testament Apocrypha. Vol. 1: Gospels and Related Writings*. W. Schneemelcher (ed.) and R. McL. Wilson (tr.); Louisville, KY: Westminster-John Knox Press, 1991, 9–75.

Thundy, Z., *Buddha and Christ: Nativity Stories and Indian Traditions*. SHR 60; Leiden: E.J. Brill, 1993.

Trombley, R. and A. Carr, "Birth of the Virgin," *ODB* (1991) 1.291.

———, "Presentation of the Virgin," *ODB* (1991) 3.1715.

Vielhauer, P., *Geschichte der urchristlichen Literatur*. New York: Walter de Gruyter, 1975.

The Emergence of the Infancy Gospels

About 70 C.E. some unknown Christian author made a momentous decision. He decided to make Jesus the subject of a narrative complete with setting, cast of characters, plot, motivations, etc. No one else, so far as we know, had thought of doing so before then. Only non-narrative forms such as creeds, hymns, collections of teachings, and letters had been used to express the significance of Jesus for Christians. But around 70, someone wrote the Gospel of Mark.

Mark's innovative narrative was soon revised and often expanded. About 80 or 90 C.E. the authors of the Gospels of Matthew and Luke revised Mark, preserving much of his narrative, to be sure, but also expanding it in several ways. They wove many teachings of Jesus into the narrative framework of Mark, drawing on a hypothetical collection of Jesus' teachings, now identified as Q. They also expanded Mark at both ends. Mark's narrative ended with some women disciples finding Jesus' tomb empty. Matthew and Luke extend Mark's narrative beyond this story to include Jesus' appearances to his disciples. In fact, Luke carried the narrative forward into a second volume, the Acts of the Apostles, which presents the first thirty years or so of Christian history. Other Acts followed, such as those about Andrew and Thomas or even about a woman follower of Paul named Thecla.

Of greater interest to us is Matthew's and Luke's expansion of Mark's narrative backward. Mark begins with Jesus as a young man, though he does identify him as the Son of God. Matthew and Luke, however, begin farther back—with Jesus' birth. Both narrate in very different ways how Jesus came to be the Son of God. These prompted further interest in Jesus' mother Mary, her parents, her birth and upbringing. By the mid-second century new narratives, now called infancy gospels, took the story back to the time of Mary's parents, as in the Infancy Gospel of James, or filled in gaps in Jesus' childhood, as in the Infancy Gospel of Thomas.

The emergence of the Infancy Gospels of James and Thomas, therefore, should be seen within this broader literary history in which an initial narrative, the Gospel of Mark, was revised and expanded in a number of directions, including backward in time. Taken as a whole, the Gospels and Acts constructed a complex and appealing narrative world with which Christians could identify, a world that had its own cast of characters, dramatic events, and signs of divine favor. The Infancy Gospels of James and Thomas, though focused on Jesus as a mere infant and child, contribute to this narrative world by showing that the virtue and piety of Jesus' family as well as the precocious wisdom and power evident in his own childhood anticipate and confirm his later role as savior and lord.

The Infancy
Gospel
of Thomas

INTRODUCTION

1. Infancy Gospels of Childhood

Christian piety and imagination focused not only on the circumstances of Jesus' birth and specifically on the life of his mother Mary, as we have seen in the Infancy Gospel of James, but also on the childhood years of Jesus himself, prompted in part by the story in Luke's gospel in which a twelve year old Jesus is found seated with the teachers in the Temple at Jerusalem (see Luke 2:41–52). This story in fact is used as the conclusion to another infancy gospel, the Infancy Gospel of Thomas, which leads up to that story by narrating a series of stories about Jesus from the age of five to twelve, all of them illustrating in one way or another the extraordinary power and knowledge that Jesus possessed even as a youngster.

2. The Infancy Gospel of Thomas

2.1 Title

Although the name Infancy Gospel of Thomas is widely accepted today, it is by no means as established as that for the Infancy Gospel of James, which, as we have seen, derives from the Latin *Protevangelium Jacobi*, a title that Postel used when reintroducing this document to the West in the early sixteenth century. In fact, the Infancy Gospel of Thomas was not published until the early eighteenth century,[1] and its name throughout the nineteenth and early twentieth centuries was *Evangelium Thomae Israelitae* or simply *Evangelium Thomae*.[2] The word "infancy" was not added consis-

1. See Fabricius, *Codex Apocryphus*, 1.159–67.
2. Such are the names used in the important 19th c. editions of Thilo, *Codex Apocryphus*, 275, and Tischendorf, *Evangelia Apocrypha*, 140. Such is also the title used in the standard English translation of this gospel (see James, *Apocryphal New Testament*, 49).

tently until recently, and in large part due to the Nag Hammadi discoveries in the mid-1940s of another Gospel of Thomas, the now famous collection of 114 of Jesus' sayings.[3] The two gospels are unrelated, but in order to distinguish them, the narrative gospel has come to be called the Infancy Gospel of Thomas.[4]

This title, even if widely used to designate this gospel, is, of course, not found in the MSS themselves. They display a variety of titles, such as that of Tischendorf A: An Account by Thomas the Israelite Philosopher concerning the Boyhood Deeds (τὰ παιδικά) of the Lord.[5] This title, however, is itself late, so that A. de Santos Otero has sought to recover the original title in earlier MSS. In his work on the much earlier 10th century Greek *Vorlage* of the Slavonic version, he argues on the basis of the title at this time— Boyhood Deeds of our Lord and God and Savior Jesus Christ—that the original was: Boyhood Deeds (Παιδικά) of our Lord Jesus Christ.[6] This title has gained approval,[7] and in any event, the principal word in both (παιδικά) will provide an important clue for determining the purpose of the gospel as a whole (see below 4:1).

2.2 Summary of the Contents

The contents of the Infancy Gospel of Thomas not only differ materially from the Infancy Gospel of James, but also formally, in that the Infancy Gospel of Thomas is not a lengthy and coherent narrative but a collection of largely self-contained stories that are only loosely held together by a series of indications of Jesus' age—five years (2:1),[8] six (11:1), eight (12:4), nine (18:1), and finally twelve (19:1). To be sure, there are other indications of coherence—for example, cycles of stories (2:1-3:4; 4:1-5:5; 6:1-8:4; 14:1-15:7) and occasional cross-references (8:4; cf. 3:3; 4:2; 5:4; and 15:7; cf. 14:4)[9]—but these features are not enough to establish a genuine narrative thread nor to obliterate the gospel's character as a collection of stories.

3. See Elliott, *Aprocryphal New Testament*, 123–47.
4. Voicu ("L'histoire du texte," 119) remarks that this apocryphon is best known under its recent title: The Infancy Gospel of Thomas. See also Gero, "Thomas," 46; Koester, *Gospels*, 311; and Elliott, *Aprocryphal New Testament*, 68. It should be noted that in German scholarship the title used is "Kindheitserzählung" or "Kindheitsgeschichte" (des Thomas), words which seem to translate the word παιδικά in the Greek MSS (see Hennecke, *Neutestamentliche Apokryphen*, 67; Bauer, *Leben Jesu*, 88; Michaelis, *Apokryphen Schriften*, 96; and Vielhauer, *Geschichte*, 672). The translation then would be: The Infancy Story of Thomas (so Cullmann, "Thomas," 439).
5. See further the first note to the Greek text.
6. See de Santos, *Evangelium*, 37–38. Cf. also Voicu, "L'histoire du texte," 122.
7. See, e.g., Cullmann, "Thomas," 449 n. 1, and Koester, *Gospels*, 311 n. 1.
8. As in the Infancy Gospel of James, so here all references to the Infancy Gospel of Thomas will make use of the traditional chapter numbers, but a new versification system will be used that will allow more precise referencing.
9. Vielhauer, *Geschichte*, 674.

One consequence of such a loose collection of stories is that the contents of the Infancy Gospel of Thomas were quite fluid, as some individual stories appear in one MS but are absent from another. For example, in the Greek MSS there are two versions, one with nineteen chapters, termed A by its editor C. von Tischendorf, and one with only eleven, termed B by him.[10] Similar fluidity of contents appears in MSS discovered since Tischendorf's day as well as in the many versions,[11] and some scholars have even proposed an original, more gnostic gospel that was later purged of clearly heretical stories in order to make it acceptable to the church as a whole.[12] In any case, for purposes of the summary of the Infancy Gospel of Thomas given here Tischendorf A will be used, with significant departures from this, now standard, text duly noted. The story at times recalls incidents and language from the canonical stories, but what is most noticeable is a strikingly different Jesus from the one in the canonical portraits—a vindictive, arrogant, unruly child "who," as J. K. Elliott puts it, "seldom acts in a Christian way."[13]

The Infancy Gospel of Thomas opens with a prologue identifying the author as Thomas the Israelite and giving his purpose in writing as wanting to make known to non-Jews the extraordinary deeds Jesus did while growing up in Nazareth (1).[14]

The gospel then opens with a series of episodes in which Jesus is five years old (2:1–10:4).[15] The first story involves Jesus out playing with other

10. See Tischendorf, *Evangelia Apocrypha*, 140–57 (Evangelium Thomae graece A) and 158–63 (Evangelium Thomae graece B).

11. For discussion of these MSS and versions, see below Introduction 6.

12. See Bauer, *Leben Jesu*, 94; Michaelis, *Apokryphen Schriften*, 98; Vielhauer, *Geschichte*, 676; and Elliott, *Apocryphal New Testament*, 69.

13. Elliott, *Apocryphal New Testament*, 68. This assessment is frequently made (see, e.g., Vielhauer, *Geschichte*, 675; Koester, *Gospels*, 313; and Cullmann, "Thomas," 442).

14. See Voicu, "L'histoire du texte," 130–32, and below Introduction 6, for the view that this opening chapter as well as chapters 10 and 17–18 may not have belonged to the earliest forms of the gospel.

15. In one Greek MS, abbreviated here as Greek C (for details, see below Introduction 6), there is a short cycle of stories about Jesus as a two year old in Egypt (see Delatte, "Évangile," 264, 1–265, 15). This cycle, which begins with a heavenly messenger telling Joseph to flee to Egypt (264, 1–5), is obviously prompted by the canonical story of the flight of Joseph, Mary, and Jesus from Bethlehem to Egypt in the light of Herod's designs on all children under two (see Matt 2:13–16), and it is brought to a close with a divine messenger instructing Mary to leave Egypt with Joseph and Jesus and return to Judea, which they do (265, 11–15), an episode that parallels that in Matt 2:19–23. In between, however, the contents have no relation to the canonical accounts (though a similar set of stories also appears in the Latin version [see Tischendorf, *Evangelia Apocrypha*, 164–66, translation in Elliott, *Aprocryphal New Testament*, 82–83]). At any rate, this cycle contains three stories, the first about Jesus, now two years old, plucking and eating grain en route to Egypt where his family stays for a year in the house of a widow (264, 5–8), the second about him reviving a salted fish while playing with children (264, 9–14), and the third about him laughing at a teacher in the streets who was disrupted by sparrows fighting over grain and falling into his bosom; Jesus' laughter angers the teacher and results in his being driven from the city (264, 14–265, 11).

children by a rushing stream[16] one Sabbath and making ponds to collect water (2:1-2). He purifies the water with a mere command (2:2). Then he takes the water and mixes it with clay to mold twelve sparrows (2:3), an action that a man sees and reports to Joseph as a violation of the sabbath (2:4). When Joseph arrives to reprimand his son, Jesus claps his hands together and the clay sparrows come alive and fly away (2:5-7).

One child who was with Jesus drains the ponds (3:1), angering Jesus and prompting him to cause the child to wither up and die (3:2-3). The bereaving parents blame Joseph (3:4).

On another occasion Jesus is walking through the village when he is bumped on the shoulder by another boy (4:1).[17] Jesus' anger again brings about the death of the boy (4:2) and prompts a startled populace to blame Joseph again, this time with an ultimatum: either teach him to bless and not to curse or leave the village (4:4). Joseph's attempt to admonish him (5:1) only induces Jesus to blind his accusers (5:2). The populace is again amazed at Jesus' powerful words (5:3), and Joseph, now angry, grabs Jesus by the ear but gets a sharp reprimand himself (5:4).

A teacher with a name familiar from Luke 19:2, that is, Zacchaeus,[18] overhears Jesus' words and asks Joseph to hand him over to him, so that he can teach him to read and thereby not be unruly (6:1-2). Joseph is doubtful, thinking that only God can rule him (6:3). Jesus agrees (6:4), however, and then tells the teacher that he knows more than he does, including such things as knowing where the teacher came from and how many years he will live; in fact, he claims that his wisdom is divine (6:5-8). Such claims amaze those standing by, to which Jesus adds another claim: he existed before the creation of the world (6:9-10).

Surprisingly, Zacchaeus still wants to get Jesus into his classroom (6:13), and when Joseph takes him there, the teacher starts at the beginning, teaching him the letters of the alphabet (6:14-15). Jesus, however, is unwilling to cooperate, so that Zacchaeus hits him over the head (6:16). Jesus' reply is a withering attack on Zacchaeus, calling him a clashing cymbal, a phrase used by Paul (1 Cor 13:1), and then reversing roles by reciting the entire alphabet with facility and asking the teacher to give the real meaning of the letter alpha (6:16-21). When Zacchaeus cannot answer, Jesus gives a detailed, if largely incomprehensible, description of the letter (6:21-23).

Zacchaeus now recognizes the profound knowledge that Jesus possesses and gives a lengthy lament, recognizing Jesus' divine origin and power and

16. Tischendorf B and Greek C explain, adding that the rushing water was caused by a thunderstorm.
17. Tischendorf B says that a boy threw a stone and hit Jesus on the shoulder.
18. At this point even Tischendorf A is sharply abbreviated, so that the summary of chapter 6 is taken from Greek C.

expressing his own shame and despair at ever being able to hold his head up as a teacher (7:1–11). Jesus laughs at the humiliated Zacchaeus (8:1), but at least revokes the curses he made earlier (8:2–3; cf. 3:3; 4:1; 5:2).

In the following days Jesus continues the benign use of his power. On one occasion he and some other children are playing on a roof when one boy, named Zeno, falls from this height and dies (9:1). When all the other children flee, leaving Jesus all by himself, the parents of the dead boy come and accuse Jesus of deliberately pushing him (9:2) but Jesus denies the charge (9:3).[19] He then jumps down to the ground and calls to Zeno to get up and say whether he pushed him (9:4). Zeno arises and exonerates Jesus (9:5), causing the parents now to glorify God and worship Jesus (9:6).

On another occasion Jesus hears a commotion over a young man who has cut his foot with his axe (10:1–2). Jesus forces his way through the crowd and with only a touch heals the young man's foot (10:2–3). The man goes back to work, and the crowd worships Jesus since he possesses the spirit of God (10:4).

In the next episode Jesus is six years old (11:1). He is sent by his mother to fetch water from a well (11:1). The pitcher he has for the water falls to the ground, however, and breaks. To fulfill his task Jesus must devise another way to carry the water back home; he does so by using his clothing to hold the water (11:2–3). Mary responds to this miracle by kissing Jesus and keeping to herself the mysteries which Jesus has accomplished (11:4)— language which recalls Luke 2:19, 51.

The following two episodes have Jesus helping his father, though now as an eight year old (12:4). In the first episode Jesus helps with the planting of grain and sows one measure of seed (12:1). At harvest time the seed sowed produces a hundred measures, an amount which not only recalls that in the parable of the sower (Matt 13:8; Mark 4:8; Luke 8:8) but also allows Jesus enough to give to the poor in the village with some left over for Joseph to take home (12:2–3).

In the next episode Jesus helps his father in the carpentry shop when a rich man orders a bed and Joseph's boards are not the right lengths (13:1–2).[20] Jesus instructs his father to lay the boards side by side (13:2). Jesus then grabs hold of the shorter one and stretches it until it is the same length as the other (13:3). Like Mary, Joseph responds with a hug and kiss, cognizant that his son is a gift from God (13:4).[21]

19. The accusation and denial are missing in Tischendorf, a lacuna filled in by appeal to the Greek *Vorlage* of the Slavonic version (on which see below Introduction 6).
20. Tischendorf B differs considerably, expanding the story with dialogue and even changing the setting from the workshop to the woods where Joseph has gone out to get his wood.
21. Tischendorf B ends at this point.

At this point Joseph decides that Jesus should learn to read and takes him to another teacher (14:1). Once again, however, the lessons get no farther than the letters of the alphabet when Jesus asks the teacher for the meaning of the letter alpha (14:2–3; cf. 6:19–20). And once again the teacher strikes him on the head (14:4; cf. 6:16), but Jesus responds with a curse that leaves the teacher flat on his face (14:4–5). When Jesus returns home, Joseph orders Mary not to let him out of the house (14:5).

One of Joseph's friends offers to teach Jesus (15:1) and takes him to his classroom with understandable fear and trepidation (15:2). Once in the classroom, however, Jesus quickly takes up a book but does not read the letters in it; rather, he speaks in the holy spirit and amazes all with his command of the law (15:3), an incident somewhat reminiscent of Luke 4:16–17. At any rate, unlike Zacchaeus, this teacher readily admits that Jesus is already filled with grace and wisdom and so sends him back to Joseph (15:6). The teacher's good sense is rewarded by a smile from Jesus and by a revocation of the curse on the second teacher (15:7; cf. 14:4).

In the next story Jesus' brother James is sent out to gather firewood (16:1). Jesus tags along, which is fortunate, since James is bitten on the hand by a viper—an incident that recalls a similar story about the apostle Paul on the island of Malta (Acts 28:2–6). In any case, James, unlike Paul, is quickly near death when Jesus comes and merely blows on the bite and restores him to good health (16:2).

Jesus' powers are soon needed again, as an infant in the neighborhood dies (17:1). A grieving mother and wailing crowd soon arouse Jesus, who comes and touches the baby's chest and orders it to live (17:2). The baby laughs and Jesus instructs the mother to feed it—a detail that recalls similar instructions in the story of the raising of Jairus' daughter (Mark 5:43; Luke 8:55). In any case, the crowd regards Jesus as a god or heavenly messenger (17:3–4).

A year later there is another death in the village, as a construction worker falls to his death (18:1). Jesus hears the commotion and soon arrives at the site, where he grabs the dead man's hand and orders him to get up and get back to work. The man gets up and worships Jesus, prompting another claim from the crowd about Jesus' heavenly origin (18:2–3).

The Infancy Gospel of Thomas then concludes by only slightly reworking a story from Luke's gospel, the visit of Jesus at age twelve to Jerusalem (see Luke 2:41–52). The occasion is Passover, and Jesus and his family journey with many others to the city for the celebration (19:1). On the return trip, however, Joseph and Mary realize that Jesus is not in the travel party and so return to Jerusalem to locate him (19:2–3). After days of searching they find him in the Temple, seated with the teachers listening to the law and asking questions (19:4). All are marveling at how a mere child could interrogate his elders when Mary asks him why he has done what he did (19:6), to which Jesus replies: "Don't you know that I must be in my father's house?" (19:7).

At this point the story diverges most sharply from its Lukan source by having the scholars and Pharisees ask Mary whether she is the boy's mother and then pronounce a blessing on her in words reminiscent of Luke 1:42: "You more than any woman are to be congratulated, for God has blessed the fruit of your womb" (19:8–10). Jesus then arises and obediently follows his mother, after which, it says, he progressed in wisdom and stature and grace (19:11–12).

A short doxology draws the Infancy Gospel of Thomas to a close (19:13).[22]

3. Authorship, Dating, and Provenance

3.1 Authorship

Attribution of this gospel to Thomas, presumably the Thomas named in the Synoptic gospels (Matt 10:3; Mark 3:18; Luke 6:15) but especially prominent in John's gospel (John 11:16; 14:5; 20:24–28; 21:2) and even later understood to be the twin brother of Jesus (Gospel of Thomas, Acts of Thomas), is most certainly incorrect. Historical arguments are not necessary because the MSS themselves undercut the ascription.[23] Thus Greek C attributes authorship of this gospel to James,[24] and even if this ascription is a slip by the copyist (since the story about James in chap. 16 is narrated in the third person),[25] the various versions do not name Thomas as the author at all, including the oldest MS of all, a Syriac MS in the British Museum from the sixth century.[26] S. Gero is of the opinion that the ascription to Thomas did not originate until the middle ages and specifically prior to the Greek *Vorlage* of the Slavonic version around the tenth century.[27]

The Infancy Gospel of Thomas is thus a pseudonymous, or better anonymous, work, whose author recedes quickly from view. From the internal evidence of the gospel, however, a few characteristics of the author

22. So ends the gospel in Tischendorf A, Greek C, and the Latin, but in other versions, notably the Slavonic, the gospel continues with various other stories, conveniently listed in Gero, "Thomas," 57–58. For the Slavonic stories, such as Jesus destroying a temple of idols after a tile falls on him, Jesus becoming the student of a doctor and healing a blind man, and Jesus turning Jewish children into pigs, see de Santos, *Evangelium*, 140–46. Since he considers these stories to go back to the Greek *Vorlage* (169 n. 1), he retranslates them as well into Greek (169–71).

23. For full MS discussion, see Gero, "Thomas," 59, and Voicu, "L'histoire du texte," 121–22.

24. See Delatte, "Évangile," 265, 18.

25. On the name "James" possibly being a slip, see Gero, "Thomas," 59 n. 1.

26. See Gero, "Thomas," 57, and Wright, *Apocryphal Literature*, 6, whose title naming Thomas is corrected by Voicu, "L'histoire du texte," 121 n. 11. For the omission of chap. 1 in the versions, see Voicu p. 128.

27. Gero, "Thomas," 59.

are discernible. For example, since the author names no places in Palestine (except for Jerusalem in 19:1) and says nothing about Jewish life and customs that is not borrowed, such as the celebration of Passover from Luke 2:41, or widely known, such as sabbath observance in 2:4 and the Hebrew language in 14:2, scholars readily assume that the author was not a Jewish Christian.[28] In addition, the author wrote in Greek,[29] arguments to the contrary notwithstanding,[30] and although the literary level falls far short of classical standards,[31] it is in keeping with the Koine of the early Roman Empire and suggests that the author possessed a good education and a talent for effective narration (see further below 4.1).[32]

3.2 Dating

No precision regarding the date of the Infancy Gospel of Thomas is possible, and even the range of possible dates is unusually large, extending from the first to the sixth centuries. The latter end of this range is fixed, as it is the date of the earliest MS of this gospel, and only S. Gero has proposed dating the Infancy Gospel of Thomas at this end of the range. He uses a form critical model and proposes a long period of oral transmission before composition in the sixth century.[33]

The earlier end of this range is likewise fixed, this time by the date of Luke's gospel in the 80s of the first century because it supplied the story of Jesus in the Temple at age twelve (see 19:1–12; cf. Luke 2:41–52).[34] Most scholars, in fact, favor the lower end of the range, pointing in particular to the second century because one story from the Infancy Gospel of Thomas, the exchange between Jesus and his teacher regarding the letters alpha and beta (6:19–20; 14:3), is already attested in a mid-second century document, the *Epistula Apostolorum*, and it is also known, says Irenaeus, to have circulated in a second century gnostic group called Marcosians.[35] Conse-

---

28. See, e.g., Michaelis, *Apokryphen Schriften*, 97; Vielhauer, *Geschichte*, 675–76; and Cullmann, "Thomas," 442.

29. So correctly Michaelis, *Apokryphen Schriften*, 97; Vielhauer, *Geschichte*, 673; and Cullmann, "Thomas," 439.

30. The claim that the original language was Syriac has been effectively met by de Santos, *Evangelium*, 148–51. Gero, "Thomas," 55, and Elliott, *Apocryphal New Testament*, 69, however, leave the question open.

31. For a thorough discussion of the Greek of Tischendorf A in relation to classical Greek, see Weissengruber, "Untersuchungen," 209–25.

32. So Weissengruber, "Untersuchungen," 225–26.

33. See Gero, "Thomas," 56 and 73, as well as his later survey, "Apocryphal Gospels," 3982.

34. For detailed evidence showing the dependence of the Infancy Gospel of Thomas on Luke's version of this story, see de Jonge, "Sonship," 342–48, esp. 347–48.

35. See *Ep. Apos.* 4 (translation in Gero, "Thomas," 63: "This is what our Lord Jesus did who was delivered by Joseph and Mary his mother to where he might learn letters. And he who taught him said to him as he taught him 'Say Alpha.' He answered and said to him, 'First tell me what Beta is.'") and Irenaeus, *Adv. haer.* 1.13.1 (translation in Gero,

quently, the second century, perhaps the late second century, is "not certain, but also not improbable" as the date of the Infancy Gospel of Thomas.[36]

3.3 Provenance

Situating the author of the Infancy Gospel of Thomas is also difficult. The stories contain an unusual amount of detail about village life which may contain a clue. But these details—flash floods (2:1), village leaders (2:7), willow branches (3:1), elementary teachers (6:1), rooftop play (9:1), chopping wood (10:1), fetching water (11:1), growing grain (12:1), making plows and yokes and beds (13:1), etc.—point to no region in particular, as they could apply anywhere.[37] Even the suggestion of eastern Syria on account of the prominence of Thomas in this region[38] is made doubtful by the original anonymous character of the work. Consequently, we are left with the large area known as the Greek East of the Roman Empire when trying to situate the author of the Infancy Gospel of Thomas.

4. Literary Forms and Functions

4.1 Literary Forms of the Individual Narratives

The Infancy Gospel of Thomas, as we have indicated and as the summary of its contents has shown, is a collection of short narratives which are largely self-contained and only minimally made part of a larger whole by being subsumed under various ages of Jesus, gathered into short cycles of stories, or given occasional cross references. In addition, the narratives themselves, being so loosely attached to the whole, were subject to quite remarkable reworking, as a comparison of the various MSS displays considerable paraphrasing, expansion, condensation, even deletion of some stories and the addition of new ones (see above 2.2).

With such a minimal overall structure to the Infancy Gospel of Thomas scholars have understandably tended to focus on the individual narratives rather than on the whole. Thus, besides generalizations about the forms of

---

"Thomas," 63: "They [the Marcosians] propose, among others, the falsehood that the Lord, when he was a child and learning the alphabet, being asked by the teacher, as was customary, 'tell me Alpha,' said, 'Alpha.' Being then commanded by the teacher to say Beta, the Lord answered, 'Tell me first what is Alpha, then I will tell you what Beta is.' And this they explain as meaning that he alone knew the unknown, which he revealed in the form of Alpha."). Gero ("Thomas," 56 n. 1) argues that such minimal knowledge of the Infancy Gospel of Thomas in these writings is hardly enough to establish the gospel's existence. But the closeness of Irenaeus' account of this story to the corresponding part of the Infancy Gospel of Thomas seems sufficient to argue its existence.

36. So Koester, *Gospels*, 311. See also Vielhauer, *Geschichte*, 673; Cullmann, "Thomas," 442. Michaelis (*Apokryphen Schriften*, 97) suggests the first half of the second century.

37. See Michaelis, *Apokryphen Schriften*, 97.

38. See Elliott, *Apocryphal New Testament*, 69.

individual narratives—for example, all the stories are Novelle, except for
the story of Jesus at twelve years in the Temple (19:1–12), which is a
Personal Legend[39]—there have been some more sustained formal analyses.
For example, Gero has provided a Bultmannian form critical analysis of all
the individual narratives.[40] Many of the stories are easily classified into
three forms. The first includes short miracle stories with no saying of Jesus,
some of which have no reaction from bystanders (chaps. 11, 12, 16), but
others do (chap. 13). Gero adds that these stories have no Synoptic
parallels.[41] The second includes healings with a saying of Jesus attached
(chaps. 10,17, 18). These stories do have Synoptic parallels (cf. Matt 9:23–
26; Mark 2:11–12). The third involves imprecations, or curses (chaps. 3, 4).
Their model is the cursing of the fig tree (Mark 11:20–26).[42]

Other stories require fuller discussion to establish their form. For
example, the story about the sparrows (chap. 2), says Gero, is a typical
apophthegm, modeled on the Synoptic healings on the Sabbath (Mark 3:1–
6), as is clear once the secondary details are eliminated, such as the
gathering and purifying of the water (2:1–2) and the introduction of Joseph
(cf. 2:4–5). The miracle itself may have been prompted by the saying of
Mark 3:4: "Is it permissible on the Sabbath to do good or evil, to save a life
or to kill?"[43]

Gero argues similarly about the stories of Jesus' clash with his teachers
over the alphabet (chaps. 5–7, cf. also 14–15), saying that these stories, too,
are apophthegms, but not in the forms in which they appear in the Infancy
Gospel of Thomas. In the gospel they are considerably expanded by
dialogue (5:1–6:12; 7:1–11) and by esoteric descriptions of the letter alpha
(6:22–23). The simpler and original apophthegm (cf. 6:19–20) is found in
the two second century sources of this story cited above, in the *Epistula
Apostolorum* and in Irenaeus' comments on the Marcosians (see above
3.2).[44]

Gero also analyzes a number of Jesus' sayings in the Infancy Gospel of
Thomas (2:6; 5:2, 5; 6:19–20; 10:3; 17:3; 18:2), seeking amid the variety of
wordings in the MSS the wording that is most likely original. He frequently
detects a tripartite form among the options (2:6; 10:3; 17:3; 18:2) and argues
for its originality—for example, "Be off, fly away, and remember me!" (2:6).
Other examples need not be given here, as they are incorporated in the
Greek Text and the Notes to the Greek Text.

39. Vielhauer, *Geschichte*, 674.
40. See Gero, "Thomas," 56–64
41. Gero ("Thomas," 64) is hesitant to classify the story of the raising of Zeno (chap. 9)
into any of these categories, but it seems to fall into the second of these subtypes, having a
model not in the Synoptics but in the story of Eutychus in Acts 20:9–12.
42. See Gero, "Thomas," 59–61.
43. See Gero, "Thomas," 61–62.
44. See Gero, "Thomas," 62–64.

One story, however, has been overlooked, and that is Zacchaeus' lament (chap. 7). It is an exception to Vielhauer's generalization, and it is pushed aside in Gero's concern with original forms. W. Michaelis has taken note of its distinctive style in comparison with the gospel as a whole,[45] but he does not elaborate. In this chapter Zacchaeus laments his being made a fool of by Jesus who had turned the tables on him, revealing himself to be wiser than his teacher, possessing not only a facility with the alphabet he was supposed to be learning (6:18) but also a divine wisdom and status (6:5–8, 16–7) and an esoteric understanding of the letter Alpha (6:19–23).

To this series of humiliations Zacchaeus responds at some length (7:1–11). A careful reading of this lengthy lament shows that it transcends the usual oral categories of form criticism. Instead, it is a much more literary form, and specifically one of the forms learned at the tertiary, or rhetorical, stage of education—the $\dot{\eta}\theta o\pi o\iota\acute{\iota}a$, or speech-in-character. This form, like the $\delta\iota\dot{\eta}\gamma\eta\mu a$, or narrative, and the $\dot{\epsilon}\gamma\kappa\dot{\omega}\mu\iota o\nu$, or encomium, in the Infancy Gospel of James, was learned during instruction in pre-rhetorical composition by means of manuals called *Progymnasmata*.[46] Coming eleventh in the series of fourteen exercises, the $\dot{\eta}\theta o\pi o\iota\acute{\iota}a$ is defined rather cryptically as "an imitation of the character of a person,"[47] but the examples soon make clear that it is a speech that is meant. Aphthonius gives these as examples: "What words Herakles might say after the commands of Eurystheus," or "What words Hecuba might say as Troy lay in ruins," or "What words a man from the country might say on first seeing the ocean."[48] Various classifications and sub-classifications are given,[49] but what interests us are the instructions on how to compose an $\dot{\eta}\theta o\pi o\iota\acute{\iota}a$, both stylistic and structural. Among the stylistic recommendations is appropriateness, or language that fits the person's character and the occasion—for example, language that is appropriate to a young man or an old man.[50] Structurally, the $\dot{\eta}\theta o\pi o\iota\acute{\iota}a$ is to be built along the three times and in this order: present, past, and future.[51]

Aphthonius' model $\dot{\eta}\theta o\pi o\iota\acute{\iota}a$, what words Niobe might say as her children lay dead,[52] shows how these stylistic and structural recommendations work out in practice. Niobe—whose earlier boast that she was a better mother than the goddess Leto has led to the killing of her sons and

45. See Michaelis, *Apokryphen Schriften*, 98.
46. On the *progymnasmata*, see Kennedy, *Rhetoric*, 52–73 and esp. Hunger, *Literatur*, 1.92–120.
47. Hermogenes, *Progymn.* 9 (p. 20, 7–8 Rabe), and Aphthonius, *Progymn.* 11 (p. 34, 2–3 Rabe).
48. See Aphthonius, *Progymn.* 11 (pp. 34, 7–8; 35, 3–4, 5–6 Rabe).
49. See, e.g., Aphthonius, *Progymn.* 11 (p. 35, 1–10 Rabe), which subdivides $\dot{\eta}\theta o\pi o\iota\acute{\iota}a\iota$ into those that express deep emotions, characteristic dispositions, or a combination of both; and Hermogenes, *Progymn.* 9 (pp. 20, 24–21, 5 Rabe), which subdivides $\dot{\eta}\theta o\pi o\iota\acute{\iota}a\iota$ into those addressed only to the speaker and those addressed to an audience.
50. See Hermogenes, *Progymn.* 9 (p. 21, 6–9 Rabe).
51. Aphthonius, *Progymn.* 11 (p. 35, 11–14 Rabe).
52. See Aphthonius, *Progymn.* 11 (pp. 35, 15–36, 20 Rabe).

Introduction 95

daughters by Leto's children, Apollo and Artemis[53]—speaks now in this model ἠθοποιία by dividing her thoughts into the three times. First she laments her present state, being robbed of her children, grieving, and being more unfortunate than those who never bore children. Then she compares her present state with her past, when she was happy and admired for her abundant offspring, although even then, as a descendant of Tantalus, she should have expected some dire misfortune. Then she turns to the future, asking what she can do, what she can take pride in. Even death is no option, she says, since she fears that even then she will continue to weep, an allusion to her eventual fate of being turned into stone that continues to weep. Stylistically, this ἠθοποιία reflects appropriately a mother's deep grief for her lost children, and that grief is expressed in the use of the interjection "Poor me!," of self-pitying vocatives, and of rhetorical questions.

When we turn to Zacchaeus' speech its character as an ἠθοποιία becomes clear. This classification can also be made more precise, fitting the subdivisions of an ἠθοποιία that expresses deep emotion, and one that is addressed to an audience (7:2). In addition, its structure follows the time sequence of present, past, and future. Thus, Zacchaeus expresses the shame he feels at having having been reduced to silence over the meaning of the letter Alpha (see 6:21), all the result of having admitted Jesus into his school, a boy he now realizes is not born on earth but was in fact born before the creation of the world, and to what sort of mother he does not know (7:2–6). Then Zacchaeus admits that when he had accepted Jesus as a student, he had deceived himself, for he had really taken on a teacher (vv. 7–8). Finally, Zacchaeus turns to the future, thinking of the shame and despair that he must live with. He does not know what he will say to people once they find out he has been defeated by a mere boy. What is more, his ignorance will continue, regarding both the meaning of the letter Alpha and the real identity of Jesus (vv. 9–11). Throughout, moreover, the style of the speech is appropriate to a teacher by showing shame for being ignorant—note, for example, the repeated use of "I don't know" (vv. 5, 10, 11). And, as in Niobe's lament, we find in Zacchaeus' ἠθοποιία the interjection "Poor me!" (vv. 2, 6), the self-pitying vocatives—for example, "wretch that I am" (v. 2), and the rhetorical questions—"What sort of womb bore him?" "What sort of mother nourished him?" "What can I say?" "What can I report?" (vv. 5, 10). Formally speaking, therefore, Zacchaeus' speech is a virtual textbook example of an ἠθοποιία.

4.2 Literary Function of the Whole

The form critical emphasis on the individual stories in the Infancy Gospel of Thomas has left the whole largely uninvestigated.[54] At most, the

---

53. For a full account of this myth, see Ovid, *Metamorphoses*, 6.145–312.
54. See also Lowe's attempt ("IOYΔAIOI," 75–78) to identify the original "whole" of the

statements made about the whole are negative. The reticence to use the word "gospel" in the title betrays an awareness that the Infancy Gospel of Thomas is not a gospel.[55] The order of the stories is not important.[56] Despite the growth in Jesus' age from five to twelve and even the mention of progress in his wisdom and stature (19:12), there is in fact no development of Jesus' personality.[57]

While these statements are all true enough, they need to be stated more positively for the purpose of the Infancy Gospel of Thomas to emerge. And the clue to this purpose may well be a word found in both the title and the prologue (1), namely: παιδικὰ (πράγματα), or "boyhood (deeds)." When used in these places within the whole, its characterizing role becomes apparent. What did the readers of the Infancy Gospel of Thomas expect to find when they began reading about Jesus' boyhood deeds? To answer this question, we need to digress briefly and consider what childhood at this time involved and specifically what childhood meant for those whose childhoods were later remembered and put down in writing.

Recent research has not only investigated the actual experiences of children during the early Roman empire, but has also explored the way childhood, in particular that of famous political, military, and religious leaders, was portrayed by biographers and rhetoricians. T. Wiedemann, for example, has studied the lives of important individuals, mostly Roman emperors, and paid particular attention to the way their childhood functions in the biographies written about them.[58] Several of his results have a bearing on the Infancy Gospel of Thomas. Although biographies of individuals, which were decisively shaped according to the prescriptions of rhetorical handbooks,[59] dealt with ancestry, birth, childhood, and adulthood, they were not about changes and development in their subjects' fortunes and personalities, but about their character, and that character was assumed to have been fixed from birth.[60] Consequently, anecdotes about birth and childhood were expected to anticipate the qualities and virtues that characterized adult life. Signs of divine favor or even parentage are noted for the birth, and precocious achievement in school as well as intimations of future qualities in childhood play and chores are often cited. Wiedemann illustrates these features with copious evidence. He notes that already in the Alexander-Romance we find "suspected filiation from a god, miracles at the time of birth, games which reveal the boy as a natural leader,

---

Infancy Gospel of Thomas; by taking seriously the date of the MSS, the duplications, and the order of stories, he arrives at the following nucleus: Chaps. 2–6, 9, 11, and 13.

55. Gero, "Thomas," 59.
56. Gero, "Thomas," 58–59.
57. Vielhauer, Geschichte, 674.
58. See Wiedemann, Adults and Children, esp. 49–83. Much primary material also collected in Talbert, "Future Greatness," 132–37.
59. Wiedemann, Adults and Children, 52.
60. Wiedemann, Adults and Children, 49–50.

acclamation by a wise man, and great learning at school."[61] And these features continue to appear in biographies of emperors and others throughout the imperial period.[62]

The Infancy Gospel of Thomas conforms to the patterns Wiedemann has identified for the portrayal of childhood in biographies, and in fact he mentions the infancy gospels of Jesus in passing.[63] In any case, the παιδικὰ πράγματα of Jesus would have an expected form and function for ancient readers. These people would expect to read stories that anticipate the qualities of Jesus as an adult, of him as the powerful miracle worker and divine teacher that was so familiar from the canonical gospels. And the Infancy Gospel of Thomas does not fail them, for here are the incidents of Jesus as a child, spanning the years from five to twelve. The reader finds him playing with other children—alongside a rushing stream (2:1) or on a rooftop (9:1)—or helping his parents—fetching water (11:1), helping in the fields and workshop (12:1; 13:1), or gathering firewood (16:1). And whether Jesus is playing or helping out his divine power is clearly, if not always correctly, displayed: clay sparrows come alive (2:6); seeds produce miraculous harvests (12:2); and falls, accidents, snakebites, and sickness (9:4; 10:3; 16:2; 17:2) are all subject to Jesus' restorative divine power. As the people of Nazareth conclude: "This child's from heaven—he must be, because he has saved many souls from death and he can go on saving all his life" (18:3).

In addition, as a child the schooling of Jesus is germane, and once again his experiences at school (6–8; 14–15) demonstrate his precocious learning (6:18; 15:6) and superiority over his teachers (7:10) as well as point to the divine origin of his wisdom (7:4–5; 19:10).[64] In short, the Infancy Gospel of Thomas confirms what Christian readers already assumed, not just from the Lukan account of him at twelve but also from cultural expectations, that the παιδικὰ πράγματα of their Lord and Savior anticipated his adult achievements as miracle worker and divine teacher.

5. Borrowings and Backgrounds

5.1 Literary Borrowings

The Infancy Gospel of Thomas is nowhere near as dependent on earlier literature, whether the Septuagint or the writings that would make up the

---

61. Wiedemann, *Adults and Children*, 54–55.
62. See further Wiedemann, *Adults and Children*, 55–80. See also Talbert, "Future Greatness," 132–35, esp. 135: "It was commonplace . . . to relate tales of the precocious intelligence and of the unusual power and authority of the youths of destiny," with many references. On the religious side the most precocious of the gods was Hermes, who, as patron deity of thieves, is said to have stolen Apollo's cattle while a new-born infant (see Homeric Hymn 4: to Hermes, and Burkert, *Religion*, 156–59).
63. Wiedemann, *Adults and Children*, 55.
64. Even though this gospel is about Jesus' childhood and not his birth, the divine origin of Jesus is often mentioned in passing (see 7:4–5, 11; 10:4; 13:4; and 18:3).

New Testament, as is the Infancy Gospel of James. The Septuagint is not a source, and even the New Testament writings are used far less often and far less directly. The one exception is the concluding story of Jesus at age twelve in the Temple in Jerusalem (19:1–12), which, as we have said (see above 2.2), is literarily dependent on the story in Luke 2:41–52. Only the question put to Mary and the blessing pronounced over her are significant departures from the Lukan version (vv. 8–10), and even here the blessing at least is modeled on another passage from this gospel (see Luke 1:42).

Elsewhere, however, the New Testament is used more as a source for details, phraseology, or even merely as a point of departure. Only a few examples need be cited here,[65] as they are also indicated in the Notes to the English Translation. Thus, details taken from the New Testament writings include: the names Annas (3:1; cf. Luke 3:2) and Zaccheus (6:1; cf. Luke 19:2), the hundred-fold harvest (12:2; cf. Matt 13:8), Joseph's trade as a carpenter (13:1; cf. Matt 13:55), and giving the revived infant something to eat (17:3; cf. Mark 5:43). Borrowed phrases include: references to God as the one who sent me (6:6; cf. John 4:34; 5:24; etc.), the clashing cymbal (6:16; cf. 1 Cor 13:1), and Mary's keeping what Jesus did to herself (11:4; cf. Luke 2:51). Points of departure for new stories include: cursing a fig tree (3:2; cf. Matt 21:18–19), falling from an upper storey (9:1; cf. Acts 20:9–12), and being bitten on the hand by a viper (16:1; cf. Acts 28:3). In a word, readers of the Infancy Gospel of Thomas would find much in the stories that reminded them of the writings that at that time were increasingly being considered authoritative and canonical.

5.2 Cultural Backgrounds

While borrowings from Christian writings are numerous and unmistakable, scholars have tended to emphasize even more the broader cultural arena of the Greco-Roman world, including Egypt and India, as the context for reading the various stories in the Infancy Gospel of Thomas. Again, only a sampling is necessary, as some of the material has already been cited (see above 4.2) and fuller discussions, especially of the history of religions material, are readily available.[66] At any rate, history of religions parallels to Jesus being taught letters are often drawn with Indian stories of instruction in which one young prince at age eight is taught various alphabets (see 14:2) and recites the letters perfectly from the very beginning (see 6:18).[67]

But, as we have already noted, we need not go as far as the schools of India to find parallels of precociousness at school (see above 4.2). Such

---

65. See also Bauer, *Leben Jesu*, 90–91, 93–94; Michaelis, *Apokryphen Schriften*, 110–11; Vielhauer, *Geschichte*, 674; Koester, *Gospels*, 313; and Cullman, "Thomas," 450–51.
66. See especially Bauer, *Leben Jesu*, 95–97, and Vielhauer, *Geschichte*, 676.
67. See, e.g., Vielhauer, *Geschichte*, 676–77, and Cullmann, "Thomas," 442. Sources quoted in Bauer, *Leben Jesu*, 96–97, and Thundy, *Buddha and Christ*, 120–21.

behavior was commonplace in Greco-Roman biography, and this topos also undercuts the claims of some scholars to see in Jesus' precociousness (6–8, 14–15), especially in the esoteric meaning he gives to the letter Alpha (6:19–23; cf. 14:3), a gnostic origin for these stories and perhaps a gnostic origin for the entire gospel (see above 2.2). To be sure, the story about the alphabet was susceptible to a gnostic interpretation, as Irenaeus notes (see above 4.1), but both in its original form as an apophthegm and in its later expanded form this story is easily understood as merely showing Jesus' superiority over his teachers. And other gnostic features, such as a docetic Christology, are lacking in the gospel, since Jesus clearly feels the pain of having his shoulder bumped (4:1), his ear pulled (5:4) or his head struck (6:16; 14:4).[68] The immediate context of these stories is not so much religious as social, specifically the educational conventions of the elementary classroom. These conventions involve beginning with the letters of the alphabet, learning to read in more than one language, reciting to the teacher, being susceptible to corporal punishment for misbehavior, and so on. The evidence, however, is best reserved for the appropriate Notes to the Translation.

6. The Greek Text

The Infancy Gospel of Thomas was first edited by J. Fabricius in the early eighteenth century.[69] Other editions followed,[70] but the edition by C. von Tischendorf, first published in 1854 and then in 1876, has become the standard scholarly text. Because of the wide divergences in the MS tradition, however, Tischendorf grouped the MSS and printed three texts, two in Greek—a longer text, termed A and based on two MSS, and a shorter one, termed B and based on one MS—and a third text in Latin.[71] Of these three Tischendorf A has become the standard text for translations and studies of the Infancy Gospel of Thomas.

After more than a century, however, a new critical text is sorely needed, and one in fact has long been announced[72] and another at least hinted at more recently.[73] But in the meantime we must still work from Tischendorf A, taking into account the discoveries of new MSS as well as the developments in the daunting task of sorting out the relationships among these MSS, both Greek and versional.[74]

---

68. See Gero, "Thomas," 75–76.
69. Fabricius, *Apocryphus Novi Testamenti*, 1.159–67.
70. See further Elliott, *Apocryphal New Testament*, 71–73.
71. See Tischendorf, *Evangelia Apocrypha*, 140–57, 158–63, 164–80 respectively.
72. See Noret, "L'enfance selon Thomas," 472.
73. So Voicu, "L'histoire du texte," 132.
74. For full discussion of the MSS, see Gero, "Thomas," 48–56, and Voicu, "L'histoire du texte," 122–32.

Tischendorf knew of five Greek MSS of the Infancy Gospel of Thomas, and one of those was already lost. Today, however, that number has risen to eleven, according to J. Noret.[75] The most important textual discovery to date was A. Delatte's publication in 1927 of a fifteenth century MS, known as Atheniensis 355.[76] Generally speaking, this MS is close to Tischendorf A in contents and wording, but it also shows an occasional independence, especially at the beginning where it narrates the flight of Jesus and family to Egypt, complete with three miracles by the two year old child.[77]

This MS, as de Santos has shown, is also very similar to the Slavonic tradition.[78] For example, like the Slavonic version, this MS has the long form of Jesus' encounter with Zacchaeus (chap. 6), which in Tischendorf A is clearly truncated. Consequently, de Santos regards this MS as an important witness to the tenth century Greek *Vorlage* upon which the Slavonic version is based. In fact, de Santos has worked back from the Slavonic version and reconstructed the Greek of this *Vorlage*.[79] De Santos' work has had mixed reviews,[80] but he has clearly made a number of improvements on the text of Tischendorf A and his retranslation of the Slavonic is helpful in getting back to an approximation of the Greek text in the tenth century.

Work on the MSS continues, especially on the many versions[81] but also on an important new Greek MS, a Jerusalem MS known as Sabaiticus 259, which, however, has not yet been published.[82] Sorting out the MSS continues as well, with S. Voicu's proposals the most recent and provocative.[83] This scholar has tabulated the contents of the various Greek MSS (including Sabaiticus 259, according to Noret's collation) as well as the versions (Syriac, Georgian, Ethiopic, and Latin) and then has analyzed them according to which stories are missing. Chaps. 17–18 (using the chapter divisions of Tischendorf A) are in all the Greek MSS except Sabaiticus 259. The latter MS contains chap. 10, but it is placed just before chap. 19. The versions all omit chap. 1. Voicu concludes from these omissions and displacements that the extant Greek MSS represent a later, more interpolated stage of the textual tradition than do the Syriac, Georgian, Ethiopic, and Latin, which represent the more ancient tradition.

Clearly, then, the text of the Infancy Gospel of Thomas may soon have, and require, an edition that breaks away from Tischendorf's A text, as has

75. Noret, "L'enfance selon Thomas," 472. So also Voicu, "L'histoire du texte," 125.
76. See Delatte, "Évangile," 264–71.
77. See Delatte, "Évangile," 264, 1–265, 15 and n. 15 above.
78. See de Santos, *Evangelium*, esp. 147–58.
79. See de Santos, *Evangelium*, 159–68.
80. Most critical are Gero, "Thomas," 53 n. 6, and Voicu, "L'histoire du texte," 126.
81. See Voicu, "L'histoire du texte," 120–21, 125–26.
82. See Voicu, "L'histoire du texte," 125.
83. For what follows, see Voicu, "L'histoire du texte," 126–32. Cf. also the stemma of Gero ("Thomas," 56).

happened in the case of the Infancy Gospel of James. But in the meantime we are still dependent on Tischendorf's work of more than a century ago. Accordingly, the text presented here starts with Tischendorf A, but I have also changed it at a number of places—over twenty five in all—where recent work has shown it to be faulty, and I have used Atheniensis 355, termed Greek C in the apparatus, for the longer form of chapter 6. In addition, the many variants found in various Greek texts are also provided throughout, at least where translation differences or meaning would change. These variants will make it clear to any reader that the text of the Infancy Gospel of Thomas remained extremely fluid throughout the centuries.

Besides Tischendorf A, I have incorporated, where possible, the text of Tischendorf B. At times it is impossible to compare the two, but readers can consult Tischendorf's text where necessary (and a translation is available).[84] The reason for incorporating Tischendorf B into the text of Tischendorf A is to make it more apparent how different the two really are, which is not as easy to see when they are printed in seqence. In addition, I have used Greek C not just in chapter 6 but throughout the gospel, as well as de Santos' retranslation into Greek of the Slavonic version, termed here Greek-Slav. Finally, on occasion Tischendorf's Latin text is cited as is the Syriac (although only by reference to W. Wright's English translation),[85] where their readings help resolve a textual problem or underscore the variety of readings at some point.

The intentions of this text are modest: not to claim to offer the earliest text—that, as we have seen, awaits a thorough collation of the published and unpublished Greek texts and of the versions—but merely to present a text and apparatus that the reader can use, and therefore be more aware of the numerous variants that exist and hence very much aware of how insecure the text of any one passage might be.

---

84. See Elliott, *Apocryphal New Testament*, 80–82.
85. See Wright, *Apocryphal Literature*, 6–11.

Moral Instruction in Schools

The teacher Zacchaeus offers not only to teach Jesus how to read but also how to behave (6:2). Moral instruction was a principal task of education, and it began early. As soon as students were able to read their first sentences, they were assigned to read short maxims which inculcated values and attitudes along with the pride of reading for the first time (see Quintilian, 1.1.35). As with letters and alphabets, these schoolroom maxims have also survived on papyri, ostraca, and tablets (see Cribiore, *Writing*, 331–44). One teacher's manual preserved on papyrus from the 4th c. C.E., contains a maxim for each letter of the alphabet (see Ziebarth, *Schule*, 23). A sample of this schoolroom morality follows. Note that the initial Greek letters of the maxims are in alphabetical order.

A
Ἀρχὴ μεγίστη τοῦ φρονεῖν τὰ γράμματα.
The ABC's are the great beginning of wisdom.

B
Βίος βίου δεόμενος οὐκ ἔστιν βίος.
A life that needs a livelihood is no life.

Γ
Γέροντα τίμα τοῦ θεοῦ τὴν εἰκόνα.
Honor an old man like the statue of a god.

Δ
Δένδρον παλαιὸν μεταφυτεύσειν δύσκολον.
It is difficult to transplant an old tree.

E
Ἔρως ἁπάντων τῶν θεῶν παλαίτατος.
Eros is the oldest of the gods.

Z
Ζήσεις βίον κράτιστον, ἢν θυμοῦ κρατῇς.
You will live the freest life if you free yourself of strong emotion.

H
Ἦθος πονηρὸν φεῦγε καὶ κέρδος κακόν.
Avoid an evil person and wicked gain.

Θ
Θάλασσα καὶ πῦρ καὶ γυνὴ τρίτον κακόν.
Along with the sea and fire a woman (or wife) is a third evil.

I
Ἴση λεαίνης καὶ γυνακὸς ὠμότης.
The savagery of a lioness and a woman (or wife) is the same.

Facing page: Codex Atheniensis 355, a 15th century MS that includes the Infancy Gospel of Thomas, was first published in 1927 by A. Delatte. This Greek MS is important for reconstructing the text of the gospel because it provides the original longer form of chapter 6 that was unavailable to Tischendorf in the 19th century. Shown here is a photograph of folio 64ʳ which contains a portion of the sixth chapter in which Jesus confronts the teacher Zacchaeus (=6:13–22). *Photograph courtesy of the Department of Manuscripts, The National Library of Greece, Athens.*

The Infancy Gospel of Thomas

Prologue

1 Ἀναγγέλλω ὑμῖν ἐγὼ Θωμᾶς Ἰσραηλίτης πᾶσι τοῖς ἐξ ἐθνῶν ἀδελφοῖς γνωρίσαι τὰ παιδικὰ καὶ μεγαλεῖα τοῦ κυρίου ἡμῶν Ἰησοῦ Χριστοῦ, ὅσα ἐποίησεν γεννηθεὶς ἐν τῇ χώρᾳ ἡμῶν. οὗ ἡ ἀρχὴ οὕτως.

Jesus and the sparrows

2 Τοῦτο τὸ παιδίον Ἰησοῦς πενταέτης γενόμενος παίζων ἦν ἐν διαβάσει ῥύακος, ²καὶ τὰ ῥέοντα ὕδατα συνήγαγεν εἰς λάκκους, καὶ ἐποίει αὐτὰ εὐθέως καθαρά, καὶ λόγῳ μόνῳ ἐπέταξεν αὐτά. ³καὶ ποιήσας πηλὸν τρυφερὸν ἔπλασεν ἐξ αὐτοῦ στρουθία δώδεκα· καὶ ἦν σάββατον ὅτε ταῦτα ἐποίησεν. ἦσαν δὲ καὶ ἄλλα παιδία πολλὰ παίζοντα σὺν αὐτῷ.

Title: Παιδικὰ τοῦ κυρίου ἡμῶν Ἰησοῦ Χριστοῦ. On this form of the title as most likely original, see de Santos, *Evangelium*, 37–38. Παιδικὰ τοῦ κυρίου καὶ θεοῦ καὶ σωτῆρος ἡμῶν Ἰησοῦ Χριστοῦ: Greek-Slav. Θωμᾶ Ἰσραηλίτου φιλοσόφου ῥητὰ εἰς τὰ παιδικὰ τοῦ κυρίου: Tischendorf A. Σύγγραμμα τοῦ ἁγίου ἀποστόλου Θωμᾶ περὶ τῆς παιδικῆς ἀναστροφῆς τοῦ κυρίου: Tischendorf B. Greek C omits. **1.** (=Chapter 1 in Tischendorf B.) **1.** ἐγὼ Θωμᾶς Ἰσραηλίτης: Tischendorf A and B (adding ὁ before Ἰσραηλίτης). ἐγὼ Θωμᾶς Ἰσραηλίτης ὁ ἐκλεκτός: Greek-Slav. κἀγώ (=Ἰάκωβος): Greek C, on which see Delatte, "Evangile," 265, 18, and the corresponding note to the English translation. **1.** τὰ παιδικὰ καὶ μεγαλεῖα . . . ὅσα: Tischendorf A, Greek-Slav, and Tischendorf B. ὅσα: Greek C. **1.** γεννηθείς: Tischendorf A, Greek C, and Greek-Slav. ἀναστρεφόμενος σωματικῶς: Tischendorf B. **1.** ἐν τῇ χώρᾳ ἡμῶν: Tischendorf A. ἐν τῇ χώρᾳ ἡμῶν Βηθλεὲμ καὶ ἐν κώμῃ Ναζαρέτ: Greek C. ἐν τῇ χώρᾳ ἡμῶν τῇ λεγομένῃ Βηθλεέμ, ἐν τῇ πόλει Ναζαρέτ: Greek-Slav. ἐν πόλει Ναζαρέτ: Tischendorf B, after which it continues: ἐλθὼν ἐν πέμπτῳ ἔτει τῆς αὐτοῦ ἡλικίας. (In Tischendorf A, Greek C, and Greek-Slav, however, this reference to Jesus' age is not given until the beginning of the next chapter.) **1.** οὗ ἡ ἀρχὴ οὕτως: Tischendorf A. οὗ ἡ ἀρχή ἐστιν αὕτη: Greek C. Tischendorf B omits. Greek-Slav mistranslates (see de Santos, *Evangelium*, 40 n. 8). **2:1–2.** (=Chapter 2:1 in Tischendorf B, which, however, is narrated so differently that it requires separate presentation: μιᾷ τῶν ἡμερῶν βροχῆς γενομένης ἐξελθὼν τοῦ οἴκου οὗ ἦν ἡ μήτηρ αὐτοῦ ἔπαιζεν ἐν τῇ γῇ, ἔνθα κατέρρεον ὕδατα· καὶ ποιήσας λάκκους, κατήρχοντο τὰ ὕδατα, καὶ ἐπλήθησαν οἱ λάκκοι ὕδατος. εἶτα λέγει· θέλω ἵνα γένησθε καθαρὰ καὶ ἐνάρετα ὕδατα. καὶ εὐθέως ἐγένοντο.) **2:1.** παίζων ἦν: Tischendorf A. γενομένης βροχῆς ἔπαιζεν: Greek C and Greek-Slav. facta est pluvia magna super terram, et deambulavit puer Iesus per eam: Latin. **2:1.** ἐν διαβάσει ῥύακος: Tischendorf A. ἐπὶ διάβασιν ῥύακος: Greek C. ἐν διαβάσει τῶν ἐκ τῆς βροχῆς ῥυάκων: Greek-Slav. **2:2.** λόγῳ μόνῳ: Tischendorf A. τῷ λόγῳ αὐτοῦ: Greek C. λόγῳ δὲ μόνῳ καὶ οὐκ ἔργῳ: Greek-Slav. **2:3–7.** (=Chapter 3:1–2 in Tischendorf B.) **2:3.** καὶ ποιήσας πηλὸν τρυφερόν: Tischendorf A. εἶτα πάλιν ἐπάρας πηλὸν καθαρὸν ἐκ λάκκου: Greek C. εἶτα πάλιν ἐπάρας ἐκ τῆς ὕλης πηλὸν τρυφερόν: Greek-Slav. **2:3.** ἦσαν δὲ καὶ ἄλλα παιδία πολλὰ παίζοντα σὺν αὐτῷ: Tischendorf A and Greek-Slav. παίζων μετὰ τῶν παίδων τῶν Ἑβραίων: Greek C. inter pueros Iudaeorum: Latin. Tischendorf B omits.

1 I, Thomas the Israelite, am reporting to you, all my non-Jewish brothers and sisters, to make known the extraordinary childhood deeds of our Lord Jesus Christ—what he did after his birth in my region. This is how it all started:

Prologue

2 When this boy, Jesus, was five years old, he was playing at the ford of a rushing stream. ²He was collecting the flowing water into ponds and made the water instantly pure. He did this with a single command. ³He then made soft clay and shaped it into twelve sparrows . He did this on the sabbath day, and many other boys were playing with him.

*Jesus and
the sparrows*

• **1.** The opening chapter identifies the author, subject, and purpose of the document.

• **1.** *Thomas* is merely a name in the Synoptic tradition (Matt 10:3; Mark 3:18; Luke 6:15; cf. Acts 1:13). In John, however, Thomas plays a more prominent role, culminating in the "doubting" Thomas story (20:24–28; cf. also John 11:16; 14:5; 21:2). He assumes an even larger role in apocryphal literature, most notably in the Gospel of Thomas and the Acts of Thomas. The name "James" in Greek C (see note to Greek text) is due to the fact that this MS has attempted to connect this gospel with the Infancy Gospel of James. On this and other issues of authorship, see the Introduction 2.1.

• **2:1–10:4.** A series of episodes about Jesus as a five-year-old.

• **2:1–3:4.** A cycle of episodes initiated by Jesus' directing some water from a rushing stream into ponds and then fashioning sparrows from this water and clay, and doing all this on the sabbath day (2:1–3). First, his "working" on the sabbath is reported to Joseph, whose reprimand of his boy leads Jesus to clap his hands and turn the clay sparrows into real and noisy birds (2:4–7). Second, one of Jesus' playmates empties the ponds Jesus had made, and he

responds to this destructive act by causing his playmate to shrivel up and die (3:1–2). Third, the stricken boy's parents bury him and accuse Joseph for Jesus' actions (3:3–4).

• **2:1.** *he was playing*: Greek C and Greek-Slav expand on this clause, saying that Jesus played "after a thunderstorm" (similarly the Latin version). Tischendorf B is even fuller and deserves to be quoted: "One day after a thunderstorm Jesus went out of the house where his mother was and was playing on the ground where water was flowing down. He fashioned ponds and as the water came down it filled the ponds."

• **2:2.** *made the water instantly pure*: Jesus' control over nature appears again at 7:4. See also the Synoptic account of the stilling of the storm (Matt 8:23–27; Mark 4:35–41; Luke 8:22–25).

• **2:3.** *sparrows*: Sparrows are mentioned in Matt 10:29, 31; Luke 12:6–7, but there they function as symbols of something of little value. Consequently, this saying is not related to this story. Sparrows, however, have a variety of other connotations, and the one most relevant here is their association with rainy weather (see Pollard, *Birds*, 112).

⁴Ἰδὼν δέ τις Ἰουδαῖος ἃ ἐποίει ὁ Ἰησοῦς ἐν σαββάτῳ παίζων, ἀπῆλθε παραχρῆμα καὶ ἀνήγγειλε τῷ πατρὶ αὐτοῦ Ἰωσήφ· Ἰδοὺ τὸ παιδίον σού ἐστιν ἐπὶ τὸ ῥυάκιον, καὶ λαβὼν πηλὸν ἔπλασεν πουλία δώδεκα, καὶ ἐβεβήλωσεν τὸ σάββατον.

⁵Καὶ ἐλθὼν Ἰωσὴφ ἐπὶ τὸν τόπον καὶ ἰδὼν ἀνέκραξεν αὐτῷ λέγων· Διὰ τί ταῦτα ποιεῖς ἐν σαββάτῳ ἃ οὐκ ἔξεστι ποιεῖν;

⁶Ὁ δὲ Ἰησοῦς συγκροτήσας τὰς χεῖρας αὐτοῦ ἀνέκραξε τοῖς στρουθίοις καὶ εἶπεν αὐτοῖς· Ὑπάγετε, πετάσατε καὶ μιμνήσκεσθέ μου οἱ ζῶντες. καὶ πετασθέντα τὰ στρουθία ὑπῆγον κράζοντα.

⁷Ἰδόντες δὲ οἱ Ἰουδαῖοι ἐθαμβήθησαν, καὶ ἀπελθόντες διηγήσαντο τοῖς πρώτοις αὐτῶν ὅπερ εἶδον πεποιηκότα τὸν Ἰησοῦν.

The curse on Annas' son

3 Ὁ δὲ υἱὸς Ἄννα τοῦ γραμματέως ἦν ἑστὼς ἐκεῖ μετὰ τοῦ Ἰησοῦ, καὶ λαβὼν κλάδον ἰτέας ἐξέχεε τὰ ὕδατα ἃ συνήγαγεν ὁ Ἰησοῦς. ²Ἰδὼν δὲ ὁ Ἰησοῦς τὸ γινόμενον ἠγανάκτησε, καὶ εἶπε πρὸς αὐτόν· Σοδομίτα, ἀσεβὲς καὶ ἀνόητε, τί ἠδίκησάν σε οἱ

2:4. ἰδὼν δέ τις Ἰουδαῖος ἃ ἐποίει ὁ Ἰησοῦς ἐν σαββάτῳ παίζων: Tischendorf A and Greek-Slav. καὶ δραμὼν ἐν παιδίον: Tischendorf B. Greek C has a different construction, but see previous note: μετὰ τῶν παίδων τῶν Ἑβραίων. **2:4.** ἀπῆλθε παραχρῆμα καὶ ἀνήγγειλε τῷ πατρὶ αὐτοῦ Ἰωσήφ: Tischendorf A and Greek-Slav (omitting παραχρῆμα and adding λέγων after Ἰωσήφ). ἀπήγγειλε τῷ Ἰωσὴφ λέγων: Tischendorf B. ἀπῆλθον (i.e., τὰ παιδία) δὲ πρὸς Ἰωσὴφ τὸν πατέρα αὐτοῦ λέγοντες: Greek C. **2:6.** ὑπάγετε, πετάσατε καὶ μιμνήσκεσθέ μου οἱ ζῶντες: Greek C. πετάσθητε καὶ μέμνησθέ μου οἱ ζῶντες: Greek-Slav. ὑπάγετε πετάσθητε καὶ μιμνήσκεσθέ μου ζῶντα: Tischendorf B. ὑπάγετε: Tischendorf A. Full discussion in Gero, "Thomas," 64–65. **2:7.** ἰδόντες δὲ οἱ Ἰουδαῖοι ἐθαμβήθησαν: Tischendorf A and Greek-Slav. καὶ ἰδὼν Ἰωσὴφ ἐθαύμασεν: Tischendorf B. Greek C omits. **2:7.** διηγήσαντο τοῖς πρώτοις αὐτῶν: Tischendorf A. ἀπήγγειλαν πᾶσι: Greek C. διηγήσαντο τοῖς ἄλλοις: Greek-Slav. nuntiantes: Latin. Tischendorf B omits. **2:7.** ὅπερ εἶδον πεποιηκότα τὸν Ἰησοῦν: Tischendorf A and Greek-Slav (adding σημεῖον after εἶδον). τὸ σημεῖον ὃ ἐποίησεν ὁ Ἰησοῦς: Greek C. signa quae fecit Iesus: Latin. Tischendorf B omits. **3:1–4.** (=Chapter 2:2–3 in Tischendorf B.) **3:1.** ὁ δὲ υἱὸς Ἄννα τοῦ γραμματέως: Tischendorf A and Greek-Slav. τις παῖς Ἄννα τοῦ γραμματέως: Tischendorf B. Ἄννας δὲ γραμματεύς: Greek C. Pharisaeus: Latin. **3:1.** μετὰ τοῦ Ἰησοῦ: Greek C. μετὰ τοῦ Ἰωσήφ: Tischendorf A and Greek-Slav. Tischendorf B omits. **3:2.** Σοδομίτα, ἀσεβὲς καὶ ἀνόητε: Greek C and Greek-Slav. Sodomita impie et nesciens: Latin. Ἄδικε, ἀσεβὴ καὶ ἀνόητε: Tischendorf A. Ἀσεβὴ καὶ παράνομε: Tischendorf B. See further de Santos, *Evangelium*, 49 n. 9. On the vocative form ἀσεβή, see Weissengruber, "Untersuchungen," 209. **3:2.** οἱ λάκκοι καὶ τὰ ὕδατα: Tischendorf A. οἱ λάκκοι οἱ ἐμοὶ καὶ τὰ ἐμὰ ὕδατα: Greek C and Greek-Slav. οἱ λάκκοι: Tischendorf B, after which it alone continues: καὶ ἐξεκένωσας αὐτούς; οὐ μὴ ἀπελεύσει τὴν ὁδόν σου. **3:2.** καὶ οὐ μὴ ἐνέγκῃς φύλλα οὔτε ῥίζαν οὔτε καρπόν: Tischendorf A and Greek-Slav. καὶ μὴ ἔχῃς ῥίζαν μήτε κεφαλὴν μήτε καρπόν: Greek C. Tischendorf B omits.

⁴But when a Jew saw what Jesus was doing while playing on the sabbath day, he immediately went off and told Joseph, Jesus' father: "See here, your boy is at the ford and has taken mud and fashioned twelve birds with it, and so has violated the sabbath."

⁵So Joseph went there, and as soon as he spotted him he shouted, "Why are you doing what's not permitted on the sabbath?"

⁶But Jesus simply clapped his hands and shouted to the sparrows: "Be off, fly away, and remember me, you who are now alive!" And the sparrows took off and flew away noisily.

⁷The Jews watched with amazement, then left the scene to report to their leaders what they had seen Jesus doing.

3 The son of Annas the scholar, standing there with Jesus, took a willow branch and drained the water Jesus had collected. ²Jesus, however, saw what had happened and became angry, saying to him, "Damn you, you irreverent fool! What harm did the ponds of water do to you? From this moment you, too, will

The curse on Annas' son

• **2:4.** *a Jew*: The identity of the person(s) reporting Jesus' actions to his father varies. Tischendorf A and Greek-Slav have "a Jew," but Tischendorf B has "a child" and Greek C assumes (from 2:3) "children of the Hebrews" (so also the Latin). Lowe ("IOYΔAIOI," 83 and n. 101) argues that "the child" (παιδίον) of Tischendorf B is original and that the "certain Jew" (τις Ἰουδαῖος) of Tischendorf A is a later change, modeled on the analogous case of a Jew reporting Jesus' behavior in John 3:25–30. Context also points to a child (or to children).

• **2:4.** *violated the sabbath*: Doing work instead of resting on the seventh day, as required (Exod 20:8–11; Deut 5:12–15), is a charge that anticipates similar charges made against Jesus later by the authorities (see, e.g., Mark 2:23–28; 3:1–6; Luke 13:10–17; 14:2–6; John 5:2–16; 9:1–17).

• **2:6.** *sparrows took off*: Michaelis (*Apokryphen Schriften*, 110) suggests that the twelve sparrows may be a symbol for the twelve apostles.

• **3:1.** *Annas* is a name familiar from the New Testament, though there it designates a high priest (see Luke 3:2; John 18:13, 24; Acts 4:6). Here, however, Annas is identified as a *scholar* (γραμματεύς), as also in the Inf James (15:1). Incidentally, in Greek C it is Annas the scribe and not his son who drained Jesus' ponds. In the Latin it is a Pharisee.

• **3:1.** *with Jesus*: Michaelis (*Apokryphen Schriften*, 110) suspected that originally the story had Jesus, not Joseph (as in Tischendorf A), standing by Annas. Greek C confirms his suspicion, as does the Syriac (see Wright, *Apocryphal Literature*, 6).

λάκκοι καὶ τὰ ὕδατα; ἰδοὺ νῦν καὶ σὺ ὡς δένδρον ἀποξηρανθῇς, καὶ οὐ μὴ ἐνέγκῃς φύλλα οὔτε ῥίζαν οὔτε καρπόν.

³Καὶ εὐθέως ὁ παῖς ἐκεῖνος ἐξηράνθη ὅλος. ὁ δὲ Ἰησοῦς ἀνεχώρησε καὶ ἀπῆλθεν εἰς τὸν οἶκον Ἰωσήφ. ⁴οἱ δὲ γονεῖς τοῦ ξηρανθέντος ἐβάστασαν αὐτὸν θρηνοῦντες τὴν νεότηταν αὐτοῦ, καὶ ἤγαγον πρὸς τὸν Ἰωσήφ, καὶ ἐνεκάλουν αὐτὸν ὅτι τοιοῦτον ἔχεις παιδίον ἐργαζόμενον τοιαῦτα.

Curse on a clumsy child

4 Εἶτα πάλιν ἐπορεύετο διὰ τῆς κώμης, καὶ παιδίον τρέχων διερράγη εἰς τὸν ὦμον αὐτοῦ. καὶ πικρανθεὶς ὁ Ἰησοῦς εἶπεν αὐτῷ· Οὐκ ἀπελεύσει τὴν ὁδόν σου. ²καὶ παραχρῆμα πεσὼν ἀπέθανεν.

³Ἰδόντες δέ τινες τὸ γινόμενον εἶπον· Πόθεν τοῦτο τὸ παιδίον ἐγεννήθη, ὅτι πᾶν ῥῆμα αὐτοῦ ἔργον ἐστὶν ἕτοιμον;

⁴Καὶ προσελθόντες οἱ γονεῖς τοῦ τεθνεῶτος τῷ Ἰωσὴφ κατεμέμφοντο λέγοντες· Σὺ τοιοῦτον παιδίον ἔχων οὐ δύνασαι μεθ᾽ ἡμῶν οἰκεῖν ἐν τῇ κώμῃ, ἢ δίδασκε αὐτῷ εὐλογεῖν καὶ μὴ καταρᾶσθαι· τὰ γὰρ παιδία ἡμῶν θανατοῖ.

3:3. ἐξηράνθη: Tischendorf A, Greek C, and Greek-Slav. arefactus: Latin. ἀπέψυξε: Tischendorf B.   **3:3.** ὁ δὲ Ἰησοῦς ἀνεχώρησε καὶ ἀπῆλθεν εἰς τὸν οἶκον Ἰωσήφ: Tischendorf A and Greek-Slav (substituting αὐτοῦ for Ἰωσήφ). Tischendorf B and Greek C omit.   **3:4.** θρηνοῦντες τὴν νεότηταν αὐτοῦ: Tischendorf A and Greek-Slav. Tischendorf B, Greek C, and Latin omit.   **3:4.** ὅτι τοιοῦτον ἔχεις παιδίον ἐργαζόμενον τοιαῦτα: Tischendorf A. ὅτι ἔχεις τοιοῦτον παιδίον: Greek-Slav. ὅτι ἔχεις τοιοῦτον παιδίον καὶ ἰδὲ τί ποιεῖ ἡμῖν· δίδαξον αὐτὸ εὐλογεῖν καὶ μὴ καταρᾶσθαι: Greek C. ecce quod fecit filius tuus: doce eum orare et non blasphemare: Latin. Tischendorf B omits the explicit accusation, merely saying ἐγκαλῶν τῷ Ἰωσήφ.   **4:1–4.** (=Chapter 4 in Tischendorf B.)   **4:1.** διὰ τῆς κώμης: Tischendorf A and Greek-Slav. εἰς τὴν κώμην: Greek C. per villam: Latin. μέσον τῆς πόλεως: Tischendorf B. The same split between κώμη and πόλις occurs again at 4:4.   **4:1.** παιδίον τρέχων διερράγη εἰς τὸν ὦμον αὐτοῦ: Tischendorf A. δραμὸν ἐν παιδίον ἔδωκε τὸν Ἰησοῦν ἐπὶ τὸν ὦμον: Greek C. παιδίον δραμὼν ὥρμησε εἰς τὸν ὦμον: Greek-Slav. παιδίον τι ῥῖψαν λίθον κατ᾽ αὐτοῦ ἔπληξεν αὐτοῦ τὸν ὦμον: Tischendorf B.   **4:1.** ἀπελεύσει: On this second person singular ending for the future middle, see Weissengruber, "Untersuchungen," 210.   **4:3.** τινες: Tischendorf A. οἱ δὲ τυχόντες: Tischendorf B. οἱ δὲ Ἰουδαῖοι: Greek C. οἱ ἄλλοι: Greek-Slav.   **4:3.** ὅτι πᾶν ῥῆμα αὐτοῦ ἔργον ἐστὶν ἕτοιμον: Tischendorf A and Greek-Slav (substituting γίνεται for ἐστιν). ὅπως πᾶν ῥῆμα ὃ λέγει ἔργον γίνεται ἕτοιμον: Tischendorf B. Greek C omits.   **4:4.** οἱ γονεῖς τοῦ τεθνεῶτος: Tischendorf A. οἱ γονεῖς τοῦ πεσόντος: Greek-Slav. Tischendorf B, Greek C, Latin omit any reference to parents, keeping the same subject as in 4:3, namely οἱ τυχόντες and οἱ Ἰουδαῖοι.   **4:4.** κατεμέμφοντο: Tischendorf A. ἀπειλοῦντες: Greek-Slav. ἐγκάλουν: Tischendorf B. Greek C omits.   **4:4.** δίδασκε αὐτῷ εὐλογεῖν: On this unusual dative, see Weissengruber, "Untersuchungen," 212.   **4:4.** θανατοῖ: Tischendorf A. ξηραίνει: Greek-Slav. ὡς ἀνάπηρα ἐποίησεν: Greek C. θανατοῖ: Tischendorf B, after which it alone adds: καὶ πᾶν ὃ λέγει ἔργον γίνεται ἕτοιμον.

dry up like a tree, and you'll never produce leaves or root or bear fruit."

³In an instant the boy had completely withered away. Then Jesus departed and left for the house of Joseph. ⁴The parents of the boy who had withered away picked him up and were carrying him out, sad because he was so young. And they came to Joseph and accused him: "It's your fault—your boy did all this."

4 Later he was going through the village again when a boy ran by and bumped him on the shoulder. Jesus got angry and said to him, "You won't continue your journey." ²And all of a sudden he fell down and died.

Curse on a clumsy child

³Some people saw what had happened and said, "Where has this boy come from? Everything he says happens instantly!"

⁴The parents of the dead boy came to Joseph and blamed him, saying, "Because you have such a boy, you can't live with us in the village, or else teach him to bless and not curse. He's killing our children!"

- **3.2.** *dry up like a tree*: This metaphor may derive from the story of Jesus cursing the fig tree (Matt 21:18–19; Mark 11:12–14). At any rate, the point here seems to be: just as the boy had caused the ponds to dry up, so now Jesus causes him to dry up and die—an analogy that is explicitly made in the Syriac (see Wright, *Apocryphal Literature*, 6–7). See also Michaelis, *Apokryphen Schriften*, 110.
- **3:3.** *withered*: The same word (ξηραίνειν) is used in a Synoptic miracle story (Matt 12:9–14; Mark 3:1–6; Luke 6:6–11), although there it is only the man's hand which is withered.
- **3.4.** *carrying him out*: The word used here for carrying out (βαστάζειν) is a technical term for carrying a body out for burial. The burial ritual also includes lamenting his youth en route to the grave, a not infrequent theme for mourners (see, e.g., *Greek Anthology* 7.468, 482, 507b, 515).
- **4:1–5:5.** Another cycle of episodes prompted by Jesus being accidentally bumped on the shoulder by another boy (4:1a). As with

the son of Annas, the boy is punished by Jesus with death (4:1b-3). The parents once again blame Joseph (4:4), and Joseph reprimands his son (5:1–2a). Jesus accepts his father's admonishment but then blinds his accusers (5:2b). Joseph, in turn, gives Jesus' ear a hard tug and receives a sharp reprimand from Jesus (5:3–5).
- **4:1.** *through the village*: Tischendorf B has "in the middle of the city," a variant which does not, however, suggest a different locale for this story. In fact, Tischendorf B is consistent in this usage (see textual notes to 1 and 13:4).
- **4:1.** *a boy ran by and bumped him on the shoulder*: Tischendorf B has an entirely different occasion: "A boy threw a stone at him and struck his shoulder."
- **4:3.** *Everything he says happens instantly*: The thought, though not the wording, is paralleled in Ps 33:9 (LXX 32:9), which says that God speaks and things immediately happen. The same or similar expression appears again at 5:3 and 17:4.

5 Καὶ προσκαλεσάμενος ὁ Ἰωσὴφ τὸ παιδίον κατ' ἰδίαν ἐνουθέτει αὐτὸν λέγων· "Ινα τί τοιαῦτα κατεργάζει, καὶ πάσχουσιν οὗτοι καὶ μισοῦσιν ἡμᾶς καὶ διώκουσιν; ²Εἶπε δὲ ὁ Ἰησοῦς· Ἐγὼ οἶδα ὅτι τὰ ῥήματα ταῦτα οὐκ ἔστιν ἐμά, ἅπερ ἐγὼ ἐλάλησα. ὅμως σιγήσω διὰ σέ· ἐκεῖνοι δὲ οἴσουσιν τὴν κόλασιν αὐτῶν. καὶ εὐθέως οἱ ἐγκαλοῦντες αὐτὸν ἀπετυφλώθησαν.

³Καὶ οἱ ἰδόντες ἐφοβήθησαν σφόδρα καὶ ἠπόρουν, καὶ ἔλεγον περὶ αὐτοῦ ὅτι πᾶν ῥῆμα ὃ ἐλάλει, εἴτε καλὸν εἴτε κακόν, ἔργον ἦν καὶ θαῦμα ἐγένετο. ⁴ἰδὼν δὲ ὅτι τοιοῦτον ἐποίησεν ὁ Ἰησοῦς, ὀργισθεὶς ὁ Ἰωσὴφ ἐπέλαβεν αὐτοῦ τὸ ὠτίον καὶ ἔτεινεν σφόδρα. ⁵τὸ δὲ παιδίον ἠγανάκτησε καὶ εἶπεν αὐτῷ· Ἀρκετόν σοί ἐστιν ζητεῖν καὶ μὴ εὑρίσκειν, καὶ μάλιστα οὐ σοφῶς ἔπραξας· ⁶οὐκ οἶδας ὅτι σός; μή με λύπει.

5:1–6. (=Chapter 5 in Tischendorf B, which, however, is so brief as to require separate presentation: καὶ καθίσας ὁ Ἰωσὴφ ἐπὶ τοῦ θρόνου αὐτοῦ, ἔστη τὸ παιδίον ἔμπροσθεν αὐτοῦ· καὶ κρατήσας αὐτοῦ ἐκ τοῦ ὠτίου ἔθλιψε σφοδρῶς. ὁ δὲ Ἰησοῦς ἀτενίσας αὐτῷ εἶπεν· Ἀρκετόν σοί ἐστιν.) **5.1.** κατ' ἰδίαν: Tischendorf A and Greek C. Greek-Slav omits. **5:1.** τοιαῦτα κατεργάζει: Tischendorf A. καταρᾶσαι: Greek C. οὕτως καταρᾶσαι: Greek-Slav. On κατεργάζει as denoting the second person singular, see Weissengruber, "Untersuchungen," 210. **5:1.** διώκουσιν: Tischendorf A. διώκουσιν ἐκ τῆς κώμης: Greek C and Greek-Slav (substituting ἀπό for ἐκ). **5:2.** τὰ ῥήματα ταῦτα οὐκ ἔστιν ἐμά, ἅπερ ἐγὼ ἐλάλησα: Greek-Slav. τὰ ῥήματά σου ταῦτα οὐκ εἰσὶν σά: Tischendorf A. τὰ ῥήματα οὐκ ἔστιν ἐμά, ἀλλὰ σά εἰσιν: Greek C. See de Santos, *Evangelium*, 58 nn. 7 and 8. For a different view, one favoring Greek C, see Gero, "Thomas," 67. **5:4.** ἰδών: Greek C and Greek-Slav. ἰδόντες: Tischendorf A. See de Santos, *Evangelium*, 61 n. 17. **5:4.** ὀργισθείς: Greek-Slav (Greek C also has ὀργισθείς, but it is used of Jesus in the next sentence). cum furore: Latin. So also the Syriac (see Wright, *Apocryphal Literature*, 7). ἐγερθείς: Tischendorf A. See de Santos, *Evangelium*, 62 n. 18. **5:4.** ἔτεινεν: Greek C and Greek-Slav. ἔτιλεν: Tischendorf A. See de Santos, *Evangelium*, 62 n. 19. **5:5–6.** The MSS diverge even more than usual regarding Jesus' response to Joseph, and Gero ("Thomas," 68–69) cannot resolve the confusion. Consequently, Tischendorf A is given, and only major divergences from it will be noted. For full textual evidence, see Gero, "Thomas," 68. **5:5.** ζητεῖν καὶ μὴ εὑρίσκειν: Tischendorf A and Greek-Slav. Greek C omits. **5:5.** μάλιστα: Tischendorf A. The Slavonic version reads "you robber," which is a misreading of μάλιστα (as though it were μὰ λῇστα). This translation error, which is common to all Slavonic MSS, is the chief proof that they go back to single translation from the Greek. Greek C omits. See de Santos, *Evangelium*, 63 n. 23 and 147, and Gero, "Thomas," 68 n. 3. **5:5.** οὐ σοφῶς ἔπραξας: Tischendorf A. Greek C and Greek-Slav omit. **5:6.** ὅτι σός: Tischendorf A. ὅτι σός εἰμι καὶ πρὸς σὲ πάρειμι: Greek Slav. τίς εἰμι καὶ πρὸς σὲ πάρειμι: Greek C. **5:6.** μή με λύπει: Tischendorf A. λοιπὸν μή με λύπει: Greek-Slav. βλέπεις με καὶ μή με λοπιάζεις: Greek C. Delatte emends the *hapax legomenon* λοπιάζεις to λοπίζῃς, but Gero ("Thomas," 68 n. 4) more plausibly suggests λύπῃς.

5 So Joseph summoned his child and admonished him in private, saying, "Why are you doing all this? These people are suffering and so they hate and harass us." [2]Jesus said, "I know that the words I spoke are not my words. Still, I'll keep quiet for your sake. But those people must take their punishment." There and then his accusers became blind.

[3]Those who saw this became very fearful and at a loss. All they could say was, "Every word he says, whether good or bad, has became a deed—a miracle, even!" [4]When Joseph saw that Jesus had done such a thing, he got angry and grabbed his ear and pulled very hard. [5]The boy became infuriated with him and replied, "It's one thing for you to seek and not find; it's quite another for you to act this unwisely. [6]Don't you know that I don't really belong to you? Don't make me upset."

• **5:2.** *I know that the words I spoke are not my words*: Jesus' response has many textual problems and is far from secure. See the corresponding note to the Greek text.

• **5:5.** Jesus' response again has textual problems and is far from secure. See the corresponding note to the Greek text.

Jesus and
the teacher

6 Διδάσκαλος δέ τις ὀνόματι Ζακχαῖος ἠκροᾶτο πάντα ὅσα ἐλάλει Ἰησοῦς πρὸς τὸν Ἰωσὴφ καὶ ἐθαύμαζε λέγων ἐν ἑαυτῷ· τοιοῦτον παιδίον ταῦτα φθέγγεται. ²καὶ προσκαλεσάμενος τὸν Ἰωσὴφ λέγει αὐτῷ· φρόνιμον παιδίον ἔχεις καὶ καλὸν νοῦν ἔχει, ἀλλὰ παράδος μοι αὐτὸν ἵνα μάθῃ γράμματα καὶ διδάξω αὐτὸν πᾶσαν ἐπιστήμην ἵνα μὴ ᾖ ἀνυπότακτον.

³Ἀποκριθεὶς δὲ Ἰωσὴφ εἶπεν αὐτῷ· οὐ δύναταί τις τοῦτον ὑποτάξαι, εἰ μὴ μόνος θεός· μὴ μικρὸν σταυρὸν νομίσῃς αὐτὸν εἶναι, ἀδελφέ.

⁴Ὡς δὲ ἤκουσεν ὁ Ἰησοῦς τοῦ Ἰωσὴφ τοῦτο λέγοντος ἐγέλασε καὶ εἶπε πρὸς τὸν Ζακχαῖον· ἀληθῶς, καθηγητά· ὅσα εἴρηκέ σοι ὁ πατήρ μου ἀληθές ἐστι. ⁵καὶ τούτων μὲν ἐγώ εἰμι κύριος καὶ πρὸς σὲ πάρειμι καὶ ἐν ὑμῖν ἐγεννήθην καὶ μεθ' ὑμῶν εἰμι. ⁶ἐγὼ οἶδα ὑμᾶς πόθεν ἐστὲ καὶ πόσα ἔτη ἔσται τῆς ζωῆς

6:1–23. In this chapter we break with our practice of using the text of Tischendorf A since it is a much abbreviated version of the account found in Greek C and Greek-Slav. Instead, the text presented here is Greek C, since it is in fact a Greek MS and not a retranslation, as is Greek-Slav (for an English translation of the latter, see Cullmann, "Thomas," 449–50). Tischendorf B is also much shorter and will be incorporated, along with Tischendorf A, where relevant.   **6:1–2.** (=Chapter 6:1–2 in Tischendorf A; Tischendorf B omits.)   **6:1.** Ζακχαῖος ἠκροᾶτο: Greek C. Ζακχαῖος ἦν ἑστὼς ἐκεῖ καὶ ἤκουσε: Greek-Slav and Tischendorf A (substituting ἐν μέρει τινί for ἐκεῖ).   **6:2.** (cf. Chapter 6:1b in Tischendorf B: παράδος μοι αὐτό, καθηγητά, κἀγώ διδάξω τὴν γραφήν, καὶ πείσω εὐλογεῖν πάντας καὶ μὴ καταρᾶσθαι.)   **6:2.** καὶ προσκαλεσάμενος: Greek C. καὶ μεθ' ἡμέρας τινὰς προσήγγισε: Greek-Slav and Tischendorf A.   **6:2.** καλὸν νοῦν: Greek C and Greek-Slav. νοῦν: Tischendorf A.   **6:2.** πᾶσαν ἐπιστήμην ἵνα μὴ ᾖ ἀνυπότακτον: Greek C. πᾶν ὅτι πρέπει εἰδέναι· τιμᾶν τοὺς πρεσβυτέρους ὡς προπάτορας καὶ πατέρας, ἀγαπᾶν τοὺς συνηλικιώτας μετὰ πραότητος, καὶ φοβεῖσθαι καὶ ἐντρέπεσθαι τοὺς γονέας ἵνα καὶ αὐτὸς ὑπὸ τῶν ἰδίων καὶ ὑπ' ἀλλοτρίων τέκνων ἀγαπᾶται: Greek-Slav. πᾶσαν ἐπιστήμην καὶ προσαγορεύειν πάντας τοὺς πρεσβυτέρους καὶ τιμᾶν αὐτοὺς ὡς προπάτορας καὶ πατέρας καὶ τοῦ ἀγαπᾶν συνηλικιώτας: Tischendorf A.   **6:3–13.** (Tischendorf A omits.)   **6:3.** ἀποκριθεὶς δὲ Ἰωσὴφ εἶπεν αὐτῷ: Greek C. ὁ δὲ Ἰωσὴφ ἠγανάκτησε σφόδρα κατὰ τοῦ παιδίου καὶ εἶπε τῷ διδασκάλῳ: Greek-Slav.   **6:3.** οὐ δύναταί τις τοῦτον ὑποτάξαι εἰ μὴ μόνος θεός: Greek C. καὶ τίς δύναται διδάσκειν αὐτό;: Greek-Slav.   **6:4.** (cf. Chapter 6:2a in Tischendorf B: καὶ ἀκούσας ὁ Ἰησοῦς ἐγέλασε.)   **6:5.** καὶ πρὸς σὲ πάρειμι: Greek C. ὑμεῖς δὲ ξένοι ἐστε, ὅτι μόνῳ ἐμοὶ ἐδόθη ἡ ἐξουσία, ἐγὼ γὰρ πρὶν ἦν καὶ νῦν εἰμι: Greek-Slav.   **6:6.** (cf. Chapter 6:2c in Tischendorf B: καὶ ἐπίσταμαι πόσα ἔτη τῆς ζωῆς ὑμῶν.)   **6:6.** ἐγὼ οἶδα ὑμᾶς: Greek C. ὑμεῖς μὲν οὐκ οἴδατε τίς ἐγώ εἰμι, ἐγὼ δὲ οἶδα ὑμᾶς: Greek-Slav.   **6:6.** πόθεν ἐστέ: Greek C. πόθεν ἐστὲ καὶ τίνες ἐστὲ καὶ πότε ἐγεννήθητε: Greek-Slav.

6 A teacher by the name of Zacchaeus was listening to everything Jesus was saying to Joseph, and was astonished, saying to
himself, "He is just a child, and saying this!" ²And so he summoned Joseph and said to him, "You have a bright child, and he
has a good mind. Hand him over to me so he can learn his
letters. I'll teach him everything he needs to know so as not to be
unruly."

*Jesus and
the teacher*

³Joseph replied, "No one is able to rule this child except God
alone. Don't consider him to be a small cross, brother."

⁴When Jesus heard Joseph saying this he laughed and said to
Zacchaeus, "Believe me, teacher, what my father told you is
true. ⁵I am the Lord of these people and I'm present with you
and have been born among you and am with you. ⁶I know where
you've come from and how many years you'll live. I swear to

• **6:1–8:4.** A cycle of stories centered around
Jesus' being taught to read by the teacher
Zacchaeus. This teacher asks Joseph to
hand his son over to him for instruction,
but Jesus gives him an earful of christological doctrine and claims to have a divine
wisdom, all of which amazes those standing
by (6:1–13). Still, Joseph takes Jesus to the
teacher's house where he gets instructions
in the alphabet, but turns the tables on his
teacher by giving the esoteric meaning of
the letter alpha (6:14–23). Zacchaeus laments ever having accepted Jesus and
expresses his humiliation at being defeated
by a young pupil (7:1–11). Jesus responds
by revealing his divine mission and making
all afraid of provoking him to anger (8:1–4).
• **6:1.** The name "Zacchaeus" is known from
Luke 19:2, but no identity is to be assumed,
since the Zacchaeus in Luke is a tax
collector, here an elementary school teacher.
• **6:2.** *Hand him over to me*: That Jesus must
be handed over to someone like Zacchaeus
for elementary schooling shows that Joseph
is assumed to be illiterate. Otherwise, he
would have assumed this responsibility.
Schooling in villages is attested but clearly
unusual (see Athenaeus, 8.354c; Longus,
Daphnis and Chloe 1.8.1), which explains
why it is only Jesus' good mind that
prompts Zacchaeus' interest in him.
• **6:2.** *learn his letters* is a standard shorthand
expression for learning to read, the principal task of elementary school. The child
first learned to pronounce and write the
letters of the alphabet, even learning to

recite the alphabet backwards (see Athenaeus, 15.671b). The child then progressed
to reading syllables, then words, then sentences, and finally short passages (Quintilian, 1.1.24–37). For actual texts from
elementary school, see Milne, "Relics,"
121–27, Ziebarth, *Schule*, 1–15, and
Cribiore, *Writing*, 167–69.
• **6:2.** *everything he needs to know*: Greek C is
especially condensed here. Tischendorf A
and Greek-Slav are much fuller, the latter
reading: "...everything that is fitting to
know: to honor his elders like ancestors and
parents, to treat those of his own age with
gentleness, and to fear and respect his
parents in order that he might be loved by
his own family and by the other children."
Such moral lessons are part and parcel of
ancient education and inculcated especially
in the first sentences students read, which
were one line maxims organized alpha-
betically—for example, "Honor your parents and benefit your friends" (Jaekel,
Sententiae, 42). See also Quintilian, 1.1.35,
and, more generally, Bonner, *Education*,
172–76.
• **6:3.** *except God alone*: It is only later, after
Jesus has been in the temple in Jerusalem
with the elders and teachers of the law (see
19:4–5), that he is said to have become
obedient to his parents (19:11).
• **6:3.** *small cross*: Seemingly an idiomatic
expression for a simple task, but later (see v.
8) it is used to refer to Jesus' eventual
crucifixion.

ὑμῶν· ἀληθῶς λέγω σοι, διδάσκαλε, ὅτε ἐγεννήθης ἐγὼ εἰμί· καὶ
εἰ θέλεις τέλειος εἶναι διδάσκαλος, ἄκουσόν μου κἀγὼ διδάξω σε
σοφίαν ἣν οὐδεὶς ἄλλος οἶδε πλὴν ἐμοῦ καὶ τοῦ πέμψαντός με
πρὸς ὑμᾶς. [7]σὺ γὰρ τυγχάνεις ἐμὸς μαθητὴς κἀγὼ οἶδά σε πόσων
ἐτῶν εἶ καὶ πόσον ἔχεις ζῆσαι. [8]καὶ ὅταν ἴδῃς τὸν σταυρόν μου ὃν
εἶπεν ὁ πατήρ μου, τότε πιστεύσεις ὅτι πάντα ὅσα εἶπόν σοι
ἀληθῆ εἰσιν.

[9]Οἱ δὲ παριόντες Ἰουδαῖοι καὶ ἀκούοντες τὸν Ἰησοῦν ἐθαύ-
μασαν καὶ εἶπον· ὦ ξένον καὶ παράδοξον πρᾶγμα· οὔπω ἐστὶν
ἐτῶν πέντε τὸ παιδίον τοῦτο καὶ τοιαῦτα φθέγγεται· τοιούτους
γὰρ λόγους οὐδέποτε ἠκούσαμεν εἰρηκότος τινὸς ὡς τὸ παιδίον
τοῦτο.

[10]Ἀποκριθεὶς δὲ ὁ Ἰησοῦς λέγει αὐτοῖς· πάνυ θαυμάζετε;
μᾶλλον δὲ ἐπιστῆτε ἐφ' οἷς εἶπον ὑμῖν· ἀληθῶς οἶδα καὶ πότε
ἐγεννήθητε ὑμεῖς καὶ οἱ πατέρες καὶ τὸ παράδοξον λέγω ὑμῖν· ὅτε
δὴ ὁ κόσμος ἐκτίσθη, ἐγὼ εἰμὶ καὶ ὁ πέμψας με πρὸς ὑμᾶς.

[11]Ἀκούσαντες δὲ οἱ Ἰουδαῖοι ὅτι οὕτως λέγει τὸ παιδίον
ἐθυμώθησαν, μὴ δυνάμενοι ἀποκριθῆναι αὐτῷ λόγον. [12]προσ-
ελθὸν δὲ τὸ παιδίον καὶ σκιρτῆσαν αὐτοῖς λέγει· ἔπαιξα ὑμᾶς·
οἶδα γὰρ ὅτι μικροθαύμαστοί ἐστε καὶ μικροὶ τοῖς φρονήμασιν.

[13]Ὡς οὖν ἔδοξαν παρηγορεῖσθαι ἐν τῇ παρακλήσει τοῦ παιδίου, εἶπεν ὁ καθηγητὴς πρὸς τὸν Ἰωσήφ· ἄγαγε αὐτὸν εἰς τὸ
παιδευτήριον κἀγὼ αὐτὸν διδάξω γράμματα.

6:6. ἐγὼ εἰμί: Greek C. ἐγὼ παρέστη καὶ πρὸ τῆς γεννήσεώς σου ἐγὼ ἦν:
Greek-Slav.   6:6. πρὸς ὑμᾶς: Greek C. πρὸς ὑμᾶς τοῦ διδάξαι ὑμᾶς:
Greek-Slav.   6:7. σὺ γὰρ τυγχάνεις ἐμὸς μαθητής: Greek C. ἐγὼ μὲν ὁ
καθηγητής σου εἰμί, εἰ καὶ σὺ ὑπ' ἐμοῦ καθηγητὴς προσαγορεύῃ: Greek-
Slav.   6:8. ἀληθῆ εἰσιν: Greek C and Greek-Slav, after which the latter
adds: ἐγὼ μὲν τούτων εἰμὶ κύριος, ὑμεῖς δὲ ξένοι ἐστέ, ὅτι ἐγὼ καὶ νῦν
αὐτὸς εἰμί.   6:9. εἰρηκότος τινὸς ὡς τὸ παιδίον: Greek C. εἰρηκότος
ἀρχιερέως ἢ γραμματέως ἢ Φαρισέως: Greek-Slav. audivimus nec audituri
sumus ab alio aliquo homine, neque a pontificibus neque a magistris
neque a Pharisaeis: Latin. See de Santos, Evangelium, 79 n. 55.   6:10–
11. (cf. Chapter 6:2b and 3 in Tischendorf B, but so condensed as to
require separate presentation: πρὸ γὰρ τῶν αἰώνων εἰμί. καὶ οἶδα πότε
ἐγεννήθησαν οἱ πατέρες τῶν πατέρων. . . . [3]καὶ πάλιν εἶπεν αὐτοῖς ὁ
Ἰησοῦς· θαυμάζετε ὅτι εἶπον ὑμῖν ὅτι οἶδα πόσα ἔτη τῆς ζωῆς ὑμῶν·
ἀληθῶς οἶδα πότε ἐκτίσθη ὁ κόσμος. ἰδοὺ οὐ πιστεύετέ μοι ἄρτι· ὅταν
ἴδητε τὸν σταυρόν μου, τότε πιστεύσετε ὅτι ἀληθῆ λέγω. οἱ δὲ
ἐξεπλήσοντο ἀκούοντες ταῦτα.)   6:10. πάνυ θαυμάζετε· μᾶλλον δὲ
ἐπιστῆτε: Greek C. ὑμεῖς μὲν θαυμάζετε, οὐ δὲ πιστεύετε: Greek-Slav.
6:11. ἐθυμώθησαν: Greek C. ἐφοβήθησαν: Greek-Slav.   6:12. σκιρτῆσαν
αὐτοῖς λέγει· ἔπαιξα ὑμᾶς: Greek C. ἔπαιζεν καὶ ἐσκίρτα καὶ κατεγέλασεν
αὐτοὺς λέγων: Greek-Slav.   6:13. ὡς οὖν ἔδοξαν παρηγορεῖσθαι ἐν τῇ
παρακλήσει τοῦ παιδίου: Greek C. ἡ γὰρ δόξα ἐλογίσθη μοὶ εἰς
παράκλησιν τοῦ παιδίου: Greek-Slav.   6:14. (cf. Chapter 6:1a in
Tischendorf B: τῇ δὲ ἐπαύριον κρατήσας αὐτοῦ τῆς χειρὸς ἤγαγε πρός
τινα καθηγητήν.)

you, teacher, I existed when you were born. If you wish to be a perfect teacher, listen to me and I'll teach you a wisdom that no one else knows except for me and the one who sent me to you. ⁷It's you who happen to be my student, and I know how old you are and how long you have to live. ⁸When you see the cross that my father mentioned, then you'll believe that everything I've told you is true."

⁹The Jews who were standing by and heard Jesus marveled and said, "How strange and paradoxical! This child is barely five years old and yet he says such things. In fact, we've never heard anyone say the kind of thing this child does."

¹⁰Jesus said to them in reply, "Are you really so amazed? Rather, consider what I've said to you. The truth is that I also know when you were born, and your parents, and I announce this paradox to you: when the world was created, I existed along with the one who sent me to you."

¹¹The Jews, once they heard that the child was speaking like this, became angry but were unable to say anything in reply. ¹²But the child skipped forward and said to them, "I've made fun of you because I know that your tiny minds marvel at trifles."

¹³When, therefore, they thought that they were being comforted by the child's exhortation, the teacher said to Joseph, "Bring him to the classroom and I'll teach him the alphabet."

• **6:6.** *wisdom*: Zacchaeus promised to teach Jesus the mundane skill of reading, but Jesus offers to teach him a divine wisdom that only he knows.

• **6:6.** *the one who sent me*: This language (see also v. 10) recalls a favorite Christological expression in John (see, e.g., 4:34; 5:24, 37; 6: 44; 7:16; 8:26; 9:4; etc.).

• **6:9.** *anyone*: Greek-Slav is more specific, mentioning high priest, scholar, and Pharisee (so also the Latin).

• **6:10.** *when the world was created, I existed*: This christological view, hinted at in 6:5–6 and repeated at 7:4 is reflected in a variety of NT writings (see John 1:1–3; Col 1:15–16; Heb 1:2; Rev 3:14).

¹⁴ Ὁ δὲ Ἰωσὴφ λαβὼν αὐτὸν ἀπὸ τῆς χειρὸς ἤγαγεν αὐτὸν εἰς τὸ διδασκαλεῖον. ¹⁵καὶ ἔγραψεν αὐτῷ ἀλφάβητον καθηγητὴς καὶ ἤρξατο ἐπιτηδεύειν καὶ εἶπε τὸ ἄλφα πλειστάκις· τὸ δὲ παιδίον ἐσιώπα καὶ οὐκ ἀπεκρίνατο αὐτὸν ἕως ὥρας πολλάς. ¹⁶ὀργισθεὶς οὖν ὁ καθηγητὴς ἔκρουσεν αὐτὸν εἰς τὴν κεφαλήν· τὸ δὲ παιδίον ἀξίως παθὸν εἶπεν αὐτῷ· ἐγώ σε παιδεύω μᾶλλον ἢ παιδεύομαι ἀπὸ σοῦ, ὅτι οἶδα γράμματα ἃ σύ με διδάσκεις καὶ πολλή σου κρίσις ἐστί· καὶ ταῦτά σοί ἐστιν ὡς χοῦς χαλκοῦς, ὡς κύμβαλον ἀλαλάζον, ἅτινα οὐ παρέχουσι διὰ τὴν φωνὴν τὴν δόξαν καὶ τὴν σοφίαν. ¹⁷οὐδέ τινος ψυχὴ συνίησι τὴν δύναμιν τῆς σοφίας μου. ¹⁸παυσάμενος δὲ ἀπὸ τῆς ὀργῆς εἶπε τὰ γράμματα ἀπὸ τοῦ ἄλφα ἕως τὸ ω μετὰ πολλῆς ὀξύτητος.

¹⁹Ἐμβλέψας δὲ εἰς τὸν καθηγητὴν λέγει αὐτόν· σὺ τὸ ἄλφα μὴ εἰδὼς κατὰ φύσιν, τὸ βῆτα πῶς μᾶλλον διδάσκεις; ²⁰ὑποκριτά, εἰ οἶδας, δίδαξόν με πρῶτον σὺ τὸ ἄλφα καὶ τότε σοι πιστεύω τὸ βῆτα. ²¹ὁ δὲ ἤρξατο ἐπερωτᾶν τὸν διδάσκαλον περὶ τοῦ πρώτου στοιχείου· καὶ οὐκ ἴσχυσεν εἰπεῖν οὐδέν.

6:15. (=Chapter 7:1a-d in Tischendorf B.)   **6:15.** καὶ ἔγραψεν αὐτῷ ἀλφάβητον: Greek C and Greek-Slav (adding τό before ἀλφάβητον). γράψας δὲ ὁ Ζακχαῖος τὴν ἀλφάβητον ἑβραιστί: Tischendorf B. Tischendorf A omits.   **6:15.** ἐπιτηδεύειν: Greek C. ἐπιτηδεύειν πείθων αὐτόν: Greek-Slav.   **6:15.** καὶ εἶπε τὸ ἄλφα πλειστάκις: Greek C. εἶτα ἐπετήδευε εἰπεῖν πλειστάκις τὰ γραφθέντα: Greek-Slav. καὶ λέγει πρὸς αὐτὸν λαβών· φησιν τὸ παιδίον ἄλφα. καὶ αὖθις ὁ διδάσκαλος ἄλφα· καὶ τὸ παιδίον ὁμοίως. εἶτα πάλιν ὁ διδάσκαλος ἐκ τρίτου τὸ ἄλφα: Tischendorf B. Tischendorf A omits.   **6:15.** ἀπεκρίνατο αὐτόν: Greek C. ἤκουσεν αὐτοῦ: Greek-Slav.   **6:16.** τὸ δὲ παιδίον ἀξίως παθὸν εἶπεν αὐτῷ: Greek C. ἀπεκρίθη δὲ τὸ παιδίον· οὐκ ἀξίως ποιεῖς: Greek-Slav.   **6:16.** καὶ πολλή σου κρίσις ἐστί· καὶ ταῦτά σοί ἐστιν: Greek C. καὶ πολλοὶ κρινοῦσίν σε ὅτι ταῦτα ἐν ἐμοί ἐστιν: Greek-Slav.   **6:16.** ὡς χοῦς χαλκοῦς: Greek C. ὡς χαλκὸς ἠχῶν: Greek-Slav. vasa de quibus non exeunt nisi voces: Latin.   **6:16–17.** παρέχουσι διὰ τὴν φωνὴν τὴν δόξαν καὶ τὴν σοφίαν. οὐδέ τινος ψυχὴ συνίησι τὴν δύναμιν τῆς σοφίας μου: Greek C. παρέχουσιν οὔτε φωνὴν τοῦ ἀκοῦσαι οὔτε τὴν δόξαν τῆς σοφίας ἢ τὴν δύναμιν τῆς ψυχῆς καὶ τοῦ νοῦ: Greek-Slav. **6:18–23.** (=Chapter 6:3-4 in Tischendorf A.)   **6:18.** (cf. Chapter 7:1f in Tischendorf B.)   **6:18.** παυσάμενος δὲ ἀπὸ τῆς ὀργῆς: Greek C. ὀργισθέν: Greek-Slav. Tischendorf A and B omit.   **6:18.** εἶπε τὰ γράμματα ἀπὸ τοῦ ἄλφα ἕως τοῦ ω μετὰ πολλῆς ὀξύτητος: Greek C. εἶπεν αὐτῷ πάντα τὰ γράμματα ἀπὸ τοῦ α ἕως τοῦ ω μετὰ πολλῆς ἐξατάσεως τρανῶς: Tischendorf A. εἶπε πάντα τὰ γράμματα ἀπὸ τοῦ A ἕως τοῦ T μετὰ πολλῆς ἐξατάσεως: Greek-Slav. καὶ ἀρξάμενος τὸ παιδίον ἀπὸ τοῦ ἄλφα εἶπεν ἀφ᾽ ἑαυτοῦ τὰ κβ γράμματα: Tischendorf B.   **6:19.** (=Chapter 7:1e in Tischendorf B.)   **6:20.** ὑποκριτά: Greek C, Greek-Slav, and Tischendorf A. Gero ("Thomas," 72), however, would like to delete this address as a later harmonization with Matt 7:5.   **6:21.** ἐπερωτᾶν: Greek C. ἀποστοματίζειν: Greek-Slav. ἀποστομίζειν: Tischendorf A.   **6:21.** περὶ τοῦ πρώτου στοιχείου: Greek C and Tischendorf A (substituting γράμματος for στοιχείου). περὶ τῆς φύσεως τοῦ πρώτου γράμματος: Greek-Slav.   **6:21.** καὶ οὐκ ἴσχυσεν εἰπεῖν οὐδέν: Greek C. καὶ οὐκ ἴσχυσεν αὐτῷ ἀνταποκριθῆναι: Tischendorf A. Greek-Slav omits.

¹⁴Joseph took him by the hand and led him to the classroom. ¹⁵The teacher wrote the alphabet for him and began the instruction by repeating the letter alpha many times. But the child clammed up and did not answer him for a long time. ¹⁶No wonder, then, that the teacher got angry and struck him on the head. The child took the blow calmly and replied to him, "I'm teaching you rather than being taught by you: I already know the letters you're teaching me, and your condemnation is great. To you these letters are like a bronze pitcher or a clashing cymbal, which can't produce glory or wisdom because it's all just noise. ¹⁷Nor does anyone understand the extent of my wisdom." ¹⁸When he got over being angry he recited the letters from alpha to omega very quickly.

¹⁹Then he looked at the teacher and told him, "Since you don't know the real nature of the letter alpha, how are you going to teach the letter beta? ²⁰You imposter, if you know, teach me first the letter alpha and then I'll trust you with the letter beta." ²¹He began to quiz the teacher about the first letter, but he was unable to say anything.

• **6:15.** *the letter alpha many times*: Tischendorf B expands considerably at this point but also changes the encounter: "(The teacher) said the letter alpha to him, and the boy responded, 'Alpha.' Again the teacher said alpha and the boy responded. Then yet again for the third time the teacher said alpha." In Herodas, 3.22–23, the pupil Kottalos does not learn the letter alpha until his teacher says it five times.

• **6:16:** *clashing cymbal*: This phrase comes from 1 Cor 13:1. In fact, Greek-Slav also has the other half of Paul's expression, replacing "bronze pitcher" with "ringing brass gong" (χαλκὸς ἠχῶν). Interestingly, the Latin does not reflect the Pauline language at all.

• **6:18.** *from alpha to omega*. Note the variants at this point. Greek-Slav says "from alpha to tau," while Tischendorf B says: "The child began with the letter alpha and said all twenty-two letters by himself." The reading "from alpha to tau" is defended by de Santos (*Evangelium*, 91 n. 26).

• **6:19–20.** This same challenge is made to another teacher at 14:3. As becomes clear from vv. 22–23, Jesus is thinking of an esoteric meaning read into the shape of the letter alpha (see further McNeil, "Alphabet," 126–28, and Thundy, *Buddha and Christ*, 120–21).

²² Ἀκουόντων δὲ πολλῶν, λέγει πρὸς Ζακχαῖον· ἄκουε, διδάσκαλε, καὶ νόει τὴν τοῦ πρώτου στοιχείου τάξιν. ²³ὧδέ πως ἔχει· δύο κανόνας καὶ χαρακτῆρας μέσον ὀξυσμένους διαμένοντας, συναγομένους, ὑψουμένους, χορεύοντας, τριστόμους, διστόμους, ἀμαχίμους, ὁμογενεῖς, παρόχους, ζυγοστόμους, ἰσομέτρους κανόνας ἔχει τὸ ἄλφα.

7 Ὡς δὲ ἤκουσεν ὁ διδάσκαλος Ζακχαῖος τὰς τοσαύτας καὶ τοιαύτας ἀλληγορίας τοῦ πρώτου γράμματος εἰρηκότος τοῦ παιδός, ἠπόρησεν ἐπὶ τοσαύτην ἀπολογίαν καὶ διδασκαλίαν αὐτοῦ, ²καὶ εἶπεν τοῖς παροῦσιν· Οἴμοι, ἠπορήθην ὁ τάλας ἐγώ,

---

6:22. καὶ νόει: Greek C and Greek-Slav. Tischendorf A and B omit. **6:23.** (cf. Chapter 7:2b in Tischendorf B: καὶ γνῶθι πόσους προσόδους καὶ κανόνας ἔχει καὶ χαρακτῆρας ξυνοὺς διαβαίνοντας συναγομένους.) **6:23.** ὧδέ πως ἔχει: Greek C. πῶς ἔχει: Greek-Slav. πρόσεχες ὧδε πῶς ἔχει: Tischendorf A. **6:23.** δύο κανόνας: Greek C and Greek-Slav. κανόνας: Tischendorf A, though de Santos (*Evangelium*, 95 n. 39) says that the δύο has simply fallen out. **6:23.** καὶ χαρακτῆρας μέσον ὀξυσμένους διαμένοντας, συναγομένους: Greek C. καὶ τοὺς χαρακτῆρας, οὓς ὁρᾷς ξυνοὺς διαβαίνοντας, συναγομένους: Greek-Slav. καὶ μεσαχαρακτῆρα οὓς ὁρᾷς ξυνοὺς διαβαίνοντα, συναγομένους: Tischendorf A. **6:23.** ὑψουμένους: Greek C and Greek-Slav. ὕψους μὲν αὐτούς: Tischendorf A, which, as de Santos (*Evangelium*, 95 n. 43) points out, is Tischendorf's emendation. **6:23.** χορεύοντας: Greek C and Greek-Slav (adding βαλεφεγιοῦντας, a word which not even de Santos [*Evangelium*, 95 n. 45] can fathom). πορεύοντος: Tischendorf A, which is again, as de Santos (*Evangelium*, 95 n. 44) points out, Tischendorf's emendation. **6:23.** τριστόμους, διστόμους: Greek C and Greek-Slav. τρισήμους: Tischendorf A. **6:23.** ἀμαχίμους: Greek C. Greek-Slav and Tischendorf A omit. **6:23.** παρόχους: Greek C and Greek-Slav. ὑπάρχους: Tischendorf A. **6:23.** ζυγοστόμους: Greek C. ὑποστάτους: Greek-Slav. ὑποστάτους: Tischendorf A. **7:1–4a.** (=Chapter 7.2c in Tischendorf B.) **7:1.** τὰς τοσαύτας καὶ τοιαύτας ἀλληγορίας: Tischendorf A. τὰς τοιαύτας προσηγορίας καὶ τοὺς κανόνας: Greek C and Greek-Slav. τὰς τοιαύτας προσηγορίας: Tischendorf B. **7:1.** τοῦ πρώτου γράμματος εἰρηκότος τοῦ παιδός: Tischendorf A, Greek C (substituting Ἰησοῦ for παιδός), and Greek-Slav (substituting στοιχείου for γράμματος). τοῦ ἑνὸς γράμματος: Tischendorf B. **7:1.** ἠπόρησεν ἐπὶ τοσαύτην ἀπολογίαν καὶ διδασκαλίαν αὐτοῦ: Tischendorf A. ἠπόρησεν ἐπὶ τὴν τοιαύτην διδασκαλίαν: Greek C. καὶ μὴ δυναμένων αὐτῶν ἀποκριθῆναι τοιαύτῃ ἀπολογίᾳ καὶ τῇ διδασκαλίᾳ αὐτοῦ: Greek-Slav. ἐκπλαγεὶς οὐκ εἶχεν ἀποκριθῆναι αὐτῷ: Tischendorf B. **7:2.** καὶ εἶπεν τοῖς παροῦσιν: Tischendorf A. εἶπεν: Greek-Slav. καὶ ἐβόησε λέγων: Greek C. καὶ στραφεὶς λέγει τῷ Ἰωσήφ: Tischendorf B. **7:2.** οἴμοι: Tischendorf A, Greek-Slav, and Greek C. Tischendorf B omits. **7:2.** ἠπορήθην: Tischendorf A. ὅτι ἠπατήθην: Greek C. ἐξέστη μου ἡ διάνοια: Greek-Slav. Tischendorf B omits. For preference given to Greek-Slav, see de Santos, *Evangelium*, 97 n. 7. **7:2.** ὁ τάλας ἐγώ: Tischendorf A and Greek C. ἐγὼ ὁ ταλαίπωρος: Greek-Slav. Tischendorf B omits.

²²Then while many were listening, he said to Zacchaeus, "Listen, teacher, and observe the arrangement of the first letter: ²³How it has two straight lines or strokes proceeding to a point in the middle, gathered together, elevated, dancing, three-cornered, two-cornered, not antagonistic, of the same family, providing the alpha has lines of equal measure."

7 After Zacchaeus the teacher had heard the child expressing such intricate allegories regarding the first letter, he despaired of defending his teaching. ²He spoke to those who were present: "Poor me, I'm utterly bewildered, wretch that I am. I've heaped

---

• **6:23.** *How it has two straight lines*: These are the only words of this most difficult and undoubtedly corrupt sentence that make sense. The rest of the translation is guesswork or simply a translation of words, if they are attested. James (*Apocryphal New Testament*, 62) aptly said of these words that they are "eight quite unintelligible descriptive phrases." Jesus is supposedly describing the letter alpha, but some words seem quite inappropriate in this context (e.g., χορεάοντας, or "dancing") and others are not even listed in lexica (e.g., ἀμαχίμους, ζυγοστόμους; cf. in Greek-Slav: βαλεφεγιοῦντας). Tischendorf (*Evangelia Apocrypha*, 145–46) and Delatte ("Evangile," 267–68) attempted some emendations, but they solved nothing. No wonder Zacchaeus despairs of taking on Jesus as a student! See further the discussion in de Santos, *Evangelium*, 94–95. For other examples of descriptions of letters, see Athenaeus, 10.454a–e, and, more generally, Frankfurter, "Magic of Writing," 210–11.

The Elementary School Classroom

On three occasions Jesus is sent to elementary school to learn to read (6:2, 13–18; 14:1–2; 15:1–3). The first step in learning to read was to learn the shapes and the sounds of the letters of the alphabet (see Quintilian, 1.1.24–29). Accordingly, we read that the teacher Zacchaeus wrote out the alphabet for Jesus (6:15). Many school texts have survived on papyri, ostraca, and wooden tablets, including some five dozen that contain teacher's models of individual letters or complete alphabets as well as students' efforts at copying them (see Cribiore, *Writing*, 292–306). For example, one ostracon (see p. 121), contemporary with the Infancy Gospel of Thomas, contains a teacher's model of an alphabet (text in Amundsen, *Ostraca*, 175). Unfortunately, it is broken off, but illustrates what a student used in school. The dimensions of what remains of the ostracon is roughly 2.5 x 2 in. Note that the letters are not always written in order.

ἐμαυτῷ αἰσχύνην παρέχων ἐπισπασάμενος τὸ παιδίον τοῦτο.
³ἆρον οὖν αὐτό, παρακαλῶ σε, ἀδελφὲ Ἰωσήφ· οὐ φέρω τὸ
αὐστηρὸν τοῦ βλέμματος αὐτοῦ οὔτε τὸν τρανῆ λόγον αὐτοῦ.
⁴τοῦτο τὸ παιδίον γηγενὴς οὐκ ἔστι, τοῦτο δύναται καὶ πῦρ
δαμάσαι· τάχα τοῦτο πρὸ τῆς κοσμοποιίας ἐστὶν γεγεννημένον.
⁵ποία γαστὴρ τοῦτο ἐβάστασεν, ποία δὲ μήτηρ τοῦτο ἐξέθρεψεν,
ἐγὼ ἀγνοῶ. ⁶οἴμοι, φίλε, ἐξέστη μου ἡ διάνοια· ⁷ἠπάτησα ἑαυτόν, ὁ τρισάθλιος ἐγώ· ἠγωνιζόμην ἔχειν μαθητήν, καὶ εὑρέθην
ἔχειν διδάσκαλον. ⁸ἐνθυμοῦμαι, φίλοι, τὴν αἰσχύνην, ὅτι γέρων
ὑπάρχων ὑπὸ παιδίου ἐνικήθην. ⁹καὶ ἔχω ἐκκακῆσαι καὶ ἀποθανεῖν διὰ τούτου τοῦ παιδός· οὐ δύναμαι γὰρ ἐν τῇ ὥρᾳ ταύτῃ
ἐμβλέψαι εἰς τὴν ὄψιν αὐτοῦ. ¹⁰καὶ πάντων εἰπόντων ὅτι ἐνικήθην ὑπὸ παιδίου μικροῦ, τί ἔχω εἰπεῖν; καὶ τί διηγήσασθαι περὶ

7:2. ἐμαυτῷ αἰσχύνην παρέχων: Tischendorf A. καὶ ἐμαυτῷ αἰσχύνην
κατέσχον: Greek C and Greek-Slav. Tischendorf B omits.   7:2.
ἐπισπασάμενος τὸ παιδίον τοῦτο: Tischendorf A. ἐφιστάμενος τῷ παιδίῳ
τούτῳ: Greek-Slav. Greek C and Tischendorf B omit.   7:3. ἆρον οὖν
αὐτό, παρακαλῶ σε, ἀδελφὲ Ἰωσήφ: Tischendorf A. ἆρον οὖν τὸ παιδίον,
ἀδελφὲ Ἰωσήφ, καὶ ἄγαγε αὐτὸ εὐθέως: Greek-Slav. ἆρον αὐτὸν ἀπ᾽ ἐμοῦ,
παρακαλῶ σε, ἀδελφέ: Greek C. ἀδελφέ, ἆρον οὖν αὐτὸ ἀπ᾽ ἐμοῦ:
Tischendorf B.   7:3. οὐ φέρω τὸ αὐστηρὸν τοῦ βλέμματος αὐτοῦ:
Tischendorf A, Greek C, and Greek-Slav (adding a γάρ after οὐ and
omitting the αὐτοῦ). Tischendorf B omits.   7:3. οὔτε τὸν τρανῆ λόγον
αὐτοῦ: Greek-Slav. οὐδὲ τοῦ λόγου αὐτοῦ: Greek C. οὐ τρανῶ τὸν λόγον
ἅπαξ: Tischendorf A. Tischendorf B omits. See de Santos, *Evangelium*,
99 n. 13.   7:4. τοῦτο τὸ παιδίον γηγενὴς οὐκ ἔστι: Tischendorf A,
Greek-Slav (adding ἀληθῶς at the beginning), and Tischendorf B (adding
ἀληθῶς after παιδίον). Greek C omits.   7:4. τοῦτο δύναται καὶ πῦρ
δαμάσαι: Tischendorf A and Greek-Slav. τοῦτο τὸ παιδίον δύναται
παραδαμάσαι πάντας καὶ χαλινῶσαι: Greek C. iste infans ignem domitare
et mare refrenare potest: Latin. Tischendorf B omits.   7:5. ποία γαστὴρ
τοῦτο ἐβάστασεν: Tischendorf A and Greek-Slav. ποία μήτηρ αὐτὸ
ἐγέννησεν: Greek C.   7:5. ποία μήτηρ ἐξέθρεψεν αὐτό: Greek-Slav.
mater: Latin. ποία μήτρα τοῦτο ἐξέθρεψεν: Tischendorf A. τίς ἐξέθρεψεν
αὐτό: Greek C.   7:4b-11. (Tischendorf B omits.)   7:6. φίλε:
Tischendorf A. φίλοι μου: Greek C. Greek-Slav omits.   7:6. ἐξέστη μου
ἡ διάνοια: Greek C and Greek-Slav. ἐξηχεῖ με, οὐ παρακολουθήσω τῇ
διανοίᾳ αὐτοῦ: Tischendorf A. See de Santos, *Evangelium*, 102 n. 21. 7:7.
ἠπάτησα ἑαυτόν: Weissengruber ("Untersuchungen," 213) notes that the
active verb with a reflexive pronoun (instead of the passive voice)
intensifies the self-rebuke.   7:8. ἐνθυμοῦμαι, φίλοι, τὴν αἰσχύνην:
Tischendorf A and Greek-Slav. τὴν αἰσχύνην οὐχ ὑποφέρω: Greek C.
7:8. γέρων ὑπάρχων: Tischendorf A and Greek C (substituting ὤν for
ὑπάρχων). Greek-Slav omits.   7:9. ἀποθανεῖν διὰ τούτου τοῦ παιδός:
Tischendorf A. On the causal use of διά + gen., see Weissengruber,
"Untersuchungen," 221–22. ἀποθανεῖν ἢ φυγεῖν τὴν κώμην διὰ τὸ παιδίον
τοῦτο: Greek C. ἀποθανεῖν: Greek-Slav.   7:9. ἐν τῇ ὥρᾳ ταύτῃ:
Tischendorf A. Greek C and Greek-Slav omit.

shame on myself because I took on this child. ³So take him away, I beg you, brother Joseph. I can't endure the severity of his look or his lucid speech. ⁴This child is no ordinary mortal; he can even tame fire! Perhaps he was born before the creation of the world. ⁵What sort of womb bore him, what sort of mother nourished him? —I don't know. ⁶Poor me, friend, I've lost my mind. ⁷I've deceived myself, I who am wholly wretched. I strove to get a student, and I've been found to have a teacher. ⁸Friends, I think of the shame, because, although I'm an old man, I've been defeated by a mere child. ⁹And so I can only despair and die on account of this child; right now I can't look him in the face. ¹⁰When everybody says that I've been defeated by a small child, what can I say? And what can I report about the lines of

---

- **7:3.** *or his lucid speech:* Reading Greek-Slav (and Greek C) rather than Tischendorf A, whose wording has long troubled scholars (see Thilo, *Codex Apocryphus*, 294). See further de Santos (*Evangelium*, 99 n. 13).

- **7:4.** *he can even tame fire:* This remark has occasioned difficulty, for it seems to refer to a specific story but there is nothing like it in this gospel. The Latin, however, is helpful at this point, for it says: "This child is able to subdue fire and to hold back the sea." In other words, Zacchaeus is acknowledging Jesus' power over nature.

- **7:4.** *Born before the creation of the world:*

Zacchaeus repeats the christological statement made earlier by Jesus (see 6:10).

- **7:5.** *what sort of mother nourished him?:* Reading Greek-Slav rather than Tischendorf A. The change is slight, μήτηρ instead of μήτρα, but one that eliminates what would have been a needless repetition of "womb." See de Santos, *Evangelium*, 101 n. 18.

- **7:6.** *I've lost my mind:* Again reading Greek-Slav rather than Tischendorf A, which is very problematic (see Thilo, *Codex Apocryphus*, 294–95).

O.Mich. 672: fragmentary ostrakon of a teacher's model of alphabet for pupils to copy. *Photograph courtesy of the Papyrology Collection, The University of Michigan.*

ὧν μοι εἶπε κανόνων τοῦ πρώτου στοιχείου; ἀγνοῶ, ὦ φίλοι· οὐ γὰρ ἀρχὴν καὶ τέλος αὐτοῦ γινώσκω. [11]τοιγαροῦν ἀξιῶ σε, ἀδελφὲ Ἰωσήφ, ἀπάγαγε αὐτὸν εἰς τὸν οἶκόν σου. οὗτος τί ποτε μέγα ἐστίν, ἢ θεὸς ἢ ἄγγελος, ἢ τί εἴπω οὐκ οἶδα.

8 Τῶν δὲ Ἰουδαίων παραινούντων τῷ Ζακχαίῳ, ἐγέλασε τὸ παιδίον μέγα καὶ εἶπεν· Νῦν καρποφορείτωσαν τὰ ἄκαρπα, καὶ βλεπέτωσαν τὰ ἄβλεπτα καὶ ἀκουέτωσαν οἱ κωφοὶ ἐν τῇ συνέσει τῆς καρδίας. [2]ἐγὼ ἄνωθεν πάρειμι ἵνα τοὺς κάτω ῥύσωμαι καὶ εἰς τὰ ἄνω καλέσω, καθὼς προσέταξέ μοι ὁ ἀποστείλας με πρὸς ὑμᾶς. [3]Καὶ ὡς τὸ παιδίον κατέπαυσε τὸν λόγον, εὐθέως ἐσώθησαν οἱ πάντες οἱ ὑπὸ τὴν κατάραν αὐτοῦ πεσόντες. [4]καὶ οὐδεὶς ἀπὸ τότε ἐτόλμα παροργίσαι αὐτόν, ὅπως μὴ καταράσεται αὐτὸν καὶ ἔσται ἀνάπηρος.

A fallen child raised

9 Καὶ μεθ᾽ ἡμέρας δέ τινας ἔπαιζεν ὁ Ἰησοῦς ἐπάνω διστέγου οἴκου καὶ ἕν τῶν παιδίων τῶν παιζόντων μετ᾽ αὐτοῦ πεσὼν ἀπὸ τῆς στέγης κάτω ἀπέθανε· καὶ ἰδόντα τὰ ἄλλα παιδία ἔφυγον, καὶ κατέστη ὁ Ἰησοῦς μόνος.

7:10. οὐ γὰρ ἀρχὴν καὶ τέλος αὐτοῦ γινώσκω: Tischendorf A and Greek-Slav (omitting αὐτοῦ). ὧν οὔτε ἀρχὴν εὑρίσκω οὔτε τέλος: Greek C, but placed after ἐνικήθην at the end of v. 8. **7:11.** τοιγαροῦν ἀξιῶ: Tischendorf A. παρακαλῶ: Greek C. On the translation error in Greek-Slav, see de Santos, *Evangelium*, 104 n. 33. **7:11.** ἢ θεὸς ἢ ἄγγελος ἢ τί εἴπω οἶδα: Tischendorf A. ἢ θεὸς ἢ ἄγγελος ἢ κτίστης τῶν ἀπάντων: Greek C. ἢ θεὸς ἢ κτίστης τῶν ἀπάντων ἢ τί εἴπω οὐκ οἶδα: Greek-Slav. **8:1–4.** (Tischendorf B omits.) **8:1.** παραινούντων: Tischendorf A and Greek C. παραστάντων: Greek-Slav. **8:1.** τὸ παιδίον: Tischendorf A and Greek-Slav. ὁ Ἰησοῦς: Greek C. **8:1.** τὰ ἄκαρπα: Greek C and Greek-Slav. τὰ σά: Tischendorf A. See de Santos, *Evangelium*, 106 n. 2. **8:1.** τὰ ἄβλεπτα: Greek C and Greek-Slav. οἱ τυφλοὶ τῇ καρδίᾳ: Tischendorf A. See de Santos, *Evangelium*, 106 n. 3. **8:1.** καὶ ἀκουέτωσαν οἱ κωφοὶ ἐν τῇ συνέσει τῆς καρδίας: Greek-Slav. νῦν ἀκουέτωσαν οἱ κωφοὶ τῇ καρδίᾳ: Greek C. Tischendorf A omits. See de Santos, *Evangelium*, 106 n. 4. **8:2.** ἵνα τοὺς κάτω ῥύσωμαι: Greek C and Greek-Slav. ἵνα αὐτοὺς καταράσομαι: Tischendorf A. See de Santos, *Evangelium*, 107 n. 6. **8:2.** καλέσω: Tischendorf A and Greek-Slav. βλέπω: Greek C. **8:2.** προσέταξέ μοι: Greek C and Greek Slav. διετάξατο: Tischendorf A. **8:2.** πρὸς ὑμᾶς: Greek C and Greek-Slav. δι᾽ ὑμᾶς: Tischendorf A. **8:3.** εὐθέως ἐσώθησαν οἱ πάντες οἱ ὑπὸ τὴν κατάραν αὐτοῦ πεσόντες: Tischendorf A and Greek-Slav (omitting αὐτοῦ). ἐγένοντο ὑγιεῖς πάντες ψυχῇ καὶ σώματι: Greek C. **8:4.** ὅπως μὴ καταράσεται αὐτὸν καὶ ἔσται ἀνάπηρος: Tischendorf A and Greek-Slav. Greek C omits. **9:1–6.** (=Chapter 8 in Tischendorf B.) **9:1.** ἐπάνω διστέγου οἴκου: Tischendorf B. ἔν τινι δώματι ἐν ὑπερῴῳ: Tischendorf A. ἔν τινι δώματι ὑψηλῷ: Greek-Slav. Greek C omits. **9:1.** πεσὼν ἀπὸ τῆς στέγης: Greek-Slav. πεσὼν ἀπὸ τοῦ δώματος: Tischendorf A. ἔπεσεν ἀπὸ τοῦ ἀνωγαίου: Greek C. κρημνιζόμενον ἐπὶ τῆς γῆς: Tischendorf B.

the first letter which he told me about? I just don't know, friends. For I don't know its beginning or its end. [11]Therefore, I ask you, brother Joseph, take him back to your house. What great thing he is—god or angel or whatever else I might call him—I don't know."

8 While the Jews were advising Zacchaeus, the child laughed loudly and said, "Now let the infertile bear fruit and the blind see and the deaf in the understanding of their heart hear : [2]I've come from above so that I might save those who are below and summon them to higher things, just as the one who sent me to you commanded me."

[3]When the child stopped speaking, all those who had fallen under the curse were instantly saved. [4]And from then on no one dared to anger him for fear of being cursed and maimed for life.

9 A few days later Jesus was playing on the roof of a house when one of the children playing with him fell off the roof and died. When the other children saw what had happened, they fled, leaving Jesus standing all by himself.

A fallen child raised

• **8:1.** *advising*: This participle (παραινούν-των) seems inappropriate here (see de Santos, *Evangelium*, 105 n. 1), and some have resorted to emendation, such as παροι-νούντων ("mistreating") (see Thilo, *Codex Apocryphus*, 296). This change is slight, but the context seems to require something like παραμυθουμένων ("consoling").

• **8:1-2.** This rendering of Jesus' response, taken from Greek C and Greek-Slav, differs considerably from Tischendorf A, whose wording is obviously corrupt (see Michaelis, *Apokryphen Schriften*, 110). The language echoes several gospel passages (see Matt 11:5; John 7:29; 8:23; 9:39).

• **8:1.** *the infertile*: Tischendorf A has τὰ σά, which might mean "your actions." See further de Santos, *Evangelium*, 106 n. 2.

• **8:1.** *the deaf in the understanding of their heart hear*: Tischendorf A omits, having only two of the three parts of this sentence. See de Santos, *Evangelium*, 106 n. 4.

• **8:2.** *save those who are below*: Tischendorf A has "curse them." See de Santos, *Evangelium*, 107 n. 6.

• **8:3.** *all those who had fallen under the curse*: Presumably this group includes the boy who had emptied the ponds Jesus had made (see 3:3) and the boy who bumped him on the shoulder (4:2), not to mention the group that was blinded (5:3).

• **9:1-6.** The first of several stories in which Jesus raises someone from the dead (see also chaps. 16–18). Here Jesus raises a child who has died in a fall from an upper story and in the process vindicates himself against charges that he had pushed the child. The motif of raising someone who has fallen from an upper story has no synoptic parallel, but it does occur in a story about Paul and Eutychus (see Acts 20:9–12). Gero ("Thomas," 64 n. 4) also points to a similar story in Apuleius, *Metamorphoses* 2:28–30.

²Καὶ ἐλθόντες οἱ γονεῖς τοῦ τεθνεῶτος ἐνεκάλουν τὸν Ἰησοῦν· Ταραχοποιός, σὺ αὐτὸν κατέβαλες.

³ Ὁ δὲ Ἰησοῦς ἀπεκρίνατο· Οὐκ ἐγὼ αὐτὸν κατέβαλον, ἀλλ᾽ ἐκεῖνος ἑαυτὸν κατέβαλε, οὐ γὰρ ἀκριβῶς πράττων κατεπήδησεν ἀπὸ τοῦ στέγου καὶ ἀπέθανε.

⁴Κατεπήδησεν ὁ Ἰησοῦς ἀπὸ τοῦ στέγου καὶ ἔστη παρὰ τὸ πτῶμα τοῦ παιδίου, καὶ ἔκραξε φωνῇ μεγάλῃ καὶ εἶπεν· Ζῆνον,— οὕτω γὰρ τὸ ὄνομα αὐτοῦ ἐκαλεῖτο—ἀναστὰς εἰπέ μοι, ἐγώ σε κατέβαλον;

⁵Καὶ ἀναστὰς παραχρῆμα εἶπεν· Οὐχὶ κύριε, οὐ κατέβαλας, ἀλλὰ ἀνέστησας.

⁶Καὶ ἰδόντες ἐξεπλάγησαν. οἱ δὲ γονεῖς τοῦ παιδίου ἐδόξασαν τὸν θεὸν ἐπὶ τῷ γεγονότι σημείῳ, καὶ προσεκύνησαν τῷ Ἰησοῦ.

9:2–3. καὶ ἐλθόντες οἱ γονεῖς τοῦ τεθνεῶτος ἐνεκάλουν τὸν Ἰησοῦν· Ταραχοποιός, σὺ αὐτὸν κατέβαλες. Ὁ δὲ Ἰησοῦς ἀπεκρίνατο· Οὐκ ἐγὼ αὐτὸν κατέβαλον, ἀλλ᾽ ἐκεῖνος ἑαυτὸν κατέβαλε, οὐ γὰρ ἀκριβῶς πράττων κατεπήδησεν ἀπὸ τοῦ στέγου καὶ ἀπέθανε: Greek-Slav. καὶ ἐλθόντες οἱ γονεῖς τοῦ τεθνεῶτος ἐνεκάλουν . . . ἐκεῖνος δὲ ἐπηρέαζον αὐτόν: Tischendorf A. καὶ μαθόντες οἱ γονεῖς τοῦ τεθνηκότος παιδὸς ἔδραμον μετὰ κλαυθμοῦ, καὶ εὑρόντες τὸν μὲν παῖδα κατὰ γῆς νεκρὸν κείμενον, τὸν δὲ Ἰησοῦν ἄνωθεν ἑστῶτα, ὑπολαβόντες ὡς ὑπ᾽ αὐτοῦ κατακρημνισθῆναι τὸν παῖδαν, καὶ ἀτενίζοντες ὠνείδιζον αὐτόν: Tischendorf B. ἐλθόντες δὲ οἱ γονεῖς τοῦ τεθνηκότος παιδίου ἔλεγον τῷ Ἰησοῦ ὅτι σὺ αὐτὸν κατέβαλες: Greek C. et cum venissent parentes pueri qui defunctus fuerat, dicebant adversus Iesum, Vere tu eum irruere fecisti. et insidiabantur ei: Latin. On the lacuna in Tischendorf A and its restoration, see de Santos, *Evangelium*, 111 n. 7.   **9:4.** κατεπήδησεν ὁ Ἰησοῦς ἀπὸ τοῦ στέγου: Tischendorf A. ὁ δὲ Ἰησοῦς ἰδὼν εὐθέως κατεπήδησεν ἀπὸ τοῦ διστέγου: Tischendorf B. ὡς δὲ ἐμαίνοντο κατὰ τοῦ Ἰησοῦ κατῆλθε κάτω: Greek C. Greek-Slav omits.   **9:4.** καὶ ἔστη παρὰ τὸ πτῶμα τοῦ παιδίου: Tischendorf A. καὶ ἔστη πρὸς κεφαλῆς τοῦ τεθνηκότος: Tischendorf B. καὶ στὰς ἐπάνω τοῦ πτώματος: Greek C. Greek-Slav omits.   **9:4.** ἔκραξε φωνῇ μεγάλῃ καὶ εἶπεν: Tischendorf A and Greek-Slav (adding ὁ Ἰησοῦς before ἔκραξε). ἔκραζε λέγων τὸ ὄνομα τοῦ τεθνηκότος: Greek C. καὶ λέγει αὐτῷ: Tischendorf B.   **9:4.** Ζῆνον: Tischendorf A and B and Greek Slav. Ζῆνον, Ζῆνον: Greek C. Sinoo, Sinoo: Latin.   **9:4.** οὕτω γὰρ τὸ ὄνομα αὐτοῦ ἐκαλεῖτο: Tischendorf A. οὕτως γὰρ ἐκαλεῖτο ὁ παῖς: Tischendorf B (and placed after Jesus' question). οὕτως γὰρ ἦν τὸ ὄνομα τοῦ τεθνεῶτος: Greek-Slav. Greek C omits.   **9:5.** οὐχί, κύριε, οὐ κατέβαλας ἀλλὰ ἀνέστησας: Tischendorf A. κύριε, οὐ σύ με κατέβαλες ἀλλὰ νεκρὸν ὄντα με ἐζώωσας: Tischendorf B. οὐχί, κύριε, οὐχί: Greek C. οὐχί, κύριέ μου: Greek-Slav.   **9:6.** καὶ ἰδόντες ἐξεπλάγησαν: Tischendorf A. καὶ πάντες οἱ ἰδόντες ἐξεπλάγησαν: Greek Slav. Tischendorf B omits. For Greek C, see next note.   **9:6.** οἱ δὲ γονεῖς τοῦ παιδίου ἐδόξασαν τὸν θεὸν ἐπὶ τῷ γεγονότι σημείῳ καὶ προσεκύνησαν τῷ Ἰησοῦ: Tischendorf A and Greek-Slav. ἰδόντες δὲ οἱ γονεῖς αὐτοῦ τὸ παράδοξον θαῦμα ὃ ἐποίησεν ὁ Ἰησοῦς ἐδόξασαν τὸν θεὸν καὶ προσεκύνησαν τὸν Ἰησοῦν: Greek C. cum vidissent autem parentes eius tam magnum miraculum quod fecit Iesus, glorificaverunt deum et adoraverunt Iesum: Latin. Tischendorf B omits.

²The parents of the dead child came and accused Jesus: "You troublemaker you, you're the one who threw him down."

³Jesus responded, "I didn't throw him down—he threw himself down. He just wasn't being careful and leaped down from the roof and died."

⁴Then Jesus himself leaped down from the roof and stood by the body of the child and shouted in a loud voice: "Zeno!" — that was his name—"Get up and tell me: Did I push you?"

⁵He got up immediately and said, "No, Lord, you didn't push me, you raised me up."

⁶Those who saw this were astonished, and the child's parents praised God for the miracle that had happened and worshiped Jesus.

• **9:2–3.** These two verses, beginning with "You troublemaker," are taken from Greek-Slav, as de Santos (*Evangelium*, 111 n. 7) has detected a lacuna in Tischendorf A. The Syriac also has something similar, if also briefer (see Wright, *Apocryphal Literature*, 9).

• **9:3.** *Zeno*: This name is quite popular in Greco-Roman society, its most famous bearer being the founder of the Stoic school, Zeno of Citium (see Diogenes Laertius, 7.1) In Christian tradition, however, it is rare, being found in variant readings of 2 Tim 4:19 as well as in the Acts of Paul and Thecla 3:2.

• **9:5.** *Lord*: The only time Jesus is so addressed in this gospel. This title is popular in the canonical gospels (see, e.g., Matt 7:21; 8:2, 6, 21, 25; 9:28; etc.).

• **9:6.** *Worshiped Jesus*: The parents, or the crowd, depending on the MS, worships Jesus after this miracle (so also 10:4; 18:2). Such a response to Jesus is even more frequent in the gospels (see, e.g., Matt 2:2; 8:2; 9:18; 14:33; 15:25; etc.).

*Jesus heals
a cut foot*

10 Μετ᾽ ὀλίγας ἡμέρας σχίζων τις ξύλα ἐν τῇ γειτονίᾳ νεώτερος, ἔπεσεν ἡ ἀξίνη καὶ διέσχισεν τὴν βάσιν τοῦ ποδὸς αὐτοῦ, καὶ ἔξαιμος γενόμενος ἀπέθνησκεν.

²Θορύβου δὲ γενομένου καὶ συνδρομῆς, ἔδραμε καὶ τὸ παιδίον Ἰησοῦς ἐκεῖ. καὶ βιασάμενος διῆλθεν τὸν ὄχλον, καὶ ἐκράτησεν τοῦ νεανίσκου τὸν πεπληγότα πόδαν, καὶ εὐθέως ἰάθη.

³Εἶπε δὲ τῷ νεανίσκῳ· Ἀνάστα νῦν, σχίζε τὰ ξύλα καὶ μνημόνευέ μου.

⁴Ὁ δὲ ὄχλος ἰδὼν τὸ γεγονὸς προσεκύνησαν τὸ παιδίον, λέγοντες· Ἀληθῶς πνεῦμα θεοῦ ἐνοικεῖ ἐν τῷ παιδίῳ τούτῳ.

*Jesus fetches
water*

11 Ὄντος δὲ αὐτοῦ ἐξαέτους, πέμπει αὐτὸν ἡ μήτηρ αὐτοῦ ὕδωρ ἀντλῆσαι καὶ φέρειν ἐν τῷ οἴκῳ. λελυκότος δὲ αὐτοῦ τὴν ὑδρίαν ἐν τῷ ὄχλῳ ²καὶ συγκρούσασα ἡ ὑδρία ἐκλάσθη. ³ὁ δὲ

10:1–4. (=Chapter 9 in Tischendorf B.)   **10:1.** ἐν τῇ γειτονίᾳ: Greek C and Greek-Slav (cf. Tischendorf B: τις τῶν γειτόνων). ἐν τῇ γωνίᾳ: Tischendorf A. See de Santos, *Evangelium*, 114 n. 3.   **10:1.** τὴν βάσιν τοῦ ποδὸς αὐτοῦ: Tischendorf A and B and Greek-Slav. τὸν δεξιὸν αὐτοῦ πόδα: Greek C.   **10:1.** καὶ ἔξαιμος γενόμενος ἀπέθνησκεν: Tischendorf A and Greek-Slav (substituting ἔκθαμβος for ἔξαιμος). καὶ ἔξαιμος γεγονὼς ἤμελλεν ἀποθνήσκειν: Tischendorf B. Greek C omits.   **10:2.** θορύβου δὲ γενομένου καὶ συνδρομῆς: Tischendorf A and Greek-Slav. καὶ λαοῦ συνδεδραμηκότος πολλοῦ: Tischendorf B. καὶ συνήχθη ὁ ὄχλος ἐπ᾽ αὐτῷ: Greek C.   **10:2.** τὸ παιδίον Ἰησοῦς: Tischendorf A and Greek-Slav. ὁ Ἰησοῦς: Tischendorf B. ὁ κύριος ἡμῶν Ἰησοῦς Χριστός: Greek C. **10:2.** καὶ βιασάμενος διῆλθεν τὸν ὄχλον: Tischendorf A and Greek-Slav. Tischendorf B and Greek C omit.   **10:3.** ἀνάστα νῦν, σχίζε τὰ ξύλα καὶ μνημόνευέ μου: Tischendorf A, Greek-Slav, and Greek C. ἀνάστα, σχίσον τὰ ξύλα σου: Tischendorf B, after which it alone continues: καὶ ἀναστὰς προσεκύνησεν αὐτῷ, εὐχαριστῶν καὶ σχίζων τὰ ξύλα.   **10:4.** ὁ δὲ ὄχλος ἰδὼν τὸ γεγονὸς προσεκύνησαν τὸ παιδίον λέγοντες: Tischendorf A. ἰδόντες δὲ οἱ ὄχλοι τὸ γενόμενον θαῦμα προσεκύνησαν τὸ παιδίον καὶ εἶπον: Greek-Slav. ἰδόντες οἱ ὄχλοι ὃ ἐποίησεν ὁ Ἰησοῦς σημεῖον προσεκύνησαν αὐτὸν καὶ εἶπον: Greek C. ὁμοίως καὶ πάντες οἱ ὄντες ἐκεῖ θαυμάσαντες ηὐχαρίστησαν αὐτῷ: Tischendorf B.   **10:4.** ἀληθῶς πνεῦμα θεοῦ ἐνοικεῖ ἐν τῷ παιδίῳ τούτῳ: Tischendorf A. ἀληθῶς ὁ θεὸς οἰκεῖ ἐν αὐτῷ: Greek-Slav. ἀληθῶς τάχα ὁ θεὸς οἰκεῖ ἐν τῷ παιδίῳ τούτῳ: Greek C. Tischendorf B omits.   **11:1–4.** (=Chapter 10 in Tischendorf B.)   **11:1.** ἡ μήτηρ αὐτοῦ: Tischendorf A. Μαριὰμ ἡ μήτηρ αὐτοῦ: Tischendorf B and Greek-Slav. ἡ Θεοτόκος: Greek C.   **11:1.** λελυκότος δὲ αὐτοῦ τὴν ὑδρίαν ἐν τῷ ὄχλῳ: Greek-Slav. δεδωκὼς αὐτῷ ὑδρίαν: Tischendorf A. ὄχλου δὲ ὄντος πολλοῦ ἐν τῇ πηγῇ: Greek C. πορευόμενος: Tischendorf B. See de Santos, *Evangelium*, 117 n. 4. **11:2.** καὶ συγκρούσασα ἡ ὑδρία ἐκλάσθη: Greek-Slav. ἐν δὲ τῷ ὄχλῳ συγκρούσας ἡ ὑδρία ἐρράγη: Tischendorf A. ἐκλάσθη ἡ ὑδρία αὐτοῦ: Greek C. συνετρίβη ἡ ὑδρία αὐτοῦ: Tischendorf B. See further on the grammatical constructions de Santos, *Evangelium*, 117 n. 5, and Weissengruber, "Untersuchungen," 221.

10 A few days later a young man was splitting wood in the
neighborhood when his axe slipped and cut off the bottom of his
foot. He was dying from the loss of blood.

²The crowd rushed there in an uproar, and the boy Jesus ran
up, too. He forced his way through the crowd and grabbed hold
of the young man's wounded foot. It was instantly healed.

³He said to the youth, "Get up now, split your wood, and remember me."

⁴The crowd saw what had happened and worshiped the child,
saying, "Truly the spirit of God dwells in this child."

11 When he was six years old, his mother sent him to draw
water and bring it back to the house. ²But he lost his grip on the
pitcher in the jostling of the crowd, and it fell and broke. ³So

---

• **10:1–4.** Jesus saves the life of a young man
who split open his foot with an axe and lay
dying.

• **10:1.** *in the neighborhood*: The reading of
Tischendorf A ("in the corner") makes no
sense.

• **11:1–13:4.** A small cycle of stories depicting
Jesus as giving miraculous help to his
family. At age six he fetches water for his
mother (11:1–2), and at eight he is no less
helpful to his father, working miracles in
the field and in the workshop (12:1–13:4).
In this context should also be mentioned
the miraculous help Jesus extends to his
brother when he is bitten by a viper (16:1–
2). See further Michaelis, *Apokryphen
Schriften*, 111.

• **11:1–4.** A single story about Jesus at age 6:
He fetches water for his mother by miraculously carrying it home in the folds of his
clothes.

• **11:1.** *his mother*: Jesus' mother plays a
relatively minor role in this gospel. Indeed,
this is the first time she is mentioned (see
also 14:5; 19:1–12). To be sure, in Tischendorf B she appears briefly already in 2:1,
when she lets Jesus play out in the rain,
and again in 13:4, when Joseph tells her of
Jesus' miraculous lengthening of the short

piece of wood. Note also that in Tischendorf B and Greek-Slav the proper name
Mary is used, and in Greek C she is even
identified by the exalted title of Theotokos,
or "Mother of God" (see also 11:4, where
Greek C has "the holy Mother of God").

• **11:2.** This entire verse—in wording and
punctuation—departs from Tischendorf A,
which is riddled with problems. For example, as editors since Thilo (*Codex Apocryphus*, 300) have recognized, the participle
δεδωκώς in the mss of Tischendorf A should
be feminine (δεδωκυῖα) to agree with its
obvious subject Mary. In addition, the participle συγκρούσας, if it refers to Jesus,
should be συγκρούσαντος. But de Santos
proposes a more thorough solution by
recasting the entire sentence. He first
argues that an original λελυκότος was mis-
read as δεδωκώς, and then changes συγκρούσας to συγκρούσασα, so that it modifies
ὑδρία. These changes are basic to his
overall emendation which is adopted here
(see further de Santos, *Evangelium*, 117 nn.
4 and 5). For a defense of Tischendorf's
decision to keep these two incongruous
masculine participles, see Weissengruber,
"Untersuchungen," 220–21.

Ἰησοῦς ἁπλώσας τὸ παλίον ὅπερ ἦν βεβλημένος, ἐγέμισεν αὐτὸ ὕδωρ καὶ ἤνεγκε τῇ μητρὶ αὐτοῦ.

⁴Ἰδοῦσα δὲ ἡ μήτηρ αὐτοῦ τὸ γεγονὸς σημεῖον κατεφίλει αὐτόν, καὶ διετήρει ἐν αὐτῇ τὰ μυστήρια ἃ ἔβλεπεν αὐτὸν ποιοῦντα.

A miraculous harvest

12 Πάλιν δὲ ἐν καιρῷ τοῦ σπόρου ἐξῆλθεν τὸ παιδίον μετὰ τοῦ πατρὸς αὐτοῦ ἵνα σπείρει σῖτον εἰς τὴν χώραν αὐτῶν· καὶ ἐν τῷ σπείρειν τὸν πατέρα αὐτοῦ ἔπειρε καὶ τὸ παιδίον Ἰησοῦς ἕνα κόρον σίτου. ²καὶ θερίσας καὶ ἁλωνίσας ἐποίησε κόρους ἑκατόν, ³καὶ καλέσας πάντας τοὺς πτωχοὺς τῆς κώμης εἰς τὴν ἅλωνα ἐχαρίσατο αὐτοῖς τὸν σῖτον· καὶ Ἰωσὴφ ἔφερεν τὸ καταλειφθὲν τοῦ σίτου. ⁴ἦν δὲ ἐτῶν ὀκτὼ ὅτε τοῦτο ἐποίησε τὸ σημεῖον.

11:3. ὁ δὲ Ἰησοῦς ἁπλώσας τὸ παλίον ὅπερ ἦν βεβλημένος: Tischendorf A and Greek-Slav. καὶ ἁπλώσας τὸ πάλλιον αὐτοῦ ὃ ἐφόρει: Greek C. καὶ ἀπελθὼν ἐν τῇ πηγῇ ἥπλωσε τὸν ἐπενδύτην αὐτοῦ: Tischendorf B. **11:3.** ἐγέμισεν αὐτὸ ὕδωρ: Tischendorf A and Greek-Slav. On the accusative (ὕδωρ) instead of the genitive of material, see Weissengruber, "Untersuchungen," 213. ἔθηκεν ἐπ᾽ αὐτῷ τὸ ὕδωρ: Greek C. καὶ ἀντλήσας ὕδωρ ἐκ τῆς πηγῆς ἔπλησεν αὐτόν: Tischendorf B. **11:3.** καὶ ἤνεγκε τῇ μητρὶ αὐτοῦ: Tischendorf A and Greek-Slav. καὶ ἐπήγαγε τῇ μητρὶ αὐτοῦ Μαριάμ: Greek C. καὶ λαβὼν ἀπήγαγε τὸ ὕδωρ τῇ μητρὶ αὐτοῦ: Tischendorf B. **11:4.** ἡ μήτηρ αὐτοῦ: Tischendorf A and Greek-Slav. ἐκείνη: Tischendorf B. ἡ μήτηρ αὐτοῦ ἡ ἁγία Θεοτόκος: Greek C. **11:4.** τὸ γεγονὸς σημεῖον: Tischendorf A and Greek-Slav. ὅ τι ἐποίησεν ὁ Ἰησοῦς σημεῖον: Greek C. ἐξεπλάγη: Tischendorf B. **11:4.** κατεφίλει: Tischendorf A and Greek-Slav. καταφίλησεν: Greek C. περιπλακεῖσα κατεφίλει: Tischendorf B. **11:4.** καὶ διετήρει ἐν αὐτῇ τὰ μυστήρια ἃ ἔβλεπεν αὐτὸν ποιοῦντα: Tischendorf A (cf. Greek-Slav, which reads καὶ διετήρει αὐτόν but then breaks off). καὶ εἶπε· Κύριε, ἐλέησον τὸν υἱόν μου: Greek C. Tischendorf B omits. For the personal pronoun (ἐν αὐτῇ) used in a reflexive sense in Tischendorf A, see Weissengruber, "Untersuchungen," 214. **12:1–4.** (Tischendorf B omits.) **12:1.** ἐξῆλθεν τὸ παιδίον μετὰ τοῦ πατρὸς αὐτοῦ: Tischendorf A and Greek-Slav (adding Ἰησοῦς after παιδίον). ἀπῆλθεν ὁ Ἰωσήφ: Greek C. **12:1.** εἰς τὴν χώραν αὐτῶν: Tischendorf A and Greek-Slav. Greek C omits, but then adds this clause: ἠκολούθησε δὲ αὐτὸν ὁ Ἰησοῦς. **12:1.** τὸν πατέρα αὐτοῦ: Tischendorf A and Greek-Slav. τὸν Ἰωσήφ: Greek C. **12:1.** κόρον: Greek-Slav. κόκκον: Tischendorf C. δράκαν: Greek C. quantum pusillo tenere potuit: Latin. See de Santos, *Evangelium*, 119 n. 3. **12:2.** ἁλωνίσας: Tischendorf A. ἡλώνισεν: Greek C. τρυγήσας: Greek-Slav. **12:2.** κόρους: Tischendorf A. μεγάλους κόρους: Greek-Slav. μόδια: Greek C. modia: Latin. **12:3.** πάντας τοὺς πτωχοὺς τῆς κώμης: Tischendorf A. πάντας τοὺς πτωχούς: Greek-Slav. χήρας καὶ ὀρφανούς: Greek C. pauperes et viduas et orphanos: Latin. **12:3.** καὶ Ἰωσὴφ ἔφερεν τὸ καταλειφθὲν τοῦ σίτου: Tischendorf A. καὶ αὐτὸς ὁ Ἰωσὴφ κεκράτηκε ἀπὸ τοῦ σίτου, ὃν ἔσπειρε ὁ Ἰησοῦς: Greek-Slav. κεκράτηκε δὲ ὁ Ἰησοῦς ἐξ αὐτοῦ τοῦ σίτου ὀλίγον ἵνα ἔχωσιν εἰς εὐλογίαν τοῦ σπόρου: Greek C. **12:4.** ἦν δὲ ἐτῶν ὀκτὼ ὅτε τοῦτο ἐποίησε τὸ σημεῖον: Tischendorf A. (This reference to Jesus' age, which concludes this chapter, is placed in Tischendorf B, Greek-Slav, and Greek C at the beginning of the next one.)

Jesus spread out the cloak he was wearing and filled it with water and carried it back to his mother.

⁴His mother, once she saw the miracle that had occurred, kissed him; but she kept to herself the mysteries that she had seen him do.

12 Again, during the sowing season, the child went out with his father to sow their field with grain. While his father was sowing, the child Jesus sowed one measure of grain. ²When he had harvested and threshed it, it yielded one hundred measures. ³Then he summoned all the poor in the village to the threshing floor and gave them grain. Joseph carried back what was left of the grain. ⁴Jesus was eight years old when he did this miracle.

A miraculous harvest

• **11:3.** *filled it with water*: It is not clear whether the pitcher was full of water when it broke, so that Jesus gathered up the spilled water in his clothing, or whether the pitcher was empty, so that Jesus put well water in his clothing (see Michaelis, *Apokryphen Schriften*, 111). In Tischendorf B and the Latin, however, the latter option is explicit; the former says: ". . . he drew water from the well and filled his garment. . . ." So also the Syriac (see Wright, *Apocryphal Literature*, 9).

• **11:4.** *she kept to herself the mysteries which she had seen him do*: The language here recalls what is said of Mary in Luke 2:19, 51.

• **12:1–17:4.** A series of episodes about Jesus at age eight.

• **12:1–4.** Jesus now helps his father with the sowing, which results in a miraculously abundant harvest and hence in enough to give grain to the poor in the village.

• **12:1.** *one measure of grain*: The MSS differ at this point, but Greek C and Greek-Slav have words that denote measure (see de Santos, *Evangelium*, 119 n. 3). The amount per measure (κόρος=Heb. *kor*) is uncertain, perhaps 10–12 bushels (see Michaelis, *Apokryphen Schriften*, 111). Tischendorf A, however, reads: "one seed of grain," which seems to be a later change, made to highlight further the magnitude of the miracle.

• **12:2.** *one hundred measures*: The same expression is found at Luke 16:7, but the emphasis here on the size of the harvest more likely recalls the parable of the sower, where some seed produced one hundred times the amount sown (see Matt 13:8; Mark 4:8; Luke 8:8).

• **12:3.** *all the poor in the village*: Greek C is more specific, saying "widows and orphans."

• **12:4.** *Jesus was eight years old*: This reference to age, which concludes this story in Tischendorf A, is placed at the beginning of the next story in other MSS and versions (see corresponding notes to the Greek text).

Miraculous
woodworking

13 ʿΟ δὲ πατὴρ αὐτοῦ τέκτων ἦν, καὶ ἐποίει ἐν τῷ καιρῷ ἐκείνῳ ἄροτρα καὶ ζυγούς. ἐπετάγη αὐτῷ κράββατος παρά τινος πλουσίου ὅπως ποιήσει αὐτῷ. ²τοῦ δὲ ἑνὸς κανόνος τοῦ καλουμένου ἐναλλάκτου ὄντος κολοβωτέρου, μὴ ἔχοντ⟨ο⟩s ⟨τοῦ Ἰωσήφ⟩ τ⟨ι⟩ ποιῆσαι, εἶπεν τὸ παιδίον ὁ Ἰησοῦς τῷ πατρὶ αὐτοῦ Ἰωσήφ, Θὲς κάτω τὰ δύο ξύλα, καὶ ἐκ τοῦ μέσου μέρους ἰσοποίησον αὐτά.

³Καὶ ἐποίησεν Ἰωσὴφ καθὼς εἶπεν αὐτῷ τὸ παιδίον. ἔστη δὲ ὁ Ἰησοῦς ἐκ τοῦ ἑτέρου μέρους καὶ ἐκράτησεν τὸ κολοβώτερον ξύλον, καὶ ἐκτείνας αὐτὸ ἴσον ἐποίησεν τοῦ ἄλλου.

⁴Καὶ εἶδεν ὁ πατὴρ αὐτοῦ Ἰωσὴφ καὶ ἐθαύμασε, καὶ περιλαβὼν τὸ παιδίον κατεφίλει λέγων· Μακάριός εἰμι, ὅτι τὸ παιδίον τοῦτο δέδωκέ μοι ὁ θεός.

13:1–4. (=Chapter 11 in Tischendorf B.)   **13:1.** ὁ δὲ πατὴρ αὐτοῦ τέκτων ἦν: Tischendorf A. As mentioned in the previous note, the other MSS and versions place the reference to Jesus' age (see above 12:4) at the beginning of this chapter, as follows: ἦν δὲ ὁ Ἰησοῦς ἐτῶν η: Greek-Slav; ἐγένετο δὲ ὁ Ἰησοῦς ἐτῶν ὀκτώ: Greek C; and φθάσας δὲ ὀγδόον τῆς ἡλικίας ἔτος: Tischendorf B. So also the Syriac (see Wright, *Apocryphal Literature*, 10) See previous note and de Santos, *Evangelium*, 120 n. 1. They then pick up the narrative of Tischendorf A.   **13:1.** ἄροτρα καὶ ζυγούς: Tischendorf A and Greek C. σκεύη: Greek-Slav. Tischendorf B omits.   **13:1.** ἐπετάγη αὐτῷ κράββατος παρά τινος πλουσίου ὅπως ποιήσει αὐτῷ: Tischendorf A. λέγει αὐτῷ τις πλούσιος· κύρ᾽ Ἰωσήφ, ποίησόν μοι κλίνην ἔντιμον, καλήν: Greek C. ἐποίει σκεύη διά τινος πλουσίου: Greek-Slav. προσετάγη ὁ Ἰωσὴφ ὑπό τινος πλουσίου κράββατον οἰκοδομῆσαι αὐτῷ: Tischendorf B, after which it continues as follows: καὶ ἐξελθὼν ἐν τῷ ἀγρῷ πρὸς συλλογὴν ξύλων, συνῆλθεν αὐτῷ καὶ ὁ Ἰησοῦς. καὶ κόψας δύο ξύλα καὶ πελεκίσας τὸ ἐν ἔθηκεν πλησίον τοῦ ἄλλου, καὶ μετρήσας εὗρεν αὐτὸ κολοβώτερον, καὶ ἰδὼν ἐλυπήθη, καὶ ἐζήτει εὑρεῖν ἕτερον.   **13:2.** τοῦ δὲ ἑνὸς κανόνος τοῦ καλουμένου ἐναλλάκτου ὄντος κολοβωτέρου: Tischendorf A. καὶ εἷς κανών, ὁ καλούμενος ἐνάλλακτος, ἦν κολοβώτερος: Greek-Slav. Greek C omits. **13:2.** μὴ ἔχοντ⟨ο⟩s ⟨τοῦ Ἰωσήφ⟩ τ⟨ι⟩ ποιῆσαι: Tischendorf A, as emended by me (cf. Weissengruber, "Untersuchungen," 219). μὴ ἔχοντός τι αὐτοῦ τοῦ μετρῆσαι. ἦν δὲ ὁ Ἰωσὴφ ἐν μεγάλῃ θλίψει: Greek-Slav. ὁ δὲ Ἰωσὴφ ἦν ἐν θλίψει διὰ τὸ εἶναι τὸ ἐν ξύλον στρεβλόν: Greek C. erat autem Ioseph in tribulatione, quia lignum quod habebat actum ad hoc opus erat breve: Latin. See also de Santos, *Evangelium*, 122 n. 6.   **13:2.** θὲς κάτω τὰ δύο ξύλα: Tischendorf A. θὲς τὰ δύο ταῦτα: Tischendorf B. μὴ λυποῦ, ἀλλὰ μᾶλλον θὲς τὰ ξύλα: Greek C. μὴ λυποῦ, θὲς κάτω τὰ δύο ξύλα: Greek-Slav.   **13:3.** After τοῦ ἄλλου Tischendorf A omits a further exchange between Jesus and Joseph. καὶ εἶπεν τῷ Ἰωσήφ· μὴ λυποῦ, ποίει ὅ βούλει: Greek-Slav. καὶ λέγει τῷ Ἰωσήφ· ποίει ὅ βούλει: Greek C. καί φησι πρὸς τὸν Ἰωσὴφ μηκέτι λυποῦ, ἀλλὰ ποίει ἀκωλύτως τὸ ἔργον σου: Tischendorf B.   **13:4.** καὶ εἶδεν ὁ πατὴρ αὐτοῦ Ἰωσὴφ καὶ ἐθαύμασε: Tischendorf A. ὁ δὲ Ἰωσὴφ ἰδὼν ὅτι ἐποίησεν ὁ Ἰησοῦς σημεῖον: Greek C. καὶ ἰδὼν ἐκεῖνος ὑπερεθαύμασεν: Tischendorf B. Greek-Slav omits.   **13:4.** καὶ περιλαβὼν τὸ παιδίον κατεφίλει: Tischendorf A and Greek-Slav (adding Ἰωσὴφ after περιλαβὼν and αὐτὸ after κατεφίλει). περιπλακεὶς ἐφίλησε τὸν Ἰησοῦν: Greek C. Tischendorf B omits.   **13:4.** λέγων: Tischendorf A and Greek C. καὶ εἶπεν: Greek-

13 Now Jesus' father was a carpenter, making ploughs and yokes at that time. He received an order from a rich man to make a bed for him. ²When one board of what is called the crossbeam turned out shorter than the other, and Joseph didn't know what to do, the child Jesus said to his father Joseph, "Put the two boards down and line them up at one end."

Miraculous woodworking

³Joseph did as the child told him. Jesus stood at the other end and grabbed hold of the shorter board, and, by stretching it, made it the same length as the other.

⁴His father Joseph looked on and marveled, and he hugged and kissed the child, saying, "How fortunate I am that God has given this child to me."

• **13:1–4.** Jesus' miraculous help now extends to his father's workshop where he does carpentry work.

• **13:1.** *carpenter*: This tradition about Joseph's trade goes back to the Synoptics (Matt 13:55; Mark 6:3).

• **13:1.** *ploughs and yokes*: Joseph is portrayed here as a village carpenter, making implements for locals. Michaelis (*Apokryphen Schriften*, 111; cf. 105) adds that Joseph as a rule may have made only such tools and hence was not used to making fine furniture, as he is instructed to do in this story. In Tischendorf B, however, no such distinction is in view: "Joseph was ordered by a rich man to make him a bed. For he was a carpenter." In any case, contrast the portrait of Joseph in the Infancy Gospel of James, where he is involved in large-scale construction which causes him to travel to the building sites (9:12).

• **13:1.** *a bed*: Greek C not only has another, more literary, word for "bed" (κλίνη), but also describes it as "expensive and beautiful."

• **13:2.** *one board . . . shorter*: Tischendorf B expands the story at this point, giving it a different setting: "And so Joseph went out into the countryside to gather the wood, and Jesus tagged along. And he chopped down two trees, and after he had trimmed the one with his axe he set it alongside the other. But after measuring it, he found it to be shorter, and on realizing this he became upset and was seeking another tree."

• **13:2.** *crossbeam*: This rendering of ἐνάλλακτον, a rare word not found in LSJ, is tentative. It seems to be derived from ἐναλλάσσειν, which LSJ s.v. says can mean "to cross," citing Philostratus, *Imag.* 2.7. The word is not used in Tischendorf B nor in Greek C, and de Santos (*Evangelium*, 121 n. 4) says that the Slavonic translator had no idea what the word meant.

• **13:3.** *the same length as the other*: Again, Tischendorf A seems truncated, as Greek-Slav, Greek C, and Tischendorf B all continue as follows (rendering Tischendorf B): "And Jesus said to Joseph, 'Don't be upset any longer, but do your work unhindered.'"

• **13:4.** After the beatitude Tischendorf B continues as follows: "When they returned to the city, Joseph told Mary. When she had heard and seen the extraordinary miracles of her son, she rejoiced." (For Nazareth referred to as a city, see note to 4:1.) Incidentally, Tischendorf B ends here; for the concluding doxology, see note to 19:13.

New instructors **14** Ἰδὼν δὲ Ἰωσὴφ τὴν προθυμίαν τοῦ παιδίου καὶ τὴν ἡλικίαν καὶ τὸν νοῦν, ὅτι ἀκμάζει, πάλιν ἐβουλεύσατο μὴ εἶναι αὐτὸ ἄπειρον τῶν γραμμάτων, καὶ ἀπαγαγὼν αὐτὸ παρέδωκεν ἑτέρῳ διδασκάλῳ. ²εἶπε δὲ ὁ διδάσκαλος τῷ Ἰωσήφ· Πρῶτον παιδεύσω αὐτὸ τὰ ἑλληνικά, ἔπειτα τὰ ἑβραικά. ᾔδει γὰρ ὁ διδάσκαλος τὴν πεῖραν τοῦ παιδίου, καὶ ἐφοβήθη αὐτό· ὅμως γράψας τὸν ἀλφάβητον ἐπετήδευεν αὐτὸ ἐπὶ πολλὴν ὥραν, καὶ οὐκ ἀπεκρίνατο αὐτῷ.

³Εἶπε δὲ αὐτῷ ὁ Ἰησοῦς· Εἰ ὄντως διδάσκαλος εἶ, καὶ εἰ οἶδας καλῶς τὰ γράμματα, εἰπέ μοι τοῦ ἄλφα τὴν δύναμιν, κἀγώ σοι ἐρῶ τὴν τοῦ βῆτα.

⁴Πικρανθεὶς δὲ ὁ διδάσκαλος ἔκρουσεν αὐτὸν εἰς τὴν κεφαλήν. ὁ δὲ Ἰησοῦς ἀγανακτήσας κατηράσατο αὐτόν. καὶ εὐθέως ἐλιποθύμησε καὶ ἔπεσεν χαμαὶ ἐπὶ πρόσωπον.

⁵Ἀπεστράφη δὲ τὸ παιδίον εἰς τὸν οἶκον Ἰωσήφ. Ἰωσὴφ δὲ ἐλυπήθη, καὶ παρήγγειλε τῇ μητρὶ αὐτοῦ ὅπως ἔξω τῆς θύρας μὴ ἀπολύσεις αὐτόν, διότι ἀποθνήσκουσιν οἱ παροργίζοντες αὐτόν.

Slav. καὶ λέγει καθ᾿ ἑαυτόν: Tischendorf B.   **13:4.** After the beatitude Tischendorf B continues as follows: ἀπελθόντων δὲ ἐν τῇ πόλει διηγήσατο τῇ Μαριὰμ ὁ Ἰωσήφ. ἐκείνη δὲ ἀκούσασά τε καὶ βλέπουσα τὰ παράδοξα μεγαλεῖα τοῦ υἱοῦ αὐτῆς ἔχαιρεν. For the doxology which brings Tischendorf B to a close here, see below at note to 19:13.   **14:1.** τὴν προθυμίαν τοῦ παιδίου καὶ τὴν ἡλικίαν καὶ τὸν νοῦν: Greek-Slav. τὸν νοῦν τοῦ παιδίου καὶ τὴν ἡλικιότητα ὅτι ἀκμάζει: Tischendorf A. ὀξὺν νοῦν καὶ ἡλικίαν αὐξάνει: Greek C. See de Santos, *Evangelium*, 123 n. 1. **14:1.** πάλιν ἐβουλεύσατο μὴ εἶναι αὐτὸ ἄπειρον τῶν γραμμάτων: Tischendorf A and Greek-Slav (omitting πάλιν). ἠβουλήθη δοῦναι αὐτὸν ἵνα μάθῃ γράμματα: Greek C.   **14:2.** πρῶτον παιδεύσω αὐτὸ τὰ ἑλληνικά, ἔπειτα τὰ ἑβραικά: Tischendorf A. ποῖα γράμματα θέλεις ἵνα διδάξω αὐτὸν πρῶτον; λέγει αὐτῷ ὁ Ἰωσήφ· τὰ ἑλληνικά, εἶτα τὰ ἑβραικά: Greek C and Greek-Slav (adding πρῶτον before ἑλληνικά). quales litteras desideras illum puerum docere? respondit Ioseph et dixit Primum doce ei litteras gentilicas et postea hebraeas: Latin.   **14:2.** τὴν πεῖραν: Tischendorf A and Greek C (omitting τήν). τὸν νόμον: Greek-Slav.   **14:2.** ἐπετήδευεν αὐτὸ ἐπὶ πολλὴν ὥραν, καὶ οὐκ ἀπεκρίνατο αὐτῷ: Tischendorf A. ἐπεστοίχασεν αὐτὸν ἐπὶ πολλὰς ὥρας: Greek C. ἐπετήδευεν αὐτὸ λέγων· A. ὁ δὲ Ἰησοῦς ἀπεκρίθη Α, καὶ ἔπειτα ἐσίγησεν. ὁ καθηγητὴς εἶπε Β, ἀλλ᾿ ὁ Ἰησοῦς οὐκ ἀπεκρίνατο αὐτῷ: Greek C. **14:3.** εἶπε δὲ αὐτῷ ὁ Ἰησοῦς: Tischendorf A. ὁ δὲ Ἰησοῦς ἀποκριθεὶς εἶπε πρὸς τὸν καθηγητήν: Greek C. εἶτα εἶπε Ἰησοῦς πρὸς τὸν καθηγητήν: Greek-Slav.   **14:4.** αὐτόν: Greek C and Greek-Slav. αὐτοῦ: Tischendorf A.   **14:4.** ὁ δὲ Ἰησοῦς ἀγανακτήσας: Greek C. τὸ δὲ παιδίον ἀγανακτήσαν: Greek-Slav. τὸ δὲ παιδίον πονέσας: Tischendorf A. See de Santos, *Evangelium*, 126 n. 14.   **14:4.** ἐπὶ πρόσωπον: Tischendorf A. Greek C and Greek-Slav omit.   **14:5.** ἀπεστράφη δὲ τὸ παιδίον: Tischendorf A. ὁ δὲ Ἰησοῦς ἀπῆλθεν: Greek C and Greek-Slav (omitting δέ).   **14:5.** Ἰωσὴφ δὲ ἐλυπήθη: Tischendorf A and Greek-Slav. Greek C omits.   **14:5.** διότι ἀποθνήσκουσιν οἱ παροργίζοντες αὐτόν: Tischendorf A. ἵνα μὴ καταρᾶται τοῖς ἀνθρώποις: Greek C. ἵνα μὴ οὕτως πάσχωσιν οἱ παροργίζοντες αὐτόν: Greek-Slav.

14 When Joseph saw the child's aptitude, and his great *New instructors*
intelligence for his age, he again resolved that Jesus should not
remain illiterate. So he took him and handed him over to
another teacher. ²The teacher said to Joseph, "First I'll teach
him Greek, then Hebrew." This teacher, of course, knew of the
child's previous experience ⟨with a teacher⟩ and was afraid of
him. Still, he wrote out the alphabet and instructed him for
quite a while, though Jesus was unresponsive.

³Then Jesus spoke: "If you're really a teacher, and if you
know the letters well, tell me the meaning of the letter alpha,
and I'll tell you the meaning of beta."

⁴The teacher became exasperated and hit him on the head.
Jesus got angry and cursed him, and the teacher immediately
lost consciousness and fell facedown on the ground.

⁵The child returned to Joseph's house. But Joseph was upset
and gave this instruction to his mother: "Don't let him go
outside, because those who annoy him end up dead."

- **14:1–5.** A second attempt to teach Jesus his letters again ends in failure. Joseph is upset, Jesus is to be kept at home, and the teacher is left cursed and lying on the ground. His fate, though, is reversed later (see 15:7).
- **14:2.** *First I'll teach him Greek, then Hebrew*: In Greek C and Greek-Slav the teacher's statement becomes a question and prompts more of a conversation: "'What letters do you want me to teach him first?' Joseph said to him, 'The Greek, then the Hebrew.'" In any case, Quintilian (1.1.12) recommends that Roman boys learn Greek first.
- **14:3.** *tell me the meaning of the letter alpha*: A doublet of the story of Zacchaeus (see 6:20).
- **14:4.** *hit him on the head*: Such punishment was not unusual in classrooms. Note espe-

cially one maxim learned by schoolboys: "No one learns his letters without blows" (Jaekel, *Sententiae*, 19). See also Herodas, 3.58–93; Lucian, *The Dream* 2; Alciphron, *ep.* 3.7.3–5; Bonner, *Education*, 38–46; and Cribiore, *Writing*, 167–69.
- **14:4.** *Jesus got angry*: So Greek C and similarly Greek-Slav and the Latin. Tischendorf A reads: "In pain the child. . . ." See further de Santos, *Evangelium*, 126 n. 14.
- **14:5.** *because those who annoy him end up dead*: The wording of this clause varies considerably, though not finally its import. In Greek C it reads: ". . . in order that those who annoy him not suffer so." In Greek-Slav it says: ". . . in order that he not curse people."

15 Μετὰ δὲ χρόνον τινὰ ἕτερος πάλιν καθηγητής, γνήσιος φίλος ὢν τοῦ Ἰωσήφ, εἶπεν αὐτῷ· Ἀγαγέ μοι τὸ παιδίον εἰς τὸ παιδευτήριον· ἴσως ἂν δυνηθῶ ἐγὼ μετὰ κολακείας διδάξαι αὐτὸ τὰ γράμματα.

²Καὶ εἶπεν Ἰωσήφ· Εἰ θαρρεῖς, ἀδελφέ, ἔπαρον αὐτὸ μετὰ σεαυτοῦ. καὶ λαβὼν αὐτὸ μετ᾽ αὐτοῦ μετὰ φόβου καὶ ἀγῶνος πολλοῦ, τὸ δὲ παιδίον ἡδέως ἐπορεύετο.

³Καὶ εἰσελθὼν θρασὺς εἰς τὸ διδασκαλεῖον εὗρε βιβλίον κείμενον ἐν τῷ ἀναλογίῳ, καὶ λαβὼν αὐτὸ οὐκ ἀνεγίνωσκε τὰ γράμματα τὰ ἐν αὐτῷ, ἀλλὰ ἀνοίξας τὸ στόμα αὐτοῦ ἐλάλει πνεύματι ἁγίῳ, καὶ ἐδίδασκε τὸν νόμον τοὺς περιεστῶτας.

⁴Ὄχλος δὲ πολὺς συνελθόντες παριστήκεισαν ἀκούοντες αὐτοῦ, καὶ ἐθαύμαζον ἐν τῇ ὡραιότητι τῆς διδασκαλίας αὐτοῦ καὶ τῇ ἑτοιμασίᾳ τῶν λόγων αὐτοῦ, ὅτι νήπιον ὢν τοιαῦτα φθέγγεται.

⁵Ἀκούσας δὲ Ἰωσὴφ ἐφοβήθη, καὶ ἔδραμεν εἰς τὸ διδασκαλεῖον λογισάμενος μὴ οὗτος ὁ καθηγητής ἐστιν ἄπειρος.

⁶Εἶπε δὲ ὁ καθηγητὴς τῷ Ἰωσήφ· Ἵνα εἰδῇς, ἀδελφέ, ὅτι ἐγὼ μὲν παρέλαβον τὸ παιδίον ὡς μαθητήν, αὐτὸ δὲ πολλῆς χάριτος

15:1. μετὰ δὲ χρόνον τινά: Tischendorf A. μεθ᾽ ἡμέρας δέ τινας: Greek C. μετὰ δὲ ἔτος ἕν: Greek-Slav.   15:1. γνήσιος φίλος: Tischendorf A. φίλος: Greek C. γείτων: Greek-Slav.   15:1. μετὰ κολακείας: Tischendorf A. μετὰ πολλῆς παρακλήσεως: Greek C. παρακαλῶν καὶ κολακεύων: Greek-Slav. cum multa suavitate: Latin.   15:2. ἔπαρον αὐτὸ μετὰ σεαυτοῦ: Tischendorf A. παράλαβε αὐτὸν καὶ δίδαξον: Greek C. παράλαβε αὐτὸν μετὰ προσοχῆς καὶ φόβου καὶ ἀγῶνος: Greek-Slav. 15:2. καὶ λαβὼν αὐτὸ μετ᾽ αὐτοῦ μετὰ φόβου καὶ ἀγῶνος πολλοῦ, τὸ δὲ παιδίον ἡδέως ἐπορεύετο: Tischendorf A. Greek C and Greek-Slav omit, though in the latter the reference to φόβος and ἀγών is already incorporated into the previous sentence (see preceding note).   15:3. θρασύς: Tischendorf A and Greek-Slav. Certain adjectives can be used as adverbs, but such a use of θρασύς is not otherwise attested (see Weissengruber, "Untersuchungen," 221). μετὰ πολλῆς χαρᾶς: Greek C.   15:3. λαβών: Tischendorf A. ἀνοίξας: Greek C and Greek-Slav.   15:3. τὸν νόμον τοὺς περιεστῶτας: Tischendorf A. τὸν νόμον αὐτοῦ τοὺς παρόντας καὶ ἀκούοντας: Greek C, which departs from Tischendorf and continues as follows: ὥστε καὶ ὁ καθηγητὴς πλησίον αὐτοῦ καθίσας πάνυ ἡδέως αὐτοῦ ἤκουσεν, παρακαλῶν αὐτὸν ἵνα πλείονα εἴπῃ. et magister ille iuxta illum sedebat et libenter eum audiebat, et deprecabatur eum ut amplius doceret: Latin. τὸν νόμον: Greek-Slav, which, similarly to Greek C, continues as follows: καὶ οἱ παρόντες ἤκουον αὐτοῦ καὶ παρεκάλουν αὐτὸ ἵνα πλείονα εἴπῃ.   15:5. ἐφοβήθη: Tischendorf A and Greek-Slav. timuit: Latin. Greek C omits.   15:5. λογισάμενος μὴ οὗτος ὁ καθηγητής ἐστιν ἄπειρος: Tischendorf A and Greek-Slav (substituting πειράζεται for ἐστιν ἄπειρος). There is a lacuna in the Latin. Greek C omits. Weissengruber ("Untersuchungen," 217) says that the indicative (ἐστιν) can be used in expressions of concern, if the concern is directed to something already happening.

15 After some time another teacher, a close friend of Joseph, said to him, "Send the child to my schoolroom. Perhaps with some flattery I can teach him his letters."

²Joseph replied, "If you can muster the courage, brother, take him with you." And so he took him along with much fear and trepidation, but the child was happy to go.

³Jesus strode boldly into the schoolroom and found a book lying on the desk. He took the book but did not read the letters in it. Rather, he opened his mouth and spoke by ⟨the power of⟩ the holy spirit and taught the law to those standing there.

⁴A large crowd gathered and stood listening to him, and they marveled at the maturity of his teaching and his readiness of speech—a mere child able to say such things.

⁵ When Joseph heard about this he feared the worst and ran to the schoolroom, imagining that this teacher was having trouble with Jesus.

⁶But the teacher said to Joseph, "Brother, please know that I

• **15:1–7.** Yet a third teacher attempts to teach Jesus his letters (see chaps 6–8, 14). This time, however, the teacher defers to Jesus' superiority and all ends well.

• **15:1.** *After some time*: Greek-Slav is much more definite about the time, saying "after one year," which would make Jesus nine years old at the time of this story (see also note to 18:1).

• **15:3.** *boldly*: Greek C has "with much joy."

• **15:3.** *found a book lying on the desk*: The circumstances recall those in Luke 4:16–17, though perhaps not as directly as Michaelis (*Apokryphen Schriften*, 111) thinks.

• **15:3.** *taught the law to those standing there*: Greek C is rather different at this point and also expanded: "Taught his own law to those who were standing by and listening. Consequently, the teacher who sat beside him listened to him with much pleasure and urged him on to say more."

• **15:5.** *having trouble*: So Tischendorf A, but Tischendorf himself (*Evangelia Apocrypha*, 146) suggests an emendation, namely, ἀνάπηρος ("maimed"), citing the use of this word at 8:4 and an even more dire outcome in a similarly worded sentence in Pseudo-Matthew, chap 39: "When Joseph heard this he went running to Jesus out of fear that the teacher himself had died." The emendation is ingenious and sometimes accepted (see, e.g., Michaelis, *Apokryphen Schriften*, 107 and 111), but subsequent texts and the versions have not confirmed it. Greek C omits the entire clause, as does the Syriac (Wright, *Apocryphal Literature*, 10); the Latin has a lacuna here (Tischendorf, *Evangelia Apocrypha*, 168); and Greek-Slav does not confirm the emendation either (see de Santos, *Evangelium*, 130 n. 18).

καὶ σοφίας μεστόν ἐστιν· καὶ λοιπὸν ἀξιῶ σε, ἀδελφέ, ἆρον αὐτὸ εἰς τὸν οἶκόν σου.

⁷Ὡς δὲ ἤκουσεν τὸ παιδίον ταῦτα, εὐθέως προσεγέλασεν αὐτῷ καὶ εἶπεν, Ἐπειδὴ ὀρθῶς ἐλάλησας καὶ ὀρθῶς ἐμαρτύρησας, διὰ σὲ κἀκεῖνος ὁ πληγωθεὶς ἰαθήσεται. καὶ παραυτὰ ἰάθη ὁ ἕτερος καθηγητής. παρέλαβε δὲ Ἰωσὴφ τὸ παιδίον καὶ ἀπῆλθεν εἰς τὸν οἶκον αὐτοῦ.

Jesus and the viper

16 Ἔπεμψε δὲ Ἰωσὴφ τὸν υἱὸν αὐτοῦ τὸν Ἰάκωβον τοῦ δῆσαι ξύλα καὶ φέρειν εἰς τὸν οἶκον αὐτοῦ· ἠκολούθει δὲ καὶ τὸ παιδίον Ἰησοῦς αὐτῷ. καὶ συλλέγοντος τοῦ Ἰακώβου τὰ φρύγανα, ἔχιδνα ἔδακε τὴν χεῖραν Ἰακώβου. ²καὶ κατατεινομένου αὐτοῦ καὶ ἀπολλυμένου προσήγγισεν ὁ Ἰησοῦς καὶ κατεφύσησε τὸ δῆγμα· καὶ εὐθέως ἐπαύσατο ὁ πόνος, καὶ τὸ θηρίον ἐρράγη, καὶ παραυτὰ ἔμεινεν ὁ Ἰάκωβος ὑγιής.

Raising a dead infant

17 Μετὰ δὲ ταῦτα ἐν τῇ γειτονίᾳ τοῦ Ἰωσὴφ νοσῶν τι νήπιον ἀπέθανεν, καὶ ἔκλαιεν ἡ μήτηρ αὐτοῦ σφόδρα. ἤκουσε δὲ ὁ Ἰησοῦς ὅτι πένθος μέγα καὶ θόρυβος γίνεται, καὶ ἔδραμε σπουδαίως·

15:6. καὶ λοιπὸν ἀξιῶ σε, ἀδελφέ, ἆρον αὐτὸ εἰς τὸν οἶκόν σου: Tischendorf A and Greek-Slav. λαβὲ αὐτὸν εἰς τὸν οἶκόν σου μετὰ χαρᾶς· τὸ γὰρ χάρισμα ὃ ἔχει ἀπὸ θεοῦ ἐστιν: Greek C.   15:7. τὸ παιδίον ταῦτα: Tischendorf A. ὁ Ἰησοῦς τοῦ καθηγητοῦ τούτους λόγους ⟨λέγ⟩οντος: Greek C (as corrected by Delatte). τὸ παιδίον τοῦ καθηγητοῦ ταῦτα λέγοντος τῷ πατρὶ αὐτοῦ: Greek-Slav.   15:7. ἐπειδὴ ὀρθῶς ἐλάλησας καὶ ὀρθῶς ἐμαρτύρησας: Tischendorf A. ἐπειδὴ ἀληθῶς ἐμαρτύρησας: Greek C and Greek-Slav.   15:7. παρέλαβε δὲ Ἰωσὴφ τὸ παιδίον καὶ ἀπῆλθεν εἰς τὸν οἶκον αὐτοῦ: Tischendorf A and Greek C (substituting ἤγαγεν for ἀπῆλθεν). Greek-Slav omits.   16:1. τὸν υἱὸν αὐτοῦ: Tischendorf A and Greek-Slav. Greek C omits.   16:1. τοῦ δῆσαι ξύλα: Tischendorf A. τοῦ δῆσαι φρύγανα: Greek-Slav. συλλέξαι φρύγανα τοῦ φούρνου: Greek C. ad colligendam stipulam: Latin.   16:1. καὶ φέρειν εἰς τὸν οἶκον αὐτοῦ: Tischendorf A and Greek-Slav. Greek C omits.   16:1. καὶ συλλέγοντος τοῦ Ἰακώβου τὰ φρύγανα: Tischendorf A. καὶ συλλεγόντων τὰ φρύγανα: Greek C. ἀπελθόντος δὲ αὐτοῦ καὶ συλλέγοντος τὰ φρύγανα: Greek-Slav.   16:1. τὴν χεῖραν Ἰακώβου: Tischendorf A. εἰς τὴν χεῖραν: Greek-Slav. eum: Latin. Greek C omits.   16:2. καὶ κατατεινομένου αὐτοῦ: Tischendorf A. καὶ ξηραινομένου αὐτοῦ: Greek-Slav. καὶ πεσὼν εἰς τὴν γῆν: Greek C.   16:2. καὶ ἀπολλυμένου: Tischendorf A. καὶ μέλλοντος τελευτᾶν: Greek-Slav. ἔμελλε τελευτᾶν ἐκ τοῦ πόνου τοῦ φαρμάκου: Greek C.   16:2. προσήγγισεν ὁ Ἰησοῦς καὶ κατεφύσησε τὸ δῆγμα: Tischendorf A and Greek-Slav. ὁ δὲ εὐθέως ἐμφυσήσας: Greek C.   16:2. καὶ εὐθέως ἐπαύσατο ὁ πόνος: Tischendorf A. καὶ τὸ φάρμακον ἐχαννώθη: Greek-Slav. Greek C omits.   16:2. καὶ παραυτὰ ἔμεινεν ὁ Ἰάκωβος ὑγιής: Tischendorf A. ἰάθη Ἰάκωβος: Greek C. Greek-Slav omits.   17:1. ἤκουσε δὲ ὁ Ἰησοῦς ὅτι πένθος μέγα καὶ θόρυβος γίνεται: Tischendorf A and Greek-Slav (having ἀκούσας instead of ἤκουσε). ἀκούσας δὲ ὁ Ἰησοῦς: Greek C.   17:1. καὶ ἔδραμε σπουδαίως: Tischendorf A and Greek-Slav (omitting καί). ἦλθε: Greek C.

accepted this child as a student, but already he's full of grace and wisdom. So I'm asking you, brother, to take him back home."

⁷When the child heard this, he immediately smiled at him and said, "Because you have spoken and testified rightly, that other teacher who was struck down will be healed." And right away he was. Joseph took his child and went home.

16 Joseph sent his son James to tie up some wood and carry it back to the house, and the child Jesus followed. While James was gathering the firewood, a viper bit his hand. ²And as he lay sprawled out on the ground, dying, Jesus came and blew on the bite. Immediately the pain stopped, the animal burst apart, and James got better on the spot.

Jesus and the viper

17 After this incident an infant in Joseph's neighborhood became sick and died, and his mother grieved terribly. Jesus heard the loud wailing and the uproar that was going on and quickly ran there.

Raising a dead infant

- **15:6.** *take him back home:* Greek C expands as follows: "Take him home with joy, for the grace which he has is from God."
- **15:7.** *that teacher who was struck down* is the teacher who had hit Jesus on the head and then fainted and fell to the ground after Jesus cursed him (see 14:4).
- **16:1–2.** Jesus saves his brother James from a deadly viper bite. The story has no parallels, although in Acts 28:2–6 a rather similar story is told of Paul who likewise is bitten on the hand by a viper.
- **16:1.** *his son James:* James is listed among the brothers of Jesus in Matt 13:55; Mark 6:3 and identified as "the Lord's brother" by Paul (Gal 1:19). James eventually became, to use Paul's language, a "pillar" of the church in Jerusalem (Gal 2:9, 12; cf.

Acts 12:17; 15:13; 21:18).
- **16:1.** *While James was gathering the firewood:* Jesus is depicted here as merely tagging along while his brother gathers wood, but in Greek C both are engaged in this task.
- **17:1–18:3.** Two more stories of Jesus raising the dead (see chaps 9 and 16), which complement one another since the first involves an infant (17:1–4), the second a grown man (18:1–3) (Michaelis, *Apokryphen Schriften,* 111). The first story recalls the synoptic account of the raising of Jairus' daughter (Matt 9:18–19, 23–26; Mark 5:22–24, 35–43; Luke 8:41–42, 49–56) as well as the Lukan story of the raising of the widow's son at Nain (Luke 7:11–17).

²Καὶ εὑρὼν τὸ παιδίον νεκρόν, καὶ ἥψατο τοῦ στήθους αὐτοῦ καὶ εἶπεν· Σοὶ λέγω, βρέφος, μὴ ἀποθάνῃς ἀλλὰ ζῆσον, καὶ ἔστω μετὰ τῆς μητρός σου.

³Καὶ εὐθὺς ἀναβλέψας ἐγέλασεν. εἶπε δὲ τῇ γυναικί· ᾶΑρον τὸ παιδίον σου καὶ δὸς αὐτῷ μασθὸν καὶ μνημόνευέ μου.

⁴Καὶ ἰδὼν ὁ παρεστὼς ὄχλος ἐθαύμασεν, καὶ εἶπον· Ἀληθῶς τὸ παιδίον τοῦτο ἢ θεὸς ἦν ἢ ἄγγελος θεοῦ, ὅτι πᾶς λόγος αὐτοῦ ἔργον ἐστὶν ἕτοιμον. καὶ ἐξῆλθεν ὁ Ἰησοῦς ἐκεῖθεν παίζων μετὰ καὶ ἑτέρων παιδίων.

Raising a dead laborer

18 Μετὰ δὲ ἕτερον ἔτος οἰκοδομῆς γενομένης ἄνθρωπός τις πεσὼν ἀπὸ τοῦ ὕψους ἀπέθανε. καὶ θορύβου μεγάλου, ἵστατο ὁ Ἰησοῦς καὶ ἀπῆλθεν ἕως ἐκεῖ. ²καὶ ἰδὼν ἄνθρωπον νεκρὸν κείμενον ἐπελάβετο τῆς χειρὸς αὐτοῦ καὶ εἶπεν· Σοὶ λέγω, ἄνθρωπε, ἀνάστα, ποίει τὸ ἔργον σου. καὶ εὐθέως ἀναστὰς προσεκύνησεν αὐτόν.

³Ἰδὼν δὲ ὁ ὄχλος ἐθαύμασεν καὶ εἶπεν· Τοῦτο τὸ παιδίον οὐράνιόν ἐστιν· πολλὰς γὰρ ψυχὰς ἔσωσεν ἐκ θανάτου, καὶ ἔχει σῶσαι ἕως πάσης τῆς ζωῆς αὐτοῦ.

17:2. καὶ εὑρὼν τὸ παιδίον νεκρόν: Tischendorf A. καὶ εὗρε τὸ παιδίον νεκρὸν ἐπὶ τῷ κόλπῳ τῆς μητρὸς αὐτοῦ: Greek-Slav. καὶ στὰς ἐπάνω τοῦ παιδίου: Greek C.   **17:3.** καὶ εὐθὺς ἀναβλέψας ἐγέλασεν: Tischendorf A. καὶ εὐθέως ἀνέβλεψε τὸ παιδίον: Greek C. καὶ τότε ἐγέλασε τὸ παιδίον καὶ προσεκλίθη αὐτῷ: Greek-Slav.   **17:3.** ᾶΑρον τὸ παιδίον σου καὶ δὸς αὐτῷ μασθόν: Greek C and Greek-Slav (omitting σου). ᾶΑρον αὐτὸ καὶ δὸς γάλα: Greek A. See Gero, "Thomas," 66.   **17:4.** ἔργον ἐστὶν ἕτοιμον: Tischendorf A. ἔργον γίνεται: Greek C and Greek-Slav.   **17:4.** καὶ ἐξῆλθεν ὁ Ἰησοῦς ἐκεῖθεν παίζων μετὰ καὶ ἑτέρων παιδίων: Tischendorf A. καὶ ὁ Ἰησοῦς ἦλθεν εἰς τὸν οἶκον αὐτοῦ: Greek-Slav. Greek C omits.   **18:1.** μετὰ δὲ ἕτερον ἔτος: Greek-Slav. μετὰ δὲ χρόνον τινά: Tischendorf A. Ἄλλοτε πάλιν: Greek C. See de Santos, *Evangelium*, 135 nn. 1–5.   **18:1.** οἰκοδομῆς γενομένης ἄνθρωπός τις πεσὼν ἀπὸ τοῦ ὕψους ἀπέθανε: Greek-Slav. οἰκοδόμος τις πεσὼν ἀπὸ τοῦ τείχους ἀπέθανεν: Greek C. οἰκοδομῆς γενομένης: Tischendorf A. On the suspected lacuna in Tischendorf A, see de Santos, *Evangelium*, 135 n. 2.   **18:1.** καὶ θορύβου μεγάλου, ἵστατο ὁ Ἰησοῦς καὶ ἀπῆλθεν ἕως ἐκεῖ: Tischendorf A. συνδρομῆς δὲ γενομένης καὶ θορύβου μεγάλου: Greek-Slav. Greek C omits.   **18:2.** καὶ ἰδὼν ἄνθρωπον νεκρὸν κείμενον: Tischendorf A. ἤκουσεν ὁ Ἰησοῦς καὶ ἐλθὼν εἶδε τὸν ἄνθρωπον νεκρὸν κείμενον: Greek-Slav. ἐλθὼν δὲ ὁ Ἰησοῦς: Greek C.   **18:2.** ἐπελάβετο τῆς χειρὸς αὐτοῦ καὶ εἶπεν: Tischendorf A and Greek-Slav. λέγει τῷ τεθνηκότι: Greek C.   **18:3.** ἐθαύμασεν: Tischendorf A and Greek-Slav. Greek C omits.

²When he found the child dead, he touched its chest and said, "I say to you, infant, don't die but live, and be with your mother."

³And immediately the infant looked up and laughed. Jesus then said to the woman, "Take it, give it your breast, and remember me."

⁴The crowd of onlookers marveled at this: "Truly this child was a god or a heavenly messenger of God—whatever he says instantly happens." But Jesus left and went on playing with the other children.

18 A year later, while a building was under construction, a man fell from the top of it and died. There was quite a commotion, so Jesus got up and went there. ²When he saw the man lying dead, he took his hand and said, "I say to you, sir, get up and go back to work." And he immediately got up and worshiped him.

Raising a dead laborer

³The crowd saw this and marveled: "This child's from heaven—he must be, because he has saved many souls from death, and he can go on saving all his life."

• **17:2.** *found the child dead*: Greek-Slav expands slightly but with needed clarification for what follows, saying: "found the child dead on the bosom of its mother."

• **17:3.** *Take it, give it your breast, and remember me*: This tripart form of Jesus' command is found in Greek C and Greek-Slav (only the first two parts are in Tischendorf A), which Gero ("Thomas," 66) regards as original. The detail about the baby being given milk recalls Jesus' similar command to give Jairus' newly revived daughter something to eat (Mark 5:43; Luke 8:55).

• **18:1–3.** A single episode about Jesus at age nine in which he yet again raises someone from the dead (see chaps 9, 16, 17), this time a construction worker.

• **18:1.** *A year later*: So Greek-Slav; Tischendorf A and Greek C are much vaguer.

• **18:1.** *while a building was under construction, a man fell from the top of it and died*: This setting for the story, which is the reading of Greek-Slav (cf. also Greek C), is much more vivid than Tischendorf A, where something like this sentence may in fact have dropped out (see de Santos, *Evangelium*, 135 n. 2).

• **18:1.** *from the top of it*: Greek C is specific—"from the wall."

• **18:2.** The words *I say to you, sir, get up* are very close to those found in Mark 5:41; Luke 7:14.

19 ¹Ὄντος δὲ αὐτοῦ δωδεκαετοῦς ἐπορεύοντο οἱ γονεῖς αὐτοῦ κατὰ τὸ ἔθος εἰς Ἱερουσαλὴμ εἰς τὴν ἑορτὴν τοῦ πάσχα μετὰ τῆς συνοδίας αὐτῶν, ²καὶ μετὰ τὸ πάσχα ὑπέστρεφον εἰς τὸν οἶκον αὐτῶν. καὶ ἐν τῷ ὑποστρέφειν αὐτοὺς ἀνῆλθε τὸ παιδίον Ἰησοῦς εἰς Ἱεροσόλυμα· οἱ δὲ γονεῖς αὐτοῦ ἐνόμισαν αὐτὸν ἐν τῇ συνοδίᾳ εἶναι. ³ὁδευσάντων δὲ ὁδὸν ἡμέρας μιᾶς, ἐζήτουν αὐτὸν ἐν τοῖς συγγενέσιν αὐτῶν, καὶ μὴ εὑρόντες αὐτὸν ἐλυπήθησαν, καὶ ὑπέστρεψαν πάλιν εἰς τὴν πόλιν ζητοῦντες αὐτόν.

⁴Καὶ μετὰ τρίτην ἡμέραν εὗρον αὐτὸν ἐν τῷ ἱερῷ καθεζόμενον ἐν μέσῳ τῶν διδασκάλων καὶ ἀκούοντα τοῦ νόμου καὶ ἐρωτῶντα αὐτούς. ⁵προσεῖχον δὲ πάντες καὶ ἐθαύμαζον, πῶς παιδίον ὑπάρχων ἀποστοματίζει τοὺς πρεσβυτέρους καὶ διδασκάλους τοῦ λαοῦ, ἐπιλύων τὰ κεφάλαια τοῦ νόμου καὶ τὰς παραβολὰς τῶν προφητῶν.

19:1–12. The concluding story of Jesus' visit to Jerusalem and its Temple at age twelve is based on the account in Luke 2:41–52. Where applicable the canonical text will be provided for comparison. **19:1.** εἰς τὴν ἑορτὴν τοῦ πάσχα: Tischendorf A and Greek-Slav. τῇ ἡμέρᾳ τοῦ πάσχα: Greek C. Cf. Luke 2:41: τῇ ἑορτῇ τοῦ πάσχα. **19:1.** μετὰ τῆς συνοδίας αὐτῶν: Tischendorf A and Greek-Slav. μετὰ τοῦ ὄχλου: Greek C. **19:2.** καὶ μετὰ τὸ πάσχα: Tischendorf A. καὶ κοινωνήσαντες τοῦ πάσχα: Greek-Slav. καὶ ἐκοινώνουν τὸ πάσχα: Greek C. **19:2.** ὑπέστρεφον εἰς τὸν οἶκον αὐτῶν: Tischendorf A. ὑπέστρεψαν Ἰωσὴφ καὶ Μαριὰμ εἰς τὸν οἶκον αὐτῶν: Greek-Slav. ὑποστρέψαντες δὲ ἐν τῇ πόλει αὐτῶν Ναζαρέτ: Greek C. **19:2.** καὶ ἐν τῷ ὑποστρέφειν αὐτούς: Tischendorf A. Greek-Slav and Greek C omit. Cf. Luke 2:43: ἐν τῷ ὑποστρέφειν αὐτούς. **19:2.** ἐνόμισαν αὐτὸν ἐν τῇ συνοδίᾳ εἶναι: Tischendorf A. οὐκ ἔγνωσαν νομίσαντες αὐτὸν εἶναι ἐν τῇ συνοδίᾳ: Greek-Slav. ἐνόμισαν δὲ σὺν τῷ ὄχλῳ καὶ εἰς τὴν συνοδίαν αὐτὸν εἶναι: Greek C. Cf. Luke 2:43–44: καὶ οὐκ ἔγνωσαν ... νομίσαντες δὲ αὐτὸν εἶναι ἐν τῇ συνοδίᾳ. **19:3.** ἐζήτουν αὐτὸν ἐν τοῖς συγγενέσιν αὐτῶν: Tischendorf A. ἐζήτουν αὐτὸν ἐν τῇ συγγενείᾳ ἐν τῇ συνοδίᾳ: Greek-Slav. τῇ ἑσπέρᾳ ἐζήτουν τὸν Ἰησοῦν ἐν τῷ ὄχλῳ καὶ ἐν τοῖς γνωστοῖς αὐτῶν: Greek C. Cf. Luke 2:45: ἀνεζήτουν αὐτὸν ἐν τοῖς συγγενεῦσιν καὶ τοῖς γνωστοῖς. **19:3.** πάλιν εἰς τὴν πόλιν ζητοῦντες αὐτόν: Tischendorf A. πάλιν εἰς Ἱερουσαλὴμ ζητοῦντες αὐτόν: Greek-Slav. ἐν Ἱερουσαλήμ: Greek C. **19:4.** ἐν τῷ ἱερῷ καθεζόμενον ἐν μέσῳ τῶν διδασκάλων: Tischendorf A and Greek-Slav. ἐν Ἱερουσαλὴμ καθεζόμενον: Greek C. Cf. Luke 2:46: ἐν τῷ ἱερῷ καθεζόμενον ἐν μέσῳ τῶν διδασκάλων. **19:4.** καὶ ἀκούοντα τοῦ νόμου καὶ ἐρωτῶντα αὐτούς: Tischendorf A and Greek-Slav (substituting ἐπερωτῶντα for ἐρωτῶντα). καὶ διδάσκοντα τοὺς ὄχλους: Greek C. Cf. Luke 2:46: ἀκούοντα αὐτῶν καὶ ἐπερωτῶντα αὐτούς. **19:5.** προσεῖχον δὲ πάντες: Tischendorf A. προσεῖχον δὲ πάντες τοῖς λόγοις αὐτοῦ: Greek-Slav. ἡδέως αὐτοῦ γὰρ πάντες ἤκουον οἵ τε γραμματεῖς καὶ οἱ νομοδιδάσκαλοι: Greek C. **19:5.** πῶς: Tischendorf A. ὅτι: Greek-Slav. ὅτι πῶς: Greek C. **19:5.** ἀποστοματίζει: Greek-Slav. ἀπεστόμιζεν: Greek C. ἀποστομίζει: Tischendorf A. See de Santos, *Evangelium*, 138 n. 19. **19:5.** τοὺς πρεσβυτέρους καὶ διδασκάλους τοῦ λαοῦ: Tischendorf A and Greek-Slav (putting τοῦ λαοῦ, however, after πρεσβυτέρους). πάντας τούς τε πρεσβυτέρους καὶ νομοδιδασκάλους τῶν Ἰουδαίων: Greek C. **19:5.** ἐπιλύων: Tischendorf A and Greek-Slav. ἑρμηνεύων: Greek C. **19:5.** τὰ κεφάλαια τοῦ νόμου: Tischendorf A and Greek-Slav. τὸν νόμον: Greek C. **19:5.** παραβολάς: Tischendorf A and Greek-Slav. φωνάς: Greek C.

19 When he was twelve years old his parents went to Jerusalem, as usual, for the Passover festival, along with their fellow travelers. ²After Passover they began the journey home. But while on their way, the child Jesus went back up to Jerusalem. His parents, of course, assumed that he was in the traveling party. ³After they had traveled one day, they began to look for him among their relatives. When they did not find him, they were worried and returned again to the city to search for him.

⁴After three days they found him in the temple area, sitting among the teachers, listening to the law and asking them questions. ⁵All eyes were on him, and everyone was astounded that he, a mere child, could interrogate the elders and teachers of the people and explain the main points of the law and the parables of the prophets.

Jesus in the temple

• **19:1–12.** The only story of Jesus at age twelve concludes this gospel; it is familiar from the story of Jesus remaining in the temple at Jerusalem after his parents have left for home (Luke 2:42–51). The narration here follows the Lukan account rather closely, although a few departures are apparent and will be noted.

• **19:1.** *twelve years old*: Twelve years of age meant one thing for a girl, another for a boy. The former was considered old enough for marriage and adulthood, but the latter was still regarded as a boy for two or more years. Consequently, Jesus at twelve and engaging the teachers in the temple (see vv. 4–5) further underscores how extraordinarily wise he was for his age, as is made explicit below (see v. 5: "a mere child"). For detailed presentation of this view, see de Jonge, "Sonship," 317–24.

• **19:1.** *Passover* is a Jewish festival that celebrated Israel's liberation from Egyptian rule (Exod 12:1–27). It is one of the festivals when Jews were obligated to "appear before the Lord," i.e., at the Temple in Jerusalem (Deut 16:16). Hence the need for Joseph and Mary to make the pilgrimage to Jerusalem for this feast and hence the likelihood of going with fellow

travelers. For an example of such pilgrims from Galilee traveling to Jerusalem, see John 4:45.

• **19:4.** *After three days*: de Jonge ("Sonship," 324–27) argues that "three" tends to be idiomatic for "several."

• **19:5.** This verse represents a considerable expansion of its Lukan counterpart (see Luke 2:47). In particular the paradox of a child teaching his elders is made explicit: ". . . he, a mere child, could interrogate the elders . . .," as is the sort of intelligent answers he gave: ". . . he explained the main points of the law and the parables of the prophets."

• **19:5.** *All eyes were on him*: Greek C expands considerably, adding vividness: "All the scholars and teachers of the law were listening to him gladly," an expansion that recalls Mark 6:20: ". . . listened to him gladly."

• **19:5.** *interrogate*: Reading ἀποστοματίζει (Greek-Slav and Greek C) rather than ἀποστομίζει (Tischendorf A), usually rendered "put to silence."

• **19:5.** *parables of the prophets*: The word "parable" is hardly used in its synoptic sense and may mean nothing more than "sayings," as is the case in Greek C: φωναί.

⁶Προσελθοῦσα δὲ ἡ μήτηρ αὐτοῦ Μαρία εἶπεν αὐτῷ· ῞Ινα τί τοῦτο ἐποίησας ἡμῖν, τέκνον; ἰδοὺ ὀδυνώμενοι ἐζητοῦμέν σε.

⁷Καὶ εἶπεν αὐτοῖς ὁ ᾿Ιησοῦς· Τί με ζητεῖτε; οὐκ οἴδατε ὅτι ἐν τοῖς τοῦ πατρός μου δεῖ εἶναί με;

⁸Οἱ δὲ γραμματεῖς καὶ οἱ Φαρισαῖοι εἶπον· Σὺ εἶ μήτηρ τοῦ παιδίου τούτου;

⁹῾Η δὲ εἶπεν· ᾿Εγώ εἰμι.

¹⁰Καὶ εἶπον αὐτῇ· Μακαρία σὺ εἶ ἐν γυναιξίν, ὅτι ηὐλόγησεν ὁ θεὸς τὸν καρπὸν τῆς κοιλίας σου· τοιαύτην γὰρ δόξαν καὶ τοιαύτην ἀρετὴν καὶ σοφίαν οὔτε ἴδομεν οὔτε ἠκούσαμέν ποτε.

¹¹᾿Αναστὰς δὲ ᾿Ιησοῦς ἠκολούθησεν τῇ μητρὶ αὐτοῦ, καὶ ἦν ὑποτασσόμενος τοῖς γονεῦσιν αὐτοῦ. ἡ δὲ μήτηρ αὐτοῦ διετήρει πάντα τὰ γενόμενα. ¹²ὁ δὲ ᾿Ιησοῦς προέκοπτε σοφίᾳ καὶ ἡλικίᾳ καὶ χάριτι·

¹³Αὐτῷ ἡ δόξα εἰς τοὺς αἰῶνας τῶν αἰώνων, ἀμήν.

19:7. οὐκ οἴδατε: Tischendorf A and Greek-Slav. οὐκ εἶπον ὑμῖν: Greek C. Cf. Luke 2:49: οὐκ ᾔδειτε. **19:9.** ἐγώ εἰμι: Tischendorf A and Greek-Slav. Greek C omits. **19:10.** ὅτι ηὐλόγησεν ὁ θεὸς τὸν καρπόν: Tischendorf A and Greek C. καὶ εὐλογημένος ὁ καρπός: Greek-Slav. **19:10.** τοιαύτην γὰρ δόξαν καὶ τοιαύτην ἀρετὴν καὶ σοφίαν: Tischendorf A and Greek-Slav (omitting the second τοιαύτην). τοιαύτην χάριν καὶ σοφίαν καὶ δόξαν: Greek C. **19:11.** τῇ μητρὶ αὐτοῦ: Tischendorf A and Greek-Slav. αὐτοῖς: Greek C. **19:11.** καὶ ἦν ὑποτασσόμενος τοῖς γονεῦσιν αὐτοῦ: Tischendorf A and Greek-Slav. Greek C omits. Cf. Luke 2:51: καὶ ἦν ὑποτασσόμενος αὐτοῖς. **19:11.** πάντα τὰ γενόμενα: Tischendorf A. ἐν τῇ καρδίᾳ αὐτῆς ὅσα ἐποίησεν ὁ ᾿Ιησοῦς μεγαλεῖα: Greek-Slav. ἐν τῇ καρδίᾳ αὐτῆς ὅσα ἐποίησεν ὁ ᾿Ιησοῦς ἐν τῷ λαῷ μεγαλεῖα ἰώμενος τὰς νόσους πάντων: Greek C. in corde suo quanta fecit Iesus signa magna in populo, sanando infirmos multos: Latin. Cf. Luke 2:51: πάντα τὰ ῥήματα ἐν τῇ καρδίᾳ αὐτῆς. **19:12.** χάριτι: Tischendorf A. χάριτι καὶ ἐποίησε θεραπείας, δοξαζόμενος ὑπὸ θεοῦ τοῦ πατρός: Greek-Slav. χάριτι καὶ ἐδοξάσθη παρὰ τοῦ πατρὸς αὐτοῦ: Greek C. Cf. Luke 2:52: χάριτι παρὰ θεῷ καὶ ἀνθρώποις. **19:13.** (=Chapter 11:3c in Tischendorf B.) **19:13.** αὐτῷ ἡ δόξα κτλ.: Tischendorf A and Greek-Slav. καὶ ἔστιν εὐλόγητος κτλ.: Greek C. et omnes qui videbant eum glorificabant deum patrem omnipotentem, qui est benedictus in secula seculorum, amen: Latin. Cf. Tischendorf B, which ended at 13:4 with Mary: δοξάζουσα αὐτὸν σὺν τῷ πατρὶ καὶ τῷ ἁγίῳ πνεύματι νῦν καὶ ἀεὶ καὶ εἰς τοὺς αἰῶνας τῶν αἰώνων, ἀμήν.

⁶His mother Mary came up and said to him, "Child, why have you done this to us? Don't you see, we've been worried sick looking for you."

⁷"Why are you looking for me?" Jesus said to them. "Don't you know that I have to be in my father's house?"

⁸Then the scholars and the Pharisees said, "Are you the mother of this child?"

⁹She said, "I am."

¹⁰And they said to her, "You more than any woman are to be congratulated, for God has blessed the fruit of your womb! For we've never seen nor heard such glory and such virtue and wisdom."

¹¹Jesus got up and went with his mother, and was obedient to his parents. His mother took careful note of all that had happened. ¹²And Jesus continued to excel in learning and gain respect.

¹³To him be glory for ever and ever. Amen.

• **19:7.** *in my Father's house*: The same ambiguous expression appears at Luke 2:49 and consequently has received much scholarly attention, but even so no secure interpretation has emerged. The ambiguity arises because in the phrase ἐν τοῖς τοῦ πατρός μου there is no noun for the article τοῖς. One must be supplied, and most scholars have proposed "house," as here, on the grounds that context requires a noun answering the question where. Some scholars, however, prefer to supply "affairs," so that the phrase would mean something like "concerned with my father's business." Recently, scholars are preferring to keep the ambiguity and supply both nouns: "concerned with my father's business in the temple" (see de Jonge, "Sonship," 331–37, and Sylva, "Cryptic Clause"). See further Brown, *Messiah*, 475–77, 693–94.

• **19:8–10.** These verses have no parallel in the Lukan account, although v. 10a is quite Lukan in its language, drawing on Luke 1:42. Incidentally, these verses replace v. 50 in Luke: "And they (Jesus' parents) did not understand what he was talking about," an omission which removes a negative characterization of Joseph and Mary. In contrast, at least Mary becomes the subject of an admiring beatitude (v. 10).

• **19:11.** *All that happened*: Greek C and Greek-Slav expand here, the latter, for example, saying quite appropriately: "all the extraordinary things that Jesus did." The word translated "extraordinary things" (μεγαλεῖα) was used in the opening chapter and thus its repetition here makes for a fitting conclusion.

• **19:12.** *excel in learning and gain respect*: Both Greek C and Greek-Slav expand, the former, for example, continuing as follows: "and he was glorified by his (divine) Father."

• **19:13.** *for ever and ever. Amen*: Tischendorf B also has a concluding doxology, but since it ends with chapter 13, the doxology is appended at that point. It reads: "She (Mary) glorified him (Jesus) with the Father and the holy spirit both now and always and for ever and ever. Amen."

Bookshelf of Basic Works

1. Texts, Translations, and Study Tools

(For complete listing, see Elliott, *Apocryphal New Testament*, 71–74.)

Attridge, H. and Ronald F. Hock (trs.), "The Infancy Gospel of Thomas," in *The Complete Gospels*. R. Miller (ed.); Santa Rosa, CA: Polebridge Press, rev. 1994, 369–79.

Cullmann, O. (tr.), "The Infancy Story of Thomas," in *New Testament Apocrypha. Vol. 1. Gospels and Related Writings.* W. Schneemelcher (ed.) and R. McL. Wilson (tr.); Louisville, KY: Westminster-John Knox, 1991, 439–51.

Delatte, A. (ed.), "Évangile de l'Enfance de Jacques: Manuscrit No. 355 de la Bibliothèque Nationale," *Anecdota Atheniensia. Tome 1. Textes grecs inédits relatifs à l'histoire des religions.* Paris: Edouard Champion, 1927, 264–71.

Elliott, J. K., *Apocryphal New Testament: A Collection of Apocryphal Christian Literature in an English Translation.* Oxford: Clarendon Press, 1993.

Fabricius, J. (ed.), *Codex Apocryphus Novi Testamenti.* 2 vols.; Hamburg: Schiller, 1703, 1.159–67.

Fuchs, A. and F. Weissengruber, *Konkordanz zum Thomasevangelium, Version A und B.* SNTU B4; Freistadt: Plöchl, 1978.

James, M. R., *The Apocryphal New Testament being the Apocryphal Gospels, Acts, Epistles and Apocalypses.* Oxford: Clarendon Press, 1924, 49–65.

Michaelis, W. (tr.), *Die Apokryphen Schriften zum Neuen Testament.* Bremen: Carl Schunemann, 2nd ed. 1958, 96–111.

de Santos Otero, A. (ed.), *Das Kirchenslavische Evangelium des Thomas.* PTS 6; Berlin: Walter de Gruyter, 1967.

Thilo, J. (ed.), *Codex Apocryphus Novi Testamenti.* Leipzig: Vogel, 1832, 275–315.

Tischendorf, C von (ed.), *Evangelia Apocrypha.* Leipzig: Avenarius and Mendelssohn, 2nd ed. 1876, 140–57.

Weissengruber, F., "Grammatische Untersuchungen zum Thomasevangelium A," in Fuchs and Weissengruber, *Konkordanz*, 205–26.

Wright, W. (tr.), *Contributions to the Apocryphal Literature of the New Testament.* London: Williams and Norgate, 1865.

2. Specialized Studies on the Infancy Gospel of Thomas

Gero, S., "The Infancy Gospel of Thomas: A Study of the Textual and Literary Problems," *NovT* 13 (1971) 46–80.

James, M. R., "The Gospel of Thomas," *JTS* 30 (1928) 51–54.

Lowe, M., "IOYΔAIOI of the Apocrypha: A Fresh Approach to the Gospels of James, Pseudo-Thomas, Peter and Nicodemus," *NovT* 23 (1981) 56–90.

Mc Neil, B., "Jesus and the Alphabet," *JTS* 27 (1976) 126–28.

Noret, J., "Pour une edition de l'Évangile de l'enfance selon Thomas," *AnBoll* 90 (1972) 412.

Voicu, S., "Notes sur l'histoire du texte de L'Histoire de L'Enfance de Jesus," in *La Fable Apocryphe*. 2 vols.; P. Geoltrain *et al.* (eds.); Tournhout: Brepols, 1989–91, 2.119–32.

3. Related Studies

Amundsen, L. (ed.), *Greek Ostraca in the University of Michigan Collection*. Univ. of Mich. Studies, Humanistic Series 34. Ann Arbor: University of Michigan Press, 1935.

Bauer, W., *Das Leben Jesu im Zeitalter der neutestamentlichen Apokryphen*. Tübingen: Mohr (Siebeck), 1909.

Bonner, S., *Education in Ancient Rome: From the Elder Cato to the Younger Pliny*. Berkeley: University of California Press, 1977.

Brown, R., *The Birth of the Messiah: A Commentary on the Infancy Narratives in the Gospels of Matthew and Luke*. New York: Doubleday, 2nd updated ed., 1993.

Burkert, W., *Greek Religion*. Cambridge: Harvard University Press, 1985.

Cribiore, R., *Writing, Teachers, and Students in Graeco-Roman Egypt*. Dissertation, Columbia University, 1993.

Frankfurter, D., "The Magic of Writing and the Writing of Magic: The Power of the Word in Egyptian and Greek Traditions," *Helios* 21 (1994) 189–221.

Gero, S., "Apocryphal Gospels: A Survey of Textual and Literary Problems," *ANRW* 2.25.2 (1988) 3969–96.

Hennecke, E. (ed.), *Neutestamentliche Apokryphen*. Tübingen: Mohr (Siebeck), 1904.

Hunger, H., *Die Hochsprachliche profane Literatur der Byzantiner*. 2 vols.; Munich: C.H. Beck, 1978.

Jaekel, S. (ed.), *Menandri Sententiae*. Leipzig: B.G. Teubner, 1964.

de Jonge, H., "Sonship, Wisdom, Infancy: Luke 2:41–51a," *NTS* 24 (1978) 317–54.

Kennedy, G., *Greek Rhetoric under Christian Emperors*. Princeton: Princeton University Press, 1983.

Koester, H., *Ancient Christian Gospels: Their History and Development*. Philadelphia: Trinity Press International, 1990.

———, "Überlieferung und Geschichte der frühchristlichen Evangelienliteratur," *ANRW* 2.25.2 (1984) 1463–1542.

Milne, J. G., "Relics of Graeco-Egyptian Schools," *JHS* 28 (1908) 121–32.

Pollard, J., *Birds in Greek Life and Myth*. London: Thames and Hudson, 1977.

Sylva, D., "The Cryptic Clause *en tois tou patros mou dei einai me* in Lk 2:49b," *ZNW* 78 (1987) 132–40.

Talbert, C., "Prophecies of Future Greatness: The Contribution of Greco-Roman Biographies to an Understanding of Luke 1:5–4:15," in *The Divine Helmsman: Studies on God's Control of Human Events, presented to Lou H. Silberman.* J. Crenshaw and S. Sandmel (eds.); New York: KTAV, 1980, 129–41.

Thundy, Z., *Buddha and Christ: Nativity Stories and Indian Traditions*. SHR 60; Leiden: E.J. Brill, 1993.

Vielhauer, P., *Geschichte der urchristlichen Literatur*. New York: Walter de Gruyter, 1975.

Wiedemann, T., *Adults and Children in the Roman Empire*. New Haven: Yale University Press, 1989.

Ziebarth, E. (ed.), *Aus der antiken Schule: Sammlung griechischer Texte auf Papyrus, Holztafeln, Ostraka*. Bonn: A. Marcus and E. Weber, 2nd ed. 1913.

Glossary

Apophthegm: A form critical category for a tradition, oral or written, in which a person's witty or wise saying is preserved, complete with brief context. See Form Criticism.

B.C.E./C.E.: Abbreviations for "before the common era" and "common era." These abbreviations replace B.C. and A.D., out of consideration for those from other religions who must refer to events according to the standard convention as having happened before or after the birth of Jesus.

Canonical: Belonging to the canon, or the authoritative writings of a group, as the Bible is for Christians. For example, the Gospels of Matthew, Mark, Luke, and John belong to the distinctively Christian canon, or New Testament. They are thus canonical, whereas the Infancy Gospels of James and Thomas, which do not belong to the Christian canon, are not.

Encomium: The Latin (and Anglicized) rendering of the Greek word ἐγκώμιον, one of the *Progymnasmata*, in which students learned how to praise, say, a person by following a set sequence of topics: family background, upbringing, adult pursuits, virtuous deeds, and comparison with someone worthy of equal or greater praise. The conventions of the encomium are important for the structure and contents of the Infancy Gospel of James. See *Progymnasmata*.

Form Criticism: A method of analysis in New Testament studies in which scholars seek to identify the form and function of oral traditions that have been taken up into written sources. Illustrative forms are the apophthegm and miracle story. See Apophthegm.

Gnosticism: A religious stance, sometimes called the spirit of late antiquity, in which people no longer felt at home in the world but believed themselves to belong to a higher, spiritual world and thus to have become trapped or imprisoned in this world and especially inside their bodies. Consequently, these people rejected the world and material existence, often leading an ascetic lifestyle. *Gnosis*, or knowledge, contained in esoteric myths revealed their true origin and allowed them to escape back to their true home. Gnostic ideas are reflected in various Christian writings, such as the documents from Nag Hammadi, but such ideas are also posited for the Infancy Gospel of Thomas, especially in the esoteric wisdom that comes from the precocious lips of Jesus (see 6:4–8, 22–23). See Nag Hammadi.

Infancy Gospels: A general category for a number of gospels that narrate stories about the birth and childhood of Jesus, or even about his mother Mary. They typically extend or expand materials that are found in the Gospels of Matthew and Luke. The most important Infancy Gospels are those of James and Thomas.

King Herod: Client king of Rome who ruled much of Palestine from 37 to 4 B.C.E. He is to be distinguished from his son Herod Antipas, who, while sometimes called King Herod (see Mark 6:14), was actually the tetrarch of a "fourth" of his father's kingdom, namely Galilee and Perea, from 4 B.C.E. to 39 C.E.

MS(S): Abbreviations for "manuscript(s)," the documents, written by hand, that contain, in this book, the Infancy Gospels of James and Thomas.

Nag Hammadi: Site in upper Egypt where, in 1945, a cache of Christian documents were discovered in jars. The most important of these documents is the Gospel of Thomas, a collection of 114 sayings of Jesus. See Gnosticism.

Ostraca: Plural form of ostracon, a Greek word for a broken piece of pottery. Ostraca were widely available—at home, on the street, or on rubbish heaps. They were extensively used in school, especially at the elementary level. Their small size, erasability, and indestructibility made them ideal for practicing letters, syllables, and lists of words.

Papyrus: The paper of antiquity, made from the fibers of papyrus, a reed that grew along the Nile River. Papyrus is durable, especially in the dry climate of Egypt where thousands and thousands of papyrus documents, both literary and nonliterary, have surprisingly survived from as early as the third century B.C.E. The literary papyri are particularly important, in that they often push the MS tradition of a literary work back centuries before the previously known medieval and renaissance MSS that contain that work. Papyrus Bodmer V, which contains the Infancy Gospel of James, is an example of such an important papyrus MS, dating from the early 4th c. C.E. See MS(S).

Pre-Pauline Traditions: Portions of Paul's letters that he himself did not compose but that he merely quoted from what he had learned from other Christians, such as the brief creed of 1 Cor 15:3–5 or the hymnic statements of Phil 2:6–11.

Progymnasmata: Educational textbooks used to teach students appropriate style and methods of argumentation through a series of fourteen, graded compositional exercises. These exercises were designed to prepare students for rhetorical composition. See Encomium and Speech-in-Character.

Pseudonymous: A word of Greek origin meaning "falsely named." Used to designate ancient writings whose supposed author, such as James for the Infancy Gospel of James, does not withstand critical scrutiny. Such writings are thus falsely ascribed, or pseudonymous.

Septuagint: The Greek translation of the Hebrew scriptures, made in the third century B.C.E. and used by Greek-speaking Jews and later by Greek-speaking Christians. The author of the Infancy Gospel of James was especially familiar with the Septuagint.

Source Criticism: A method of analysis in New Testament studies in which scholars seek to find the written sources that an author used in composing a literary work. For example, scholars think that the authors of the Gospels of Matthew and Luke used the Gospel of Mark as one their sources.

Speech-in-Character: A standard, if awkward, rendering of the Greek word ἠθοποιία, one of the *Progymnasmata*, in which students were taught to express a
person's character (ἦθος) by means of a short speech that responds to a specific
event and is organized according to the three times: present, past, and future.
See *Progymnasmata*.

Synoptic Gospels: A shorthand expression for the Gospels of Matthew, Mark, and
Luke, whose overall narrative structure, contents, and style are similar when
compared to the different structure, contents, and style of the Gospel of John.

Textus Receptus: A Latin phrase meaning "received text," originally applied to the
New Testament Greek text edited by Erasmus in the 16th c. which assumed a
singular authority among Christians of the succeeding centuries. The Greek
texts that C. von Tischendorf edited of the Infancy Gospels of James and
Thomas in the 19th c. have achieved a similar authority among scholars who
translate and study these gospels.

Version: The translation of a piece of literature into another language, such as the
Greek New Testament into the English of the King James Version or New
Revised Standard Version. The Infancy Gospels were translated into many
languages, or versions: Armenian, Georgian, Ethiopian, and so forth.

Vorlage: A German word used in text criticism for a "source," often hypothetical,
that can be hypothesized from peculiarities that appear in certain later MSS.
Grammatical and linguistic peculiarities in Slavonic MSS of the Infancy Gospel
of Thomas, for example, have led to the hypothesis of a Greek source, or
Vorlage, for these MSS.

Index of Ancient Writings

Index of Subjects

(except for Joseph, Mary, and Jesus)

156

Index of Modern Authors

About the Author

Ronald F. Hock is Professor of Religion at the University of Southern California in Los Angeles. He holds a Ph.D. in New Testament studies from Yale University. His research focuses on reconstructing the social and intellectual worlds of the Greek East of the early Roman Empire, which was the historical context within which earliest Christianity arose. Special interests include the Greek romances and Greek rhetoric as sources for this reconstruction. He is presently at work on a book relating the Greek romances to the Christian gospels. Professor Hock is a member of the Scholars Version translation panel.